The
Christian Experience of
God as Trinity

The
Christian Experience of
God as Trinity

JAMES P. MACKEY

SCM PRESS LTD

334 01937 0

First published 1983
by SCM Press Ltd
26–30 Tottenham Road, London N1

Photoset by Input Typesetting Ltd
and printed in Great Britain by
Richard Clay (The Chaucer Press) Ltd
Bungay, Suffolk

FOR MY CHILDREN
CIARA AND JAMES

Contents

Contents

Part Four   THE FUTURE

Introduction

In an age which combines the ever-narrowing focus of the specialist with increasing general confusion it would be a brave author indeed who would project a systematic account of any subject, and Christian theology is no exception. But if some Christian academic were to assume the courage and the ability to construct a systematic theology for our time, then those of us whose hearts harbour no such ambition – or who at least are not prepared to confess publicly that they do – would not begrudge this hardy author our advice.

I, for instance, might not be too shy to suggest that the first and foundation volume of such a system, if it is truly to be a system of Christian theology, should be a book about Jesus of Nazareth. I would not betray such inordinate pride as to suggest that my *Jesus, the Man and the Myth*[1] should be this book; and although in the course of this present work we may see reason to think that Christian theology should not begin with general tracts on God, the task of criticizing other suggested opening subjects in actual or potential systems would take up far too much time and space here. But there can hardly be anything seriously wrong with the suggestion that since it is commonly acknowledged by Christians that Jesus of Nazareth not only founded their faith, but in himself – that is, in his life, death and destiny – gave it its definitive content, any well-based system of Christian theology should really begin with a book about him.

Further, if this advice were coming from me, it would contain one particular emphasis. I argued as best I could in *Jesus, the Man and the Myth* that the study of Jesus of Nazareth must begin from the perspective of the human and the historical, must aim at a 'christology from below', as one current slogan puts it. This is not just because the human and historical perspective is now all the rage, but because there is no other way in which to take fully seriously the dogma, of incarnation of God's Word being *made flesh*, arguably the most sacrosanct dogma, and certainly the most influential in the whole of Christian history.[2]

Now it is the common experience of books on Jesus these days that so much time and space is necessarily spent on human and historical, textual and biblical matter, that little enough is normally left for an adequate account of all that the Christian tradition has to say about what may be called the godward side of Jesus. For even though one agrees with Martin Hengel 'that more happened in this period of less than two decades (after the death of Jesus) than in the whole of the next seven centuries, up to the time when the doctrine of the early church was completed',[3] it is still necessary to give an adequate account of the theological developments of these successive centuries about the person and work of Jesus. And it is to these theological developments that the doctrine of the Trinity unquestionably belongs.

One would need to anticipate too much of the argument of the present work in order to secure for the introduction the contention that the Christian doctrine of the Trinity is properly speaking a christological doctrine, that it is not at all a doctrine about God before or independently of the revelation (for those who take it as such) in Jesus, and that many of the faults and failures which the doctrine has incurred in the past have been due to the systematic exclusion from reference to key trinitarian terms, such as 'Son', of texts which dealt with 'the man' Jesus, or were alleged to deal with his 'humanity' rather than his 'divinity'. It must be sufficient to predict at this point that the Christian doctrine of the Trinity is a strictly christological doctrine, or, alternatively stated, that the Christian doctrine of the Trinity represents the most ambitious efforts of the Christian community in history to express adequately what has just now been termed the godward side of Jesus. It attempts, that is to say, to express simultaneously the full relationship of Jesus to the God he called 'Father' and, in so far as human beings still on pilgrimage can conceive of this, the nature of the God revealed by Jesus. It follows, of course, that the doctrine of the Trinity is the natural candidate for the central subject of the second volume of a projected systematic theology.

It is a little surprising, then, that at a time when books on Jesus simply pullulate, and even books which make a general case for belief in God, as we shall see, begin to mushroom once more, new works on the Trinity are relatively rare. One is tempted to say that, apart from those who think it their duty to write about everything – Karl Rahner in particular and process theologians in general – relatively few have followed the systematic indices outlined in the last paragraph with anything more than passing suggestions about the contemporary retrieval of classical trinitarian doctrine. This relative neglect of the doctrine of the Trinity is, of course, less serious in books on christology than it is in arguments for modern belief in God. For if the former are in the least adequately construed they will have much to say of Father, Son and Spirit; whereas if the latter, as we shall soon see, confine their arguments to some undifferentiated notions of God, even in the hope that these may later be trans-substantiated into a recognizable Christian entity, they may be vulnerable to the accusation that they introduce their readers to strange gods.

Whether more or less serious, however, this relative neglect of the doctrine of the Trinity is regrettable. Few doctrines of the Christian creed are more in need of recovery in terms intelligible to this time. Though undoubtedly one of the first doctrines to come to mind when the comparative religionist asks after the distinctively Christian, the doctrine probably represents in the unreflective Christian mind what Rahner has called 'a popular, unverbalized, but at bottom quite massive tritheism'.[4] To the reflective Christian mind, on the other hand, it can be at best a mystery too soon, an intellectual obstacle on the obstacle course to heaven to be taken in stride with as little thought as possible; at worst, an intellectual conundrum comprising some strange celestial mathematics, some very abstruse philosophical concepts, and some theological reasoning that is, for most people, too clever by half. Furthermore, the connection between the doctrine and the ordinary Christian life of moral endeavour, of community and worship, from which ideally the doctrine should live and breathe, is often tenuous in the extreme; too often in fact this connection is forged from simplistic moralizing analogies which depict the 'persons' of the Trinity as an unbelievably talented, mutually supportive and loving pre-existent trio (a supernumerary holy family), and thus more damage is done to the doctrine of the Trinity than could ever be compensated by whatever advantage is reaped from exhorting would-be Christian communities to follow the example of the Three.

Christians today, of course, cannot afford to think solely of their own needs and desires when they think of their doctrines (or their institutions, rituals, and codes of conduct). Faced increasingly by non-Christian cultures and by increasingly dechristianized cultures in traditionally Christian lands – faced in fact with a situation more similar than it has been for over a millenium to the one in which Christianity first made its entry and recorded, amongst others, its most pronounced doctrinal successes – Christians, if they ever were tempted to think that they existed for themselves rather than for others, cannot afford to think so now. It is most particularly true of the doctrine of the Trinity, dealing as it does with the godward side of Jesus, that anyone who would work on it and ignore, on the one hand, the current atheistic humanism and, on the other, the rival conceptions of God at least in the West (the religious positions of Jews and Muslims) could reasonably be accused of an indefensible, indeed a self-defeating chauvinism. It would take a very determined theological ostrich indeed to try to recover the substance of the Christian doctrine of the Trinity today – a substance already described as a simultaneous account of the relation of Jesus to God and of the God revealed by Jesus – while remaining blind and deaf to those who either profess to be unable to believe in any God at all or who profess a distinct preference for the God of Jesus himself before his followers made a God of Jesus.

It is probably best to begin by placing the doctrine of the Trinity in this broader context of contemporary culture and to face immediately the dilemma that the recovery of the most distinctive Christian doctrine may serve only to widen the gap between us and our theological enemies (the atheistic humanists) and potential allies (the Jews and Muslims who share a common religious background with us) alike. From there we can proceed to search out and analyse the origins of the Christian doctrine of the Trinity, its roots in the common Christian belief and Christian life, and the prospects for its recovery in theological terms more intelligible to this time.

PART ONE

The Present

1

Secular Humanism and the Death of God

Late Western civilization, it is said, is the only major civilization known to us in which atheism became an acceptable, and hence a widespread cultural option. That much said, however, the assessments of this phenomenon are about as varied as its analysts. In *A Short History of Western Atheism*,[1] for instance, James Thrower introduces an early distinction between relative atheisms (or agnosticisms), on the one hand and atheism *per se*, naturalistic or absolute atheism, on the other. The former consist of those systematic doubts or argued rejections brought to counter specific religions or religious movements and the very particular supernatural beings which these describe. The latter is fashioned more from a quite original way of looking at and interpreting the world we inhabit and the events which make up its history, a way of seeing these which is naturally incompatible with any and every form of supernaturalism. This latter form Thrower judges to be fundamentally more important, 'representing as it does one polarity in the development of the human spirit', and on it he concentrates for the rest of the book, ranging in the process from the pre-Socratic period to the modern Existentialists.

Now Thrower's distinction, like many another, is much easier to draw in the introduction than it is actually to see verified in all the material through which such analyses must inevitably pass. But there is this much at least to be said for it: the case for the relativity of atheism has been made with sufficient frequency and variety, mainly by apologists for Christianity. The case sometimes begins with the general assertion that just as there is no such thing

7

as religious faith in general, neither is there any such thing as atheism *per se*. All actual religious faith is as specific and particular as the Absolute to which it points; similarly all atheism (and agnosticism) takes its distinctive colour and shape from the specific religious tradition to which it is contrary. General notions of religious faith, as of atheism, are conceptual abstractions from the concrete realities we actually meet in the history of cultures. But whether this general premise is argued, omitted, or tacitly assumed, the next moves are fairly consistent.

An attempt is next made to show that the atheist is reacting negatively to a certain understanding of God. There follows an interval of admission that recurring human infidelity leads religious people themselves to misrepresent the one, true God. And, finally, it is alleged that all that is of positive value in the atheist's view of life points in fact to the true absolute which even the bearers of the religious tradition in question had misconstrued. Thus, not only is atheism shown to be relative, perhaps even parasitic, but the attempt of its authors to bring down the idols and yet to maintain the inalienable value of human existence is turned by the religious apologist into the strange witness of unbelief.[2] Bold, and often suspect of excessive ingenuity, the case for the relativity of atheism is thus often pressed to the point of making would-be enemies into reluctant allies. And there is no gainsaying the strength of the case.

Yet it seems just as necessary to acknowledge some real force in Thrower's distinction and in the preference which he states and substantiates with such determination. Those who rest on their oars too soon after crossing the finishing line of the argument for the relativity of atheism may not even notice that they are being carried away on another current to waters as dangerous as any they thought they had successfully navigated. For whether or not Thrower's distinction is as clear-cut and verifiable as he would wish, there is certainly a harmonious chorus from those whom Christians call atheists, and its message is clear: *the attainment of the true vision of human existence in this world is the desired end-product of all their philosophical questing; the rejection of theism in any of its forms is a mere by-product and quite inessential by comparison.* It must suffice here to illustrate this message from modern Western philosophers, to state it in its most generally accepted terms today, and to try to learn its real lessons for the contemporary possibilities of belief in God.

The message in its modern form is this: we are not atheists, we are humanists. Our *raison d'être* as philosophers and as human beings is not to be sought in our opposition to current religious beliefs but in the human and humanistic visions with which we replace these. In the course of our quest for truth, which seeks its goal in these very visions, we have simply found that religious beliefs are meaningless, irrelevant, or obsolescent, and that is all. We do not wish to devote any more time to religious belief than is necessary to state this incidental result as honestly and as une-motionally as possible. To describe us solely, or even primarily, as atheists is to misrepresent the thrust and point of our philosophy and to evade its real force.

Perhaps the least impressive form of the message comes from the linguistic analysts. In what he later termed a young man's manifesto, A. J. Ayer argued that God-talk, in company with all other metaphysical language, simply made no sense, and he drew the fullest implication of this position, namely, that it would make as little sense to call those who accepted his philosophical position atheists or agnostics as it would be to call them religious believers. If theological discourse makes nonsense, then each of these titles is as inapplicable as any of the others. The philosophers of language as a rule neither offer to the religious person the consolation of assuming that his faith might have been justified in a less-developed stage of human evolution, nor do they in their main philosophical output endorse any comparably broad vision of human existence. But the personal allegiance of some of the more prominent figures with humanist associations, and the odd remark in favour of man's future with empirical science,[3] while not quite reaching the stature of Dewey[4] in defence of a new faith in scientific humanism, clearly enough indicates the direction in which the human alternative for them lies.

In addition to these comparative inadequacies, claims about meaningfulness, though arguably prior to claims about truth (at least in the epistemological order),[5] are lesser than these, and the case against them is consequently more easily answered.

Sartre, on the other hand, who devoted some passing effort to show that the idea of a creator God was both conceptually unjustifiable and morally repugnant[6] – though he could under-stand in a way how the human *pour-soi* or self could desire to be God – is even more insistent that, if his philosophy is at all adequate to the reality of existence, God is entirely irrelevant. At the end of a long lecture designed to prove that Existentialism, far from being as inhuman a system as its detractors claimed, was humanism *par excellence*, his most emphatic assertion was this: 'Even if God did exist, that would change nothing'.[7] 'There you've got our point of view,' he added, 'Not that we believe that God exists, but we think that the problem of his existence is not the issue. In this sense existentialism is optimistic, a doctrine of action, and it is plain dishonesty for Christians to make no distinction between their own despair and ours, and then to call us despairing.' For only those who think that human happiness depends on God will conclude that the non-existence of God implies a despair which could not be overcome.

It is Marxism, however, that in the modern era has proved to be the most globally attractive alternative to traditional religious beliefs, showing in the process a power to convert even those ancient Eastern cultures that had always been more or less impervious to Christianity. Whatever the betrayals of the vision of the original prophet incurred in the various forms in which it has been institutionalized – and what prophetic vision has not been betrayed by institutionalization – Marxism has held out the most substantial human hope for a purely human future. It has most consistently refused to see itself as a reaction to religion (religion, in fact, is seen as a dying reactionary force hopelessly attempting to impede progress), and while patiently explaining the need for religious belief during the childhood and adolescence of the race, it confidently preaches the obsolescence of religion now that humanity has finally come of age.

In *The Jewish Question*,[8] for instance, Marx argued that the true liberation of the Jew from oppression by Christians could not possibly be accomplished until the common humanity of Jew and Christian alike was liberated fully from Judaism and Christianity, from religion. He exposed the false promises of the newly secular states such as France and the United States of America, by pointing out that since states were ultimately the people who made up their populations, the much-vaunted neutrality of these states *vis-à-vis* religion – the separation of church and state or, more harshly, the atheism of the state – merely meant that a man must be divided against himself and thus suffer loss instead of gain. As a citizen he behaved like a good atheist, not letting his religious convictions interfere with his political actions; but as a private individual he enjoyed the right, which as political agent he had voted for himself, to keep to his religious divisions – or class divisions or others – and inside these to engage, within the terms of the laws he had laid down for himself, in the *bellum omnium contra omnes*, the war of all against all.[9] In Marx's united humanity in eschatological peace and common prosperity, religion as it had ever been known would clearly be obsolete.

From the beginning Marx showed little or no interest in theoretical arguments for the truth or falsehood of religious beliefs;[10] he concentrated instead on religion as a force within the structures of society. So that we have in the foregoing brief selection of dominant modern philosophies an echo of the message of the positive humanist priority, first from the predominantly epistemological or analytic level (linguistic analysts), then from the predominantly moral or evaluative level (Sartre), and finally from the level of social structures and relationships (Marxism).

Now it would be quite impossible in this context to do any justice to the humanist visions of these three philosophies, but it is necessary to describe in some detail one major theme from their complex argument, if only to provide a proper basis for the assessment of what appears to be the major contemporary Christian case for belief in the one, true God. For if we are prepared to go beyond the argument for the relativity of atheism, if we are prepared to take seriously the repeated modern insistence on the primacy of the humanist motive, the clamour for recognition of what Thrower called 'one polarity in the development of the human spirit', we may find that these philosophies which we are too easily content to describe as simply atheistic do more for us in fact than rid us of the idols with which we have replaced the one, true God. They may bring us to that cutting edge where the nature and possibility of religious faith is itself at issue. For if the critics of these modern philosophies insist that they are primarily atheistic and thus relative to established theistic positions, and the exponents of these philosophies are equally insistent that their 'atheism' is either non-existent or incidental,[11] and if we are prepared to try the experiment of giving to the latter as much credence as we normally like to give to the former, we are bound to be prepared to find that more may be going on just now than the cleansing of some god-concepts. That much at least can be said for Thrower's thesis; and if we heed it we may be alerted to turbulent waters ahead. For we are being asked, if not quite forced, to go beneath the concepts of God to the ground on which

11

we could affirm any of them. Take, then, as a major theme from the modern philosophies just mentioned the theme of transcendence, and begin in reverse order with Marx.

Far too much has been made of the materialism of Marx, particularly when materialism is conceived in terms of determinism and the view of spirit as at most an epiphenomenon of the human brain. This may be partly due to Engels' more popularizing works, such as the *Dialectics of Nature* (1873–86) and the Introduction to the English Edition of *Socialism, Utopian and Scientific* (1892). In the latter context in particular he declares that 'life, from its lowest to its highest forms, is but the normal mode of existence of albuminous bodies', that 'mind is a mode of energy, a function of the brain', and that 'our juridicial, philosophical and religious ideas are the more or less remote offshoots of the economical relations prevailing in a given society'.[12] By so linking the philosophy of Marx with what he took to be the overall picture of the world emerging from the sciences of his day, Engels conveyed an impression of laws of nature and history, in flux and cycle, discovered by something called science, and determining our very thoughts.

There are those, of course, particularly amongst Marx's self-styled disciples, who maintain that the more determinist view of 'historical materialism', as Engels called it, is true to Marx's own later and more scientific writings and that only in the more 'romantic ideology' of his early works can one find any room for the free creativity of the human spirit and, consequently, for any concept of truly human transcendence. We must obviously not enter deeply at this point into such a troubled area of Marxist exegesis; the earlier writings can supply to us, and to any Marxist who still wishes it, the kind of concept of transcendence of which we are now in search.[13]

The notion of transcendence which Marx inherited came to him from Hegel, in whose system it meant the overcoming of those negative features of existence entailed in the spirit treating the world as an independent object rather than an *alter ego*, an *alienum* rather than a facet of its own conscious self. But in Hegel's view the subject who would overcome this alienation was Spirit, not the human individual either singly or in communion.

It was Ludwig Feuerbach, a pupil of Hegel's, who pointed out that Hegel in reality left human alienation intact, precisely because the subject who achieved everything in history was not a truly human subject at all, but an already constituted transcendent Spirit. As in all previous forms of religion, God did everything, man really did nothing. Hence in his almost instantly famous work *The Essence of Christianity* Feuerbach argues as follows: the fact that the human species is the only species that boasts the religious sense and also the only species that enjoys self-consciousness contains the clue to the truth, namely, that in our religious consciousness we are really conscious of self. If it is objected that the religious sense is a sense of the infinite, this can be met by saying that we are conscious of an infinite dimension of our own nature. This in turn is argued by use of the principle that a truly limited being can have no awareness of its own limitation. But there is no human limitation, real or conceivable, which we cannot see as such. And to see limitation as a limitation is to be able to see beyond it, to transcend it at least in vision. The tension between our sense of our limitations and our complementary sense of unlimitedness or infinity is relieved by the suggestion that the limits of which we appear conscious are those of our individual selves, or of our time and place, whereas the limitlessness or infinity of which we are conscious belongs to human nature itself or to the human species. Stretching this kind of argument out through anthropology and history, Feuerbach comes to the conclusion that Christianity was the definitive religion, of course, because it alone of all religions of history declared in its incarnational christology that man was God. Thus man is the subject of history and salvation, the subject who makes history and achieves salvation by going beyond all crippling limitations. Theology is anthropology in disguise: transcendence is not a name for God distinct from man, it is man's essential attribute. All future achievement will be ours, as much as all present and past failures already all too obviously are.

Marx had no quarrel with this kind of critique of religion, and certainly not with its insistence that the true subject of all history was the human subject. But he did think that Feuerbach's concept of the human subject was still itself too abstract, and this produced at once one of his major quarrels with Feuerbach and his own distinctive view of human nature and human history. 'But *man*,' he wrote, 'is no abstract being squatting outside the world. Man is the world of man, the state, society. This state, this society, produce religion.'[14] It is difficult to elaborate on this point without entering once more into the debate about creativity and determinism in Marx. So let us be satisfied to outline briefly the least that he could have meant by his theses against Feuerbach.

In his panegyric at the funeral of Marx, Engels claimed that as Darwin had discovered the laws of the evolution of life, Marx had discovered the laws of the evolution of human society, and the key to these laws was the simple principle that, before they can do anything else, human beings have to feed, clothe and shelter themselves. Human beings maintain, indeed 'produce' their own lives; and the relationships into which they enter as a result of the nature and distribution of the means of this production are certainly more determinative of what at any point in history they *are* than is any abstract notion of 'human nature' which ignores these practical and social dimensions. Marx neither regretted this basic need to work, nor, as his own life shows, did he except the academic vocation from the category of work. On the contrary, he saw in work the source of freedom and creativity and of all the dignity of being human, and his great complaint against capitalism was that it so denatured human work that it denatured man also, for by its internal logic it made of everything, even human beings themselves, commodities whose value was dictated by the rules of the market place.

> It is man's nature to be his own creator; he forms and develops himself by working on and transforming the world outside him in co-operation with his fellow men. In this progressive interchange between man and the world, it is man's nature to be in control of this process, to be the initiatior, the subject in which the process originates. However, this nature has become alien to man; that is, it is no longer his and belongs to another person or thing. In religion, for example, it is God who is the subject of the historical process and man is in a state of dependence on his grace. In economics, according to Marx, it is money and the processes of the market that manoeuver men around instead of being controlled by them.[15]

Marx did allow that religion enabled human beings to protest against their condition. In the passage which contains the far-too-often-quoted 'religion is the opium of the people', Marx also wrote, 'Religious distress is at the same time the expression of real distress and the protest against real distress. Religion is the sigh of the oppressed creature, the heart of a heartless world, just as it is the spirit of a spiritless situation.'[16] But since he had accepted the basic Feuerbachian thesis that religion is but a projection on to an empty sky of the essence of the human reality

14

on earth (or, in his own words, that religion is man's recognition of himself by a detour),[17] since he had accepted that man, not God, is the real subject active in history, he could not see religion, even in its mood of protestation, as anything other than a reactionary force preventing human beings from finding the solutions to their own problems.

The ability to transcend the limitations of the present towards a far, far better future was, for Marx, a property of the human, particularly of human labour, and the true expression of human freedom and dignity. For in Marx's prophetic vision my labour, instead of being a mere commodity to be valued at the going (market) rate, would be the creative expression in this world of my human self; it would be a contribution to the needs of others and, as such, an expression of our common humanity, arising from my own deepest natural instinct to create human life and inviting confirmation in the thought and love of another.

That would have been an extraordinary vision in any age, and in an age which offers more than usual devotion to Mammon its power is very far from depleted. But the sole feature of it which is of interest to us at this point is the repeated determination to retrieve the attribute of transcendence for human kind: to see transcendence fully explicable in human terms and containing in its conceptual index no need for a cross-reference to God.

Two general deficiencies are commonly urged against Marx's critique of Christianity, even by those who feel no need to examine it in any detail: first, that it concentrated on establishment or Constantinian Christianity to the neglect of that prophetic element which was so often critical of the *status quo* on earth and which was never altogether submerged, and second, that Marx's vision of the free, human creation of human life could not deal with life's greatest crisis, inevitable death. The first of these deficiencies, if such it is, has certainly been made good by the old Marxist, or ex-Marxist, Ernst Bloch. For it is precisely the messianic, prophetic and eschatological dimensions of Christianity that have always fascinated Bloch – though he acknowledges, significantly, that these dimensions belong to the heretical periphery more than they do to the centre of the Christian establishment – and it is precisely in these that he sees the roundabout religious recognition of what is an essential human attribute: in the title of his *opus magnum*, the principle of hope. The human being in essence is one who transcends self and circumstance towards an uncertain

15

future: the human being is, in fact, defined as hope.[18] Hope defines humanity, in short, rather than points away from it, and all the messianism, all the prophetic vision, all the eschatological imagery of past and present, is its ever-changing raiment. Those who try to answer Marx in terms of a kind of Christianity which can activate the human enterprise towards a better future on earth will simply find Bloch waiting for them at the conclusion of their work.

Nor is Bloch unaware of the second deficiency so often urged against Marxist visions of the future. As he himself puts it:

A society that is no longer antagonistic will, of course, keep all mundane fates firmly in hand. Its members are not in economic-political situations, and they have no economic-political fate. But this is just what makes them more sensitive to the indignities involved in being human, from the jaws of death down to such ebb tides of life as boredom and surfeit. The heralds of nothingness are not mere shadings any more, as in the class society; they wear new features, largely inconceivable as yet, but the train of purposes they rupture has a new way of gnawing too.[19]

If, then, the end of class struggle and of its political embodiments merely allows the nothingness which faces us to appear in newer and more unmediated form, what in face of this can hold the human race together in search of a better future? Again in Bloch's own words: 'Where is the place for the *organism* of persons (as distinct from a well managed multitude), for the *apse* and, above all, for the *apse window of solidarity* that will cast a transcending light without transcendence?'[20] He rejects the religous myths of an afterlife which have so often merely served to reinforce in heaven the states that are given on earth. And he will himself answer only in terms of the claims of the community 'that is very much in earnest about the amity that goes deep and the fraternity that is difficult',[21] in terms of the prospects that must not be foreshortened to the needs of the day.

In any case, those who believe that death, with its obvious threat of annihilation, of itself favours religion must be reminded of another influential humanist of our time, Albert Camus. Obsessed all his life by what he called the universal death penalty, Camus, from *The Myth of Sisyphus* to *The Rebel*, found in it the most persuasive reason for disbelief. But he too believed transcendence to be an attribute of human beings, and he searched for a kind of transcendence which would not truncate or restrict the human as religious versions of transcendence tended to do. 'Perhaps,' he wrote, 'there is a living transcendence, of which beauty carries the promise, which can make this mortal and limited world preferable to and more appealing than any other.'[22]

Sartre's principle that existence precedes essence is perhaps too well known: we humans are not just a 'something' fashioned by a '*Dieu Fabricateur*' such that by analysing what we are we should know how we ought to conduct ourselves. Rather, we first exist and then in the anguish of full freedom and unrelieved responsibility we make of ourselves whatever we shall be. There is no universal human nature, though there is a universal human condition, made up of limits which outline the human being's fundamental situation in the world, such as 'the necessity for him to exist in the world, to be at work there, to be there in the midst of other people, and to be mortal there'.[23] Within these limits of this condition we *are* the freedom to make of ourselves by means of them whatever we shall be, to fly by these nets, as James Joyce would say. Transcendence, for Sartre also, is a fundamental human attribute, and he is even more careful than the others to distinguish this ineradicable human transcendence from its religious counterfeit:

> Man is constantly outside of himself; in projecting himself, in losing himself outside of himself, he makes for man's existing; and, on the other hand, it is by pursuing transcendent goals that he is able to exist; man, being this state of passing-beyond, and seizing upon things only as they bear upon this passing beyond, is at the heart, at the centre of this passing beyond. There is no universe other than a human universe, the universe of human subjectivity. This connection between transcendence, as a constituent element of man – not in the sense that God is transcendent, but in the sense of passing beyond – and subjectivity, in the sense that man is not closed in on himself but is always present in a human universe, is what we call existentialist humanism. Humanism, because we remind man that there is no law-maker other than himself, and that in his forlornness he will decide by himself.[24]

I have said that representatives of the first modern philosophical movement mentioned above, linguistic analysis, seldom attempt to say what human condition or vision religions once presented in foreign costume and, apart from their membership of humanist associations, seldom offer the humanist alternative in any detail. But I may record that in the course of the American Catholic-Humanist Dialogue in New York, 5–7 May 1972, my own dialogue-partner Howard Radest pointed out to me that defiant humanism was not, as I seemed to assume, the only kind of humanism by any manner of means. He thus contributed to the point which I am trying to make here under the topic of transcendence and which can now be stated in summary fashion.

There is a kind of conception of the transcendence of the human spirit in the world which is characteristic of those modern philosophies whose exponents insist that they are primarily humanist and only incidentally atheistic. Taking the human being as it is in this world as they find it, and wishing to promise no more than human vision can truly see, they stress the creativity of the human spirit, its original and inevitable relationship with this concrete world in which it must live and die, its ability within this world to free itself from the bonds and limits which restrain and disfigure it, and they end by hinting – for hint is all one can ever do at this level – at a future in which people can be fully authentic, fully themselves, in which they will take full responsibility for what they are and do (Sartre), in which people will no longer be subjected to others through manipulation of their access to the world from which they all live, but will live instead in the full dignity of communal self-determination, and consequently in peace and prosperity (Marx). The more general Humanist Association's eschaton is characteristically more concrete and prosaic: a world government policing the peace of the world and the concrete benefits for all which modern science and technology can bring.

What is striking, and important for any Christian apologist to recognize, is that this chorus of voices from the most influential modern philosophies, whatever discordancies can otherwise be detected within it, achieves almost perfect harmony in suggesting that its humanism is no longer a protest against religion, that it is not atheistic first, as it were, and humanist as a reluctant alternative. On the contrary, it finds its strength in the positive humanist visions which it has discovered, and by reference to these it finds religious beliefs either obsolete or irrelevant – in neither case, obviously, requiring any industrious rebuttal. Put in terms of transcendence, the point is that transcendence is adequately intelligible as an essential attribute of the human being, and nothing in the structure of transcendence, despite the variety of its descriptions from these different philosophies, in itself invites any reference to a God beyond humanity. (In fact, concepts of

18

divine transcendence are found by these modern humanists to be persistently inimical to or restrictive of truly human existence: but the prior point about transcendence is the more important.)

2

Christian Secularists and the Case for God

What, in face of this, are Christian theologians doing today? In one way the answer is: as usual, everything. Many, like Hartshorne, insist that despite Kant and Hume the question of natural theology is still open, and with various modifications of procedure and weighting of results they reissue versions of the ontological argument and of those other types from which some element of the ontological is probably never entirely absent.[25] At the other extreme hardliners like Barth have kept alive the total refusal of any 'natural' contribution whatever to the human encounter with the one, true God.[26] It is not necessary to deny those portions of the truth undoubtedly contained in these two options in order to concentrate here on an option of a somewhat different kind which seems to have gained considerable currency on the contemporary scene and which seems at first sight to be specifically designed to meet the kind of secular humanism with which some previous pages have been engaged.

This option seeks a *via media* between the classical efforts to prove God's existence (or at least to prove it the more probable explanation of the world we know),[27] on the one hand, and the refusal of neo-orthodox Protestantism, on the other, to have anything whatever to do with natural theology.[28] It seeks to invite from the modern experience of secularity a positive response to what it hopes to show are intimations of divinity within that very experience itself, and to do this without the use of either the coercion of logic or the threat of damnation. It has all the more claim upon our attention because of the fact that the group which presents it straddles the boundaries of countries and churches, though lines of mutual influence cannot always be discovered between the scattered members of the group. It seems to be a reaction to the modern crisis of religious belief that has arisen spontaneously from independent sources, and that is yet sufficiently homogeneous to allow its general lines to be described as follows.

First, the experience which the new apologists hope will be recognized by all their contemporaries and from which they hope to lead some at least to religious faith is sometimes described as secularist, sometimes as humanist. And since Langdon Gilkey's *Naming the Whirlwind* is perhaps the most thorough and extensive product of this new apologetic, we may take the description of secularity from him. The secular spirit, he believes, is characterized by four basic elements: contingency, relativism, temporality and autonomy. Contingency refers to that character of things by which they just happen to be, and might just as well not be. It states at once their factuality, and that there is nothing necessary about them: as Sartre once wrote, 'uncreated, without reason for being, without any connection with another being, being-in-itself is *de trop* for eternity'.[29]

What contingency is to existence, relativism is to truth. What is thought to be true or right seems, in the light of our accumulated knowledge of history and cultures, to vary with (to be relative to) the peoples, times, places and circumstances of its origin. Some bury their dead, some eat them. To each in turn, as Herodotus once observed, the practice of the other is equally repugnant. Temporality names a more comprehensive condition which affects both existence and truth. There is a time for everything and a time-limit to everything, a time to live and a time to die, a time to sow and a time to reap, a time to build and a time to tear down. On its negative side temporality means that all things must pass. On its positive side, at least in the common linear conception of time in the West, temporality means that all things pass on to other, newer (and better?) things in an evolutionary and historical sequence towards an apparently limitless future.

Autonomy, then, names the most comprehensive condition of all, suggesting as it does that existing things, theories of truth and right, evolutionary sequences, are all a law unto themselves, independent of any higher law or entity; in Gilkey's words:

the sense that our environment, taken even in its widest sense, exhibits neither a holy eternal order, as it seemed to the Greeks, nor one eternally willed by a holy sovereign Lord, as in the Biblical tradition, and our life, therefore, is not dependent on a sacred order or a transcendent divinity for either its existence or its meaning. Rather, what is *real* in our universe is only the profane, the contingent, blind causes that have produced us, the relative social institutions within which we live, the things and artifacts that we can make, and our relations to one another.[30]

Next, the modern person is asked to inspect more closely the shape of this common experience, so that the introduction to limit language can take place and the ambivalence of limit-language can be fully exploited. If the existence which supports all we do seems itself unsupported, as Küng puts it;[31] if the partial meanings we find seem to be adrift on a larger sea of meaninglessness, and the evolution of which we are so actively and apparently purposefully a part seems ultimately aimless, we do become critically aware of limits and at the same time we become aware, as Feuerbach knew, of our ability to look beyond them. In short we become aware of our transcendence.

At this point, according to our apologists, a critical question becomes absolutely unavoidable for all; but at this point also it becomes difficult to give a common account of their progress, for some more than others attempt to shape the very question in the obvious direction of the 'answer' they desire to hear. The question, in Küng's terms, is this: is supporting reality itself supported; can partial meaning ever be complete; does evolving life have ultimate aim? Küng's terms are chosen here because Küng's stance is the most neutral. If ultimate support, meaning and goal (or value) is not immediately detectable within the premise-experience of our existence in the world – and from the usual description of that secular experience it is not – then the atheist's decision to believe that there is no such ultimate is clearly incontrovertible in itself. Küng would simply want to insist that the religious person's decision to see in that which is partial the promise of the ultimate is equally legitimate. Thus the God-question remains open and through that opening Christian discourse can gain entry to the modern debate about life.

The others are less neutral. Rahner is most simplistic of all. Having described the native transcendence of the human spirit in very general terms akin to those above, he just seems to want to move us gradually and imperceptibly, with the help of an implicit threat, to the acknowledgment that in this experience of transcendence we actually encounter, however anonymously, the Transcendent (i.e. God).[32] It would be too facetious to describe this as the argument from Capitalized Letters, but it would also be dishonest not to admit that the imperceptible progress from human transcendence to a divine Transcendent covers an enormous and unjustified leap of faith which is not at all to be taken for granted in a work which lays such stress on reason and evidence.

The threat to the effect that if we do not agree that we encounter God in our sense of transcendence we face ultimate emptiness is even less veiled and more developed in Gilkey's work. 'This dimension of ultimacy,' he writes, 'appears *directly* in the awareness of an unconditioned void, and a dim but powerful awareness of this negative context of ultimacy is the source of our common traits of fanaticism, frantic striving, meaninglessness and boredom, and terror at death and at the future.'[33] However, in that confidence of ours which survives all the limitations of and threats to our existence, meanings and values, when 'the unconditioned dimension of existence. . . is experienced indirectly in the joyful wonder, the creative meanings, and the resolute courage of life despite its obvious contingency, relativity and temporal character',[34] the source of faith in God is found.

This ineluctable confidence as a source of faith in face of ambivalent limits quite similarly described and analysed looms even larger in David Tracy's *Blessed Rage for Order*. Tracy in fact describes the faith of secularity as the fundamental attitude which affirms the ultimate significance and final worth of our lives, our thoughts and actions, here and now, in nature and history.[35] This same confidence plays the major positive role also in Ogden's argument. In fact Ogden informs us: 'I hold that the primary use or function of "God" is to refer to the objective ground in reality itself of our ineradicable confidence in the final worth of our existence.'[36]

Ogden, of course, is aware of the danger of linking the term 'God' so closely to the reality of undying human confidence: this opens up the prospect of what can only be called relativity at the top. Whatever I make the object of my most unflagging trust becomes my god. As Ogden himself remarks, 'the reason "there may be so-called gods in heaven or on earth" is that man is continually endowed with the freedom to invest any of the things in the world with the divine significance that, in reality and for the witness of Christian faith, belongs to God the Father alone'.[37] Which leads us to the third part of this new apologetic on which comment is necessary here, a part which reveals even more variation of opinion than the second part; this third part deals with the relationship to the Father of Our Lord Jesus Christ of this God in whom, it is alleged, we are enabled to believe by the experience of secularity itself, and it is therefore the part which is most important to us in this particlar context.

Küng once more is inclined to make the least claims for this God in whom our radical experience of being human in this world allows us to believe. Such secular faith, even if it should emerge, leaves our ideas of God riddled with ambiguity, and this ambiguity Küng illustrates at length from the history of philosophy and of more general culture.[38] Rahner, who is much more anxious than Küng that the experience of human transcendence should be identified with the experience of God, is not much less anxious than Küng to prevent any immediate identification of this God with the God of Christian experience. In our most fundamental encounter with God through the experience of transcendence, he argues, we are still not sure whether this Transcendent Being remains remote and indifferent, or if it does come close to us, whether it will come in loving mercy or destructive judgment. Only Christian faith can assure us on such essential issues, and reasons for accepting Christian faith are additional to those given for basic faith in God.[39] Ogden, as we saw, is painfully aware of the propensity of the human spirit, when it does believe in gods, to fashion false gods and engage in destructive idolatry. In face of this open possibility he seems satisfied to profess that belief in the God of Christianity necessarily precludes belief in other gods and lords: 'To affirm that Jesus Christ is Lord is to affirm that the *final promise* in which we place our confidence is none of the many promises of the so-called gods of heaven and earth, but solely the promise of God's unending love to all who will but receive it.'[40]

Such distinction of God-concepts or experiences of gods, such caution about the faith made possible by secularity, is not quite as evident in Gilkey, and it is almost entirely inoperative in Tracy. Gilkey shows little hesitation in describing Christian symbolism simply as 'talk about the divine as it appears in and to us in our experience of finite things as contingent, relative, temporal and autonomous beings . . . we use the "Biblical" and "Christian" verbal symbols . . . as means with which to conceive the ultimacy and sacrality that appears in all of existence. . . . Christian God-language is language descriptive of the ultimate which grounds and limits us, but that ultimate apprehended and understood through these symbols.'[41]

With Tracy the qualifying power of that last 'but' has practically disappeared. For he operates with two sources of investigation, the one working through analysis of the experience of secularity, the other through conceptual reduction of the symbols of the Christian tradition; and then he seeks a way of correlating the results. Rejecting specifically Tillich's method of correlation which allowed philosophical reflection to raise to consciousness the existential question but reserved to Christian revelation the power to offer the answering faith,[42] Tracy relates common experience and Christian faith quite neatly through the 'claim that nothing less than a proper understanding of those central beliefs – in "revelation", in "God", in "Jesus Christ" – can provide an adequate understanding, a correct "reflective inventory", or an existentially appropriate symbolic representation of the fundamental faith of secularity'.[43] The investigation of the truth-claims of experience, then, and the investigation of the inner meaning of the major symbols that make up the Christian tradition, coincide in results, the latter providing the adequate symbolism for the former. If one searches through his book for some suggestion that the Christian tradition has anything more than this to offer, one will have to be satisfied with sentences such as this: 'To speak of the truth of the proclamation of Jesus the Christ renders more factual, more representative, more human one's basic faith in the God who always and everywhere is manifested.'[44]

Undoubtedly there is a great deal to be said for this modern apologetic – and there is much more literature of a similar kind – which deserves more constructive critical comment than could possibly be offered here. In this context, our interest must be confined to one kind of query. In view of the dominant modern forms of what some Christians would simply like to call atheism, and in view of the contemporary form of Christian apologetic which appears to take this secular humanism most seriously, what opening, if any, is there for the Christian doctrine of the Trinity? Does not this doctrine now seem to represent some supererogatory credal matter of no particular urgency; not, at least, until well after basic religious faith has been secured? To put the matter more crudely, are we just a little like the barkers outside the strip-joints down Broadway in San Francisco who tell you that the first drink is free, but omit to mention that when you get inside you must accept two drinks at a time, and the 'second' one costs three times the normal price of the 'first'? Or, alternatively, is Trinity another of these 'adequate symbols' reducible by neat conceptual analysis to the basic religious faith which our Christian apologists would like to believe stems from the very experience of secularity?

It is interesting to recall that at least one philosopher of renown and one Christian theologian of almost equal renown have deplored all attempts to talk about God, even initial attempts, which do not take account of the doctrine of the Trinity. Hegel blames the 'rationalistic' philosophers of the Enlightenment, for instance, for producing to their fellow-men a God who was 'hollow, empty, and poor', stressing, as they did, his infinity in all that pertained to him, and, on the negative side, the inapplicability of all attributes humanly applied. Hegel's own philosophy, on the contrary, takes into account those concrete determinations of divinity which the Christian creeds supply, and amongst these, like a coping stone of the system, the doctrine of the Trinity.[45] Calvin anticipated one of Hegel's adjectives in making a similar, if more theologically threatening point. The revelation of the Trinity of 'persons' Calvin considers to be no less than the one, true God's own way of distinguishing himself from idols. And unless we keep this definitive understanding of God as Trinity constantly in mind, 'only the bare and empty name of God flits about in our brains, to the exclusion of the true God'.[46]

Such boldness on behalf of a distinctively Christian doctrine of God would, if taken seriously, surely encourage us to turn the tables on recent Christian apologists. If the effect of the new apologetic was to make us think of postponing any consideration of the doctrine of the Trinity, perhaps to make us feel a little embarrassed about it, embarrassed perhaps even to the point where we would consider a conceptual reduction of the doctrine to a more analytically austere and logically derived Ground of our confidence or Transcendent Horizon of our transcendence, we may now be emboldened to ask instead the following two questions.

Whether theologians specifically keep its distance from the

Triune God of the Christians (as Küng and Rahner do) or simply borrow Christian titles for it with any or no degree of logical justification (as do the others), is the idea of God directly derivable from the experience of secularity any less hollow, empty or poor than the God of the philosophers about which Hegel complained? It will not be sufficient in answer to this question to criticize roundly the god of traditional metaphysics and then to change to a more acceptable idea of God. Hartshorne, for instance, has this to say about classical theism:

> If we abstract from God's contingent qualities, with respect to the rest of his reality we can view classical theism as largely correct. Here indeed is the uncaused cause, impassible, immutable, and all the rest of it. Only it is not God, nor – in spite of Thomism – is it an actuality, 'pure' or otherwise; rather, it is a mere abstraction from the contingent and caused actuality of the divine life. To identify God with this abstraction seems a philosophical species of idolatry. God is no such abstraction. He remains entirely free, in his full reality to be receptive, enriched by his creatures, perpetually transcending himself, a genuinely active and loving subject, sympathetic companion of all existence. Eternally fixed, immune to influence, and incapable of increase is only the generic divine trait of universal interaction, unsurpassable in scope and adequacy – just what is properly meant by calling God 'all-knowing', 'all-powerful', 'ubiquitous', also unborn and immortal. These abstractions come to the same thing. But they are empty by themselves. It is vain to interact universally and always, but with nonentity, or to have unsurpassable knowledge, but of no other individual than self. But this emptiness is precisely what classical theism spoke of as God when it declared him absolutely and in all respects immutable and independent of the world. If love of the highest kind is ultimate, then so is the social interdependence of which it is the ideal form.[47]

Tracy appeals enthusiastically to Hartshorne.[48] Ogden expects from a conception of God which is 'in principle dipolar' something that traditional metaphysical conceptions could never achieve.[49]

Now this is all very well; we shall later see much reason to criticize the view that no real relation from God's side binds God to creatures (except that we shall meet this view precisely in tracing the development of the doctrine of the Trinity). But the question must still be asked – and this is the second question – how has this more relevant concept of God been derived? In Hartshorne's case it seems clear that he attempts to derive it by logical argument quite similar to that used by classical theism for its own (mistaken) concept of divinity.

Now, naturally, the suggestion that much the same logical moves as those used in classical theism will this time round yield much more acceptable results is quite problematic in itself. But the case is far worse for the modern apologist who would reject classical theism, logical moves as well as conclusion, and try to found his newly relevant concept of God squarely and solely on analysis of the experience of integral secularity. He must surely recall at this point the secular humanists of some pages back whose secular faith, in their own view, makes God either obsolete or irrelevant. He must surely anticipate that these will suspect him of changing the concept of God derived from traditional Christian arguments and evident in most traditional Christian theology, of doing this simply to avoid the 'inhuman' aspects of Christian theism which their sustained critique has forced even Christians to acknowledge, and of then finding himself reduced to the pathetic strategy of trying to derive this more relevant concept of God from the very analysis of secularity which had given rise to modern impressions of the obsolescence or irrelevance of all religious belief.

One of the most powerful philosophies produced in this modern era, we have already noted, has been Ernst Bloch's philosophy of hope. It represents the secularization of the human dimension of hope – that most neglected dimension of the human spirit's presence in the world – as men like Feuerbach and Marx had already secularized the human dimensions of faith (knowledge) and charity (practical commitment). It thus represents the completion of the secularization process, and most of the current Christian emphasis on the theology of hope and on eschatology has been derivative from or in imitation of this rather than an answer to it. Many people are at a loss to decide whether Bloch is really a Marxist or not; and one of the most intriguing introductions written for a modern book is quite at a loss to explain why he cannot be called a Christian.[50] So little does a conceptual analysis of the modern secular experience – even one which focusses specifically on the future horizons of human transcendence and the hope and trust which drives towards these – facilitate religious belief rather than lead to an agnostic or atheistic humanism.

Thrown into this world, abandoned here, as Heidegger would say, at work here, creative and free, unguided and unlimited by any absolute truths or principles, unimpressed by either promise or threat, capable of love as well as hatred and even of self-sacrifice to the causes of which it can conceive, and destined for death, the human spirit has been on pilgrimage since it first evolved in this universe and it is on pilgrimage still, sustained by a hope in its own uncertain future, a hope that is as such a part of its very make-up and as indestructible as itself (though no more indestructible than it itself is). So the modern humanist sees it, and seeing it so, sees no reason why he should not be agnostic or atheistic, though neither stance represents the primary intent of his existential analysis.

Here, then, is the first problem for the Christian doctrine of Trinity today. Will it prove an unwelcome additional complication in the Christian effort to meet the case of the contemporary secular humanist? Or could it perhaps, on the contrary, point to such an image of God, and to the adequate source for belief in such a God, as would at once correct the vagaries in the Christian presentations of God both ancient and modern, and give pause to the modern humanist who still wishes to conclude that the Christian concept of God is, like all others, obsolete or irrelevant?

3

The Living God of Judaism and of Islam

Even if the doctrine of the Trinity could be recovered so as to correct Christian mistakes and to engage the secular humanists of our time in dialogue once more, it is not at all clear that such success could be regarded as an unqualified one. It is becoming clear that we Christians owe to Judaism more than an abject apology for the utterly inhuman and entirely unjustifiable ways in which we have treated its followers down through the ages. There is, in addition, the more strictly theological problem of explaining, as they might put it, how we took a God-fearing Jewish man and made him into a new religion.

In the case of Islam we should not, of course, be motivated simply by the political desire to be associated with a religious tradition which, despite some recent aberrations, has somehow found the power in the modern world to resist the imperialism of capitalists and communists alike – though we might indeed do well to inquire more closely after the source of such power. For here again a theological problem of a very fundamental kind lies waiting for solution. For although the *Holy Qur-an* reveals that those who are nearest in love to the true Believers are 'those who say "We are Christians" ',[51] and although it appears to accept that the one, true God revealed himself and his will to Christians through Jesus (as he did to Jews through Moses), and that Christians are therefore in some sense 'people of the Book',[52] it appears equally convinced that only in itself is now to be found the perfect revelation of God's will, for Christians have corrupted this in their own traditions, not least, as we shall shortly see, in their teaching on the divinity of Jesus and their consequent doctrine of the Trinity.

In both cases, Judaism and Islam, we are surely urged by the broader ecumenical demands of our divided and dangerous world, for if the three branches of the most dominant Western religious tradition cannot come together, what hope remains that more extensive religious *rapprochement* might one day contribute to peace and unity and human fulfilment in this world?

It is significant that in both cases, Judaism and Islam, the challenge comes not directly to the doctrine of the Trinity as such, or at least not usually so,[53] but to the divinization of Jesus from which this doctrine in fact did historically develop. Pneumatology, the theology of the Holy Spirit, as we shall see later, always played a minor role, as confusing as it was nevertheless essential, in this development.

From the Jewish side Geza Vermes has recently attempted to occupy the most neutral position possible for him, arguing for 'neither the Christ of the Church, nor yet the apostate and bogey-man of Jewish popular tradition'.[54] This neutral position is the historian's hunting-ground, and although Vermes seems simply to want to distinguish the '*historical* significance of words and events recorded in the Gospels,' of which the historian is in pursuit, from what these are believed to signify, which is the preserve of the theologian, he has quite clearly convinced himself of a 'total lack of proportion between history and theology, fact and interpretation'.[55] Basing his conclusions on a life-long study of ancient sources both from Palestine and from the Diaspora roughly contemporary with the origin of Christianity, he claims that Jesus finds his true historical place amongst the venerable company of the Devout, the ancient *Hasidim*.

> The positive and constant testimony of the earliest Gospel tradition, considered against its natural background of first-century Galilean charismatic religion, leads not to a Jesus as unrecognisable within the framework of Judaism as by the standard of his own verifiable words and intentions, but to another figure: Jesus the just man, the *zaddik*, Jesus the helper and healer, Jesus the teacher and leader, venerated by his intimates and less committed admirers alike as prophet, lord, and son of God.[56]

So reads Vermes's final sentence, and by the time the reader reaches this sentence it has been made abundantly clear that the titles with which the sentence concludes were normal honorary

31

titles for such an outstanding representative of the *Hasidim*. In short, nothing in the life of the historical Jesus or in his verifiable self-understanding supports the credal view of him as 'the only-begotten Son of God, begotten of his Father before all worlds, God of God, Light of Light, very God of very God, begotten, not made, being of one substance with the Father, by whom all things were made'. The latter is the Christ of faith, not the Jesus of (his own) Jewish history, and though Christians may believe that the former is identical with, or at least legitimately developed from, the latter, such a belief cannot rest on what the historian can find to be true of the life and person of Jesus himself.

It is obvious, of course, that the founder of a religion as important and impressive as Christianity cannot be simply submerged in a group, even one as exemplary as the ancient *Hasidim*. And Jewish authors have a number of explanatory theses to cover this historic eventuality. Again amongst the more polemically neutral of these, Vermes suggests that the uniqueness of Jesus lay in his teaching, in his perception of the true relationship between God and man, and in his way of identifying himself with the pariahs of this world. In this thesis Vermes claims some precedent in the work of Joseph Klausner, who wrote fifty years earlier: 'In his ethical code there is a sublimity, distinctiveness and originality in form unparalleled in any other Hebrew ethical code; neither is there any parallel to the remarkable art of his parables.'[57]

The alternative, or perhaps the complementary thesis attributes the Christian divinization of Jesus, and hence the origin of the specifically Christian religion, to the influx of pagan, non-Jewish concepts such as that of the incarnation of a pre-existent Son of God, and often picks on Paul's theology as the prime occasion for this theological intrusion. So Schoeps sees in this Son of God belief 'the sole, albeit decisive heathen premise of Pauline thought. All that belongs to and flows from it . . . is un-Jewish and akin to heathen ideas of the time.'[58] Whatever the precise form of the thesis, most Jewish authors who have written on the subject of Jesus in modern times with as much objectivity as they thought their scholarly profession required have, like Samuel Sandmel,[59] seen in the growing belief in the divinity of Jesus the parting of the ways with Judaism and consequently with their own willingness to accept, in varying degrees, the religious significance of Jesus the Jew.

This position could be summarized quite simply by saying that

Jesus is acceptable as a true prophet of God, a true son of God issuing a true word of God in the acceptable Jewish sense of such claims, but that any attempt to divinize Jesus offends against the austere monotheism which is the very essence of their religious faith. Significantly enough, much the same summary could represent the basic attitude to christology of Islam. The *Holy Qur-an* accepts Jesus as a true apostle, one truly sent by God, and his followers, consequently, as people on the true path of salvation.

> Those who believe (in the *Qur-an*)
> And those who follow the Jewish (scriptures)
> And the Christians, and the Sabians –
> And who believe in God
> And the Last Day,
> And work righteousness,
> Shall have their reward
> With their Lord.[60]

Jesus himself was the apostle of God, and may even be called God's Word, or a Spirit proceeding from God: but no more.

> O people of the Book
> Commit no excesses
> In your religion: nor say
> Of God aught but the truth.
> Christ Jesus the son of Mary
> Was (no more than)
> An Apostle of God,
> And His Word,
> Which He bestowed on Mary,
> And a Spirit proceeding
> From Him: So believe
> In God and His Apostles.[61]

Clearly the *Holy Qur-an* considers the idea of God having a son in the literal sense quite incompatible with the strict monotheism of its own revelation – though the only problem it seems to have with Jews and Christians calling themselves sons of God metaphorically is that they are such obvious sinners.[62]

> For God is One God,
> Glory be to Him:
> (Far exalted is He) above
> Having a son. To Him
> Belong all things in the heavens
> And on earth. And enough
> Is God as a Disposer of affairs.[63]

Therefore,

> In blasphemy indeed
> Are those that say
> That God is Christ
> The son of Mary.
> Say: 'Who then
> Hath the least power
> Against God, if His will
> Were to destroy Christ,
> The son of Mary, his mother,
> And all – everyone
> That is on the earth.'[64]

And there is the key to the Muslim understanding of both Christianity and christology: the sole and sovereign divinity on whose creative will all else depends and in submission to whose will (*islam*) salvation lies. So Jesus, although he is God's Apostle, Word, and Spirit, was created like everything else.

> The similitude of Jesus
> Before God is as that of Adam;
> He created him from dust,
> Then said to him: 'Be'
> And he was.[65]

Jesus himself in fact is called to witness that he never did ask, never could ask people to worship him as a god;[66] on the contrary, Jesus himself served and worshipped God,[67] and on Jesus' own lips are placed the words:

> It is God
> Who is my Lord
> And your Lord.[68]

Finally, God will vindicate Jesus himself on the last day, and exonerate Jesus from any fault in spreading the 'falsehoods of those who blaspheme,'[69] those who 'bear witness that besides God there is another God',[70] even if they do this in the peculiarly Christian manner of having God have a Son.

It is probably worth repeating at this point that these objections drawn from modern Judaism and ancient Islam bear directly on the divinization of Jesus as the origin of the doctrine of the Trinity, rather than directly upon the developed doctrine of the Trinity itself. For the problem of reconciling the developed doctrine of the Trinity with strict monotheism is in a way a purely logical one,

34

and as our brief survey of that developed doctrine will soon indicate, by no means beyond the logical acumen of classical Christian spokesmen. The objections we have just met, however, are far more serious than that. What these objectors cannot see is not something which by some wise logician they could perhaps easily enough be shown; what they cannot see is how a doctrine of the divine Sonship and thus, ultimately, a doctrine of Trinity could ever legitimately derive from the epochal witness of Jesus of Nazareth to the one, true God.

Add one more reflection and the contemporary stage for the discussion of the Christian doctrine of the Trinity is sufficiently set. I do not have the time or the space or, to tell the truth, the expertise to draw out fully the connection between Jewish and Islamic monotheism and the catholicity of their religious goals. It must be enough here to note that the divine revelation which took the form of the very history of the Jews, is considered by Jews to be a light to the Gentiles, a light to the whole world. And Abdullah Yusuf Ali writes in his commentary on Sura III, 85:

> The Muslim position is clear. The Muslim does not claim to have a religion peculiar to himself. Islam is not a sect or an ethnic religion. In its view all religion is one, for the Truth is one. It was the religion preached by all the earlier prophets. It was the truth taught by all the inspired Books. In essence it amounts to a consciousness of the Will and Plan of God and a joyful submission to that Will and Plan.[71]

Now it is not necessary to maintain that Jews and Muslims have done any more for such human ecumenism under the one gracious and merciful God than have Christians, but in view of the specific objections here made it is necessary to ask: does the Christian doctrine of the Trinity not raise such prospects of distinctiveness of religious belief consequent upon such exclusiveness of alleged revelation that the possiblity of such ecumenism must be seriously placed in jeopardy? And is the openness of Jew and Muslim alike to the person whom Christians revere as their founder to be considered dispensable for the sake of that doctrine?

4

The Triune God?

The problem with which the last section ended now seems more like a dilemma. For even if we could make the doctrine of the Trinity point to such an idea of God and to the adequate source of belief in such a God which would at once correct the vagaries in the Christian presentations of God that secular humanists have quite rightly rejected and be of positive interest to secular humanists themselves, would we not at the same time alienate our strongest possible allies in a very secular world? The question, then, with which any contemporary treatment of the doctrine of the Trinity must begin is this: since the doctrine of the Trinity refers to the godward side of Jesus, to the relationship of Jesus to God and to the nature of the God revealed in Jesus, 1. should it put off those who can take Jesus as one sent by God, whose life and teaching revealed the one, true God, and 2. does it need some critical re-evaluation to see (a) why it did put off Jew and Muslim and (b) whether it can lay more claim to the mind of modern humanism than the idols which that humanism now rejects?

PART TWO

The Scriptures

5

The Authority of Scripture

Given the supreme authority accorded to Holy Scripture in all the Christian traditions, it might seem obvious enough that any attempt to research or to reconstruct so central a doctrine as that of the Trinity should begin with the Old and New Testaments, as Christians insist on calling them. And indeed the claims of the obvious will not be denied here. Still, it might be well to pause for some brief critical reflection on the kind of question with which we should approach the Bible, before rushing in amongst the guardian exegetes of these sacred pages and risking systematic dismemberment from their determined, if discordant, possessiveness.

On reflection, then, it is probably not a good idea to approach the Bible with the question: is the doctrine of the Trinity to be found in the Old or New Testament, or in both? For, although up to this point we have continued the convention of referring to the doctrine of the Trinity in the singular, there is probably no such thing as *the* Christian doctrine of the Trinity. One does not need to devote one's life exclusively to the study of the Christian literature of the first five centuries in order to be convinced that the plural, doctrines of the Trinity, represents more honestly than the singular the true state of trinitarian theology in the most creative and formative period. One quickly realizes also that the pluriformity of trinitarian theology is not easily contained in the twin categories, before Nicaea[1] and after Nicaea, or trinitarian theologies of the East and of the West. It is true, as we must soon see, that the Council of Nicaea in AD 325 makes a radical difference in trinitarian thought, but homogeneity is difficult to discover on ether side of it. It is also true that those theologians from East and

39

West who still argue, though more eirenically these days, as to whether the Holy Spirit proceeds from the Father and the Son or from the Father alone (the ancient and infamous *filioque* controversy), commonly find that this particular point of difference itself points to deeper and more pervasive differences in the trinitarian developments of the rival traditions,[2] and one can hardly escape the most cursory perusal of this more ecumenical modern debate about the *filioque* without the impression that both sides are still oversimplifying their inherited traditions, a prospect which seems to be an inevitable part of all controversy and which quite often outlives the more hostile years of the controversy itself.

Theologians and their theologies are noted, of course, for their tendency to differ, and often they are noted for little else. But many who would find the variety in ancient trinitarian theology not in the least surprising, and who would as a consequence prefer to look to the more solemn doctrinal formulae of the Christian church, might in their turn be more than a little surprised at the differences not only in terminology but also in content between successive creeds and numerous conciliar statements, the credal addition of the *filioque* in the West being only the most advertised of these.[3] Again it would not be at all easy to domesticate this variety by insisting on the equivalence of different terms, the necessities of translation, and, in the case of content, the increasing supplement of agreed insights.

Next, by the time the New Testament began to be written, the original revelation of God in Jesus of Nazareth (for those who can take it) was already out at interest in the theological banks. And the New Testament itself provides a further series of examples of this cumulative process. In short, there are probably as many theologies of Jesus of Nazareth in the New Testament as there are distinct authors. This means that, at the very least, our question would have to be reformulated to read: do any of the later trinitarian theologies coincide with any of the theologies of the New Testament (or of the Old Testament, or both)?

Finally, a rather disturbing range of differing opinion is found in fact amongst those authors who do try to answer our question in some such form as: is the doctrine of the Trinity scriptural? A brief but, I hope, representative selection of such authors is all that can be offered here.

A text-book in common use in Roman Catholic seminaries in the 1950s, for instance, answered our question very adamantly in the affirmative, mainly by providing 'proof' of the doctrine of the Trinity in the following manner. Monotheism was asserted, a *catena* of scriptural texts was then offered to show, in sequence, that the Son and the Spirit were (*a*) distinct from the Father and from each other, (*b*) personal beings, (*c*) divine. Ergo, the developed doctrine of the Trinity appeared as an accurate summary statement of such scattered scriptural data.[4] Some Roman Catholic exegetes writing around the same time arrived more hesitantly at much the same conclusion. Although he has no trouble in finding distinct divine personality attributed to Jesus, Ceuppens thinks it would be difficult to show from the Synoptic Gospels that the Spirit was clearly a distinct divine person – unless this could be deduced from the baptismal formula of Matthew 28.19. And although in the Acts of the Apostles and the Pauline epistles much personal language is used of the Spirit – that he examines, witnesses, and so on – Ceuppens feels that all this could be accounted personification, unless, once again, trinitarian-type formulae such as that in II Corinthians 13.13 could persuade us otherwise. But the Fourth Gospel, he feels, particularly with its talk of 'another Paraclete', removes all ambiguity and leaves us with the three distinct divine persons in what we know to be the one God.[5]

Emil Brunner, on the contrary, reads the same scriptural data as follows: 'If the Name "Father" designates the origin and content of the revelation, the Name of the "Son" designates the historic Mediator, and the "Holy Spirit" the present reality of this revelation.'[6] Undeterred by Paul's 'the Lord is the Spirit' (II Cor. 3.17), he insists on distinguishing Son and Spirit as 'the historically objective and the inwardly subjective form of the revelation',[7] and he concludes, 'Through the Spirit we see the Son as the Son of the Father, and through the Son we see the Father as the Father of the Son, and as our Father. The three Names do not stand alongside of one another but after one another.'[8] From the third century onward, however, theology began gradually to misrepresent these alleged biblical data. 'From the time of Origen. . . men's interest was deflected from the historical centre to the eternal background, and then severed from it. People then began to speculate about the transcendent relation of the Three Persons of the Trinity within the Trinity; they were set alongside one another.'[9] And the end result of this? 'The mystery of the Trinity, proclaimed by the Church, and enshrined in her liturgy, from the fifth or sixth century onwards, is a pseudo-mystery, which sprang out of an aberration of theological thought from the lines laid down in the Bible, and not from the Biblical doctrine itself.'[10]

There is hardly any need to pile up references in order to show how popular is this preference for conceiving of the Trinity in terms of a set order: the Father first as the origin and content of revelation, the Son second as the historically objective, and the Spirit third as the inwardly subjective forms of revelation; the Three thus always set, not alongside, but after one another. And there is space at this present juncture to say only this: that although this is a perfectly valid way of construing trinitarian doctrine, it has no more claim to be *the* scriptural doctrine than have many of its rivals. For one thing, subjective-objective distinctions are more than usually questionable here; for another, it is as easy to quote Scripture to the effect that the Father leads us to Jesus as to quote it to the effect that the Spirit enables us to acknowledge him. Brunner's preferred schema may in fact owe as much to Greek emanationist models, as we shall soon see, as it owes to Scripture as such. For it really does represent considerable selection and abstraction from the rich profusion of scriptural data.

Somewhere in between the position of the text-book and that of Brunner stands Barth. The doctrine of the Trinity, in Barth's view of the matter, is neither an aberration of theological thought from lines laid down in the Bible, nor is it to be derived in any direct manner from specific biblical texts. Holy Scripture, rather, testifies to divine revelation (it is not itself identical with divine revelation), and this revelation is the 'ground' of the classical doctrine of the Trinity; that is to say, when we try to interpret and understand that revelation, the result will be the doctrine of the Trinity.[11] This does not mean that we can by analysis break down the concept of revelation into three elements – the revealer, the act of revelation, and its result in the subject to whom the revelation takes place – and thus provide ourselves by our own ingenuity with a doctrine of the Trinity. Much less does it mean that we can, independently of God's revelation in Jesus to which the Bible testifies, find 'traces' of the Trinity in our human experience of being in this world.[12] Rather, the whole biblical testimony to the utter freedom of God's sovereign lordship, and to God's power in this freedom and by this revelation to become the God of concrete individuals,[13] provides the 'ground' and 'root' from which a true Christian doctrine of the Trinity must grow.

'When we ask, who is the self-revealing God? the Bible answers us in such a way that we are compelled to consider the Three-in-oneness of God.'[14] The Bible testifies to God's self-revelation in Jesus. But only God can reveal God.[15] Hence on the biblical testimony we can say that God differentiates himself into Revealer, Revealed (or event of revelation) and Revealedness (or the 'end-result' in human beings): 'to the same God . . . is also ascribed . . . this threefold mode of being'.[16] And so we are authorized to theologize God's three-in-oneness as best we can.

Finally, instead of our finding for ourselves analogies which enable us to comprehend the inner distinctions of the divinity, we shall have to realize, first, that we can never comprehend these in our mortal minds, but, second, that Scripture provides us with a language of differentiation – in terms such as creator, reconciler, redeemer or holiness, mercy, goodness – which will allow us to grasp the distinctions between the 'divine modes of being' in so far as the limits of our creaturely powers of comprehension allow us to grasp what is essentially beyond us.[17] In this rather complex manner Barth admits the biblical origin of the Christian doctrine of the Trinity. We shall have to leave until later some critical comment on Barth's trinitarian theology, if only because it is so very traditional in substance. For the moment let it be taken as yet another example of the way in which the doctrine of the Trinity may be said to be 'contained', either explicitly or implicitly, in the Scriptures.

Now even those who are blissfully unaware, or still unconvinced, of the plurality of both New Testament christologies and trinitarian theologies and doctrines, must at least be given pause by so many and such differing answers to the question about the relationship of trinitarian doctrine to the Bible. And if this pause is to be truly a reflective one it should probably take sufficient time to cover rather carefully at least the following points.

First, the reason why it must seem crucial to tackle in any form the question of the relation of trinitarian doctrine to Scripture is, as hinted at the outset of this section, the normative nature of the Scriptures in all the Christian traditions. It is true that, because of its theology of tradition[18] and its papal polity, the Roman Catholic Church has often been suspected of not accepting the Scriptures as the *supreme* norm in the formulation of doctrine. But it seems best to believe that, despite the different reasons they give for this,[19] thinkers and teachers in all the Christian traditions do accept, and do quite frequently behave as if they accepted, that the Bible provides them with the supreme norm for their faith. It seems fair to observe that the real trouble with the allegedly normative role of Scripture is not with the theories by means of which different traditions have attempted to propose it, but with that part of their practice in which representatives of all the Christian churches are really reading into the Bible doctrinal positions which they uncritically and, often, unconsciously assume to be contained in its pages, rather than reading out of it what is really in it (eisegeting, in short, instead of exegeting).

Now those who do manage in practice to follow out their theory that Scripture is the supreme norm in formulating their faith do also, as a general rule, try to point to the source of that normative status. And when they engage in this further, and very necessary exercise, they are commonly heard to say that the source of the normative status is not found in the letters or words themselves which fill the pages of the Bible, nor in any theory of inspiration conceived as divine dictation,[20] but in the Word at once behind the words and present in the Christian community, in the Spirit within the letter and operative also in the hearts and lives of the readers. It is a pity that, because of the compartmentalizing of Christian theology, such good thinking as this is so often confined to treatises on the inspiration of Scripture. For if, as even its very terms – Word and Spirit – might themselves suggest, it were transferred to our present theological context, to the problem of finding the relationship to Scripture of trinitarian doctrine, it might show us a better way of conceiving of that relationship than my old text-book, or even Barth or Brunner, have managed to do. How so?

Well, when we do take the normativeness of the Scriptures seriously, and we are wondering about the origin of or the authorization for a particular doctrine, and someone points us to the Word behind the words, the Spirit within the letters, it never does any harm to ask what precisely these very inspiring phrases are intended to denote. What is this Word behind the words? What Spirit is thought to be within the letters? Answers to the former question in terms of a 'gospel within the Gospels', or a résumé of the teaching of the Bible are too obviously invitations to arbitrary selectivity. But what of the more obvious answer, in

44

terms of the person who is called in John's Gospel the Word of God? It would still be wise to accept this answer but only as an occasion still to press the question: what precisely is denoted by this term, the Word of God, in this context?

If the reference is primarily to a pre-existent Word of God and to some doctrines about this pre-existent divine being which were either communicated through the human Jesus or derivable from some of his actions (e.g., his miracles), then we are back to some central doctrines, a gospel within the gospel, or a résumé, from which other doctrines, such as trinitarian doctrines, can be derived or of which they are the systematic expression.

If, however, the phrase 'the Word behind the words' refers first and foremost to the historical individual, Jesus of Nazareth, who is believed to be the Word of God *made flesh*, then a different account can be given of the way in which a doctrine such as that of the Trinity can be said to originate in and be authorized by Scripture. That account would run, very briefly, as follows.

Behind the Scriptures, as source of their content and their authority, lies the person of Jesus of Nazareth who is called Word of God (and given so many other titles also), because in him God was, and still is, bringing the world, in reconciliation, to his own original will for it. The pluriformity of New Testament theologies causes no real problem for this account of our inspiring phrase, as well it might do for any of the previous accounts. For nothing is more natural in the case of one who lived in history, and still lives somehow in the community which took origin from him, than that varied accounts should be given of him without any *necessary* incompatibility. Persons who live in history, as opposed to pre-existent beings who are thought to be met primarily through doctrines concerning them, simply invite pluriformity of description and assessment.

There are, of course, problems with this option which we cannot afford fully to go into here. They are varied and formidable problems which cluster under the heading: the quest of the historical Jesus. But even those who have no professional interest or expertise in this difficult quest will have gathered that modern biblical criticism has so insisted that so much of the New Testament states the faith of its authors or of communities from which units of the Jesus-tradition derived, and is so insistent on the pluriformity in the New Testament of these expressions of faith that the prospect of finding behind the New Testament the living, historical person of the Redeemer must be dim indeed.

I can only state here my own conviction that modern literary and historical criticism, which has already achieved so much, should finally find the courage fully to face up to the historical question which lies everywhere just underneath its text. I have argued already that the two most recent types of biblical criticism – form criticism and redaction criticism – are both mutually complementary and in themselves neutral to the prospects of the quest of the founding faith of Jesus of Nazareth.[21] Form criticism and redaction criticism both reveal theological theses or even whole theological systems, the former with its concentration on units of the tradition about Jesus and on their original *Sitz-im-Leben*, the latter with its concentration on the theologies of the authors of the documents we now possess in the New Testament. It is really a drastic error to restrict the quest of the historical Jesus to the few questionable units of tradition which form critics can agree as finding their *Sitz-im-Leben* in the ministry of Jesus himself. It cannot be too often repeated that if Jesus was founder of a faith, as he certainly was, and if he lived and died that faith, as he certainly did, then the only accurate historical accounts of the man's life, death and destiny (not just his teaching) must take the form of theologies, that is, statements about the God that Jesus revealed in his faith and, consequently, statements about Jesus' own relationship to that God. The over-arching task of biblical criticism, then, is to assemble those partial or more elaborate theologies (together, of course, with whatever words and deeds can be traced to Jesus himself) to see if a harmonious portrait of a man of a distinctive faith, a founder and inspirer of that faith, emerges from all the inevitable cultural differences which characterize the different theologies, from the incompatibilities and even from the detectable failures, thus showing us the founder and his faith. Biblical criticism may busy itself with many contributory tasks before facing this over-arching aim, but unless it finally orientates itself to that aim it will have refused half its responsibility.

It would clearly be impossible to go more fully into these problems here without reproducing a whole christology, but there is something that we can do in order to help us to decide how a doctrine of the Trinity might originate from the Bible, and what kind of trinitarian theology the Bible might authorize. We can take the title 'Son', so utterly central to all trinitarian thought (in which it is consistently coupled with the title 'Word'); we can look to the New Testament to see where the main New Testament emphasis lies with respect to this, and to cognate titles, whether it lies on pre-existence or on the historic life, death and destiny of Jesus; and we can in this way glean some genuine biblical directives for the answer to our question about scriptural origin and authorization for any doctrine of Trinity.

Something similar could be said in the case of 'Spirit', and in the case of that other inspiring phrase which explains the normative nature of Scripture: the Spirit behind the letters and in the hearts and lives of Christians. What, more precisely, we must once again ask, does Spirit here denote? Does Spirit here refer to the divine Spirit without more ado, operating in ways which are both indetectable and indescribable on the reader of Scripture as it once operated upon the writers of its component books and letters? And need no more be said? Surely this is not the case. Surely more must be said if the whole distinguishing character of Christianity is not to be passed over in silence at this crucial point. For if a Spirit, described as divine and no more, aids us to interpret a text it has somehow inspired, our search for origins and authorizations of doctrines will lead us back again to the statements we select from the Bible as the gospel within the gospel or as our résumé of the whole.

But the whole thrust of the Christian Scriptures is surely to present the divine Spirit as the *Spirit of Jesus* and in this way, in its pneumatologies, to secure the distinctive character of the faith which stemmed from Jesus. Certainly in presenting the Spirit as the Spirit of Jesus it is asserting the presence in Jesus of God reconciling the world to himself, but it is just as clearly giving concrete detectable content to the kind of Spirit operative in the world which is to be truly thought the Spirit of God: the Spirit behind the letters and in the hearts and lives of Christian believers is characterized by just those features which made up the life and death of Jesus of Nazareth, mainly service, supremely self-sacrificing love (Paul's description of the effects of the Spirit are virtually a character-sketch of Jesus Christ). In a phrase of James Dunn's, 'as the Spirit was the "divinity" of Jesus, so Jesus became the personality of the Spirit'.[22]

If one digs deeply enough, then, into the source of the normative role of Scripture, one may come upon a view of the development

47

of Christian doctrine quite different from that presupposed by any of the authors mentioned above, and better able to cope with the pluriformity both of scriptural christologies and of trinitarian theologies. For the source and authorization of all doctrines is found in the life, death and resurrection of Jesus of Nazareth, and *that* is discernible today primarily in the lives of those who truly follow him. In other words, the source and authorization of all doctrine is in the Spirit which was shaped and bodied forth in the life, death and resurrection of Jesus, and which is still recognizable in the communal life of Christians today. Knowing this Spirit, this life, we can discern it in Scripture, and Scripture in turn can help us discern it more clearly, approach its perfection, cleanse its imperfections. Much the same could be said of doctrines, but Scripture has a superior normative role *vis-à-vis* all subsequent doctrinal formulation, because of its place at the origins of the movement of the risen Lord, of the Spirit of Jesus, through history.

The relationship of doctrine to Scripture, though complex, can then be stated in abbreviated form. It is sometimes described as the relationship between symbolic and the conceptual (between story and system), or between the functional and the ontological (if christologies are uppermost in mind),[23] but it is possibly best to dwell here rather upon the rich variety of theologies in the Bible – if some biblical pneumatologies are, as hinted by Dunn, themselves actually christologies, the variety is even more challenging still to trinitarian doctrine – and to realize that systematic doctrinal formulations, whatever else may be said about them, operate at a certain level of abstraction from the rich profusion of data with which they normally deal, and only because of such absraction do they succeed as systems.

So in the case of trinitarian theologies, *some* of the rich profusion of data occurring round the term 'Son' in Scripture will be combined with *some* of the rich profusion of data surrounding the term 'Spirit', the combined selection abstracted perhaps from a number of different scriptural theologies, and the resulting system will not correspond exactly to any single biblical theology or to any conceivable systematization of all of them (if such a comprehensive system *is* conceivable, which I am inclined to doubt).

The New Testament, with its obvious cultural dependence upon the Old Testament and upon the Hellenistic Judaism of the time of its composition, offers a rich variety of ways of imagining and conceiving what I have termed the godward side of Jesus, the relationship of Jesus to God and the kind of God that Jesus reveals to those who can take it. It represents a specific infidelity to the professed allegiance to the supremacy of Scripture, therefore, to try to constrain that rich diversity within the confines of any systematic doctrine of the Trinity, or, if I am misled about the irreducible pluriformity of such trinitarian systems, within the system of trinitarian doctrine. It would be wrong to start with some trinitarian doctrinal formula and simply use the Scripture to substantiate this: though this is exactly what has been done and still is done by almost all practitioners of the theological art, even the great Augustine.[24] On the other hand, there should be no great difficulty about allowing that systematic doctrine of the Trinity, with its inevitable selection and abstraction from the rich variety of scriptural data (particularly from data surrounding the terms Son, Word, and Spirit), represents a valid insight into the divinity of Jesus and, with due deference to what must be said as yet about doctrine and history, a perennially valid insight.

To put the matter bluntly, a restrictive view or, worse still, an exclusivist view of the orthodoxy of a doctrine of the Trinity is likely to do far more damage to the promising variety of scriptural insights, which offers both the prospect and the example of more ways of talking about God and Jesus than the Christian traditions have as yet either explored or invented, than could ever be done to the orthodoxy of a trinitarian doctrine by the acknowledgment of the richer and more diverse scriptural options. In the final analysis, of course, one may have to recognize that it is the purpose of all doctrinal formulae, as of all scriptural teaching, to point to the living figure of the Redeemer, alive and still active in those who are his followers, and that their ultimate value depends entirely upon the efficiency and accuracy with which they so point.

Instead, then, of beginning with any too general question – is the doctrine of the Trinity contained in the Scriptures? – let us select the two titles which, in addition to the term 'Father' that Jesus used for God, form the permanent nomenclature of all trinitarian thought: Son (Word) and Spirit. Let us search the rich variety of Scripture data on these, noticing in particular, in the case of the former, how much or how little stress is laid on pre-existence, and in the case of the latter, its function in the formulation of alternative christologies. We can in this way provide

49

ourselves with the kind of biblical material which will enable us to assess, when added to other criteria, the overall worth of some of the trinities, or even binities, which we shall later find in the history of Christian theology.

6

The Problem of the Pre-existence of the Son

It is best to begin with this particular problem, not only because there are linguistic difficulties here – as soon as we recoil from the suggestion that something can pre-exist itself we must wonder what exactly, according to this term, pre-exists what else, and in what sense it does so – but because it leads directly into the main difficulties encountered in all incarnational and trinitarian theology. In addition, though biblical scholars are often not slow to suggest that the constructions of the systematic theologian show themselves to have exegetical feet of clay, it does not take a systematician of any extraordinary degree of perspicacity to notice how exegetes themselves are often the unconscious victims in the course of their most professional work of quite dogmatic (that is, uncritical) systematic assumptions.

Take, for example, Martin Hengel's short book with the long title, *The Son of God: The Origin of Christology and the History of Jewish-Hellenistic Religion*, an expanded version of his inaugural lecture at Tübingen in 1973.

Hengel wishes to rebut, once and for all, a prejudice that proved common to some Jewish scholars and some Liberal Protestants that a theology of Jesus as incarnation of a pre-existent divine being represented a Hellenistic (and probably originally a Pauline) accretion, covering over the pristine purity of the purely Jewish faith of Jesus himself, an accretion which Harnack once described as 'the suppression of the historical Christ by the pre-existent Christ'.[25] So he quotes a hymn which Paul himself, he says, quoted to one of the communities of the messianic sect which he

51

had founded in the Roman colony of Philippi (Philippians 2.6–11). Then, without any attempt whatever to say what is meant by this peculiar term pre-existence, and with no effort at all to show that whatever it means is in fact intended by this particular hymn, Hengel adds: 'The discrepancy between the shameful death of a Jewish state criminal and the confession that depicts this executed man as a pre-existent divine figure who becomes man and humbles himself to a slave's death is, as far as I can see, without analogy in the ancient world.'[26] The fact that in the context of the hymn in the actual epistle there is no mention at all of this anonymous 'pre-existent divine figure who becomes man', the fact that the subject of the hymn is specifically named as Messiah Jesus, a man like ourselves 'whose physical brother James', as Hengel remarks, 'Paul himself had personally known well,'[27] must not of course be allowed to hold up the argument.

The first major step in the argument is to show that (*a*) the title Son of God, though quite infrequent in Paul's letters, particularly when compared to the title Lord, is very significant for Paul since he used it at the most solemn moments to describe the whole content of his mission preaching; and (*b*) neither the title itself nor Paul's understanding of it was a Pauline invention. In connection with (*a*), Hengel shows how Son of God in Paul's letters indicates the redeemer of the world and the perfector of creation and history.[28] By combining the deutero-Pauline Colossians 1.13–15, where Son does occur, with I Corinthians 8.6 ('one Lord, Jesus Christ, through whom are all things and through whom we exist'), he suggests that we should understand the idea of the Son of God to include for Paul also mediation at creation; especially since II Corinthians 4.4 calls Christ the image of God, a concept which also at times occurs in the same context with the idea of mediation in creation.[29] So the title Son of God is pivotal for Paul and claims for Christ not only redemption and perfecting, but mediation at creation.

In connection with (*b*), Hengel maintains that Paul could have taken over at his conversion two formulations containing the title Son of God (and his conversion probably took place between AD 32 and 34): 1. the sending of the Son into the world (Rom. 8.3 and Gal. 4.4), for similar formulations are found in John 3.17 and I John 4.9, 10, 14; 2. the giving up of the Son to death (Romans 8.32f.), for a similar formulation is found in John 3.16. The sending of a son to death on a cross, we are then invited to think, is so similar to the thought of the hymn in Philippians (which is still assumed to contain the idea of a pre-existent divine figure) that one conclusion only can follow: Son of God in the tradition received by Paul already referred to this pre-existent divine figure who was sent into the world to the utter humiliation of the cross, and then more than exalted. In Hengel's own words, 'Jesus, the recently crucified Jew . . . is not only the Messiah whom God had raised from the dead, but much more. He is identical with a divine being, before all time, mediator between God and his creatures.'[30]

Now this is an extraordinary sequence of argumentation, not only because it is interspersed with repetition of the word pre-existent, a word that remains merely assumed, carefully undefined, and utterly unjustified, but because the argument finally depends on a hymn which does not use the title Son of God at all to argue the existence of a pre-Pauline understanding of the title which no extant Pauline usage of it reveals. A particularly aggravating example of this kind of special pleading occurs when Hengel deals with Romans 1.3f. Hengel himself reads this text to mean that *by or after his raising from the dead* Jesus Christ was appointed Son of God in 'divine' power and in a 'spirit-like', that is, heavenly mode of being.[31] And yet he insists that the formula in this text, which probably preceded Paul, is understood by Paul 'in terms of the theology of pre-existence which we find, for example, in the Philippians hymn'.[32]

But the really serious question here, of course, as in all substantial cases of biblical exegesis, is the question of the origin of the alleged idea of a pre-existent Son of God. As with all historical ideas, its origin is extremely important to the task of defining its meaning. And to followers of Jesus of Nazareth it is of most particular importance to know if it derived from him, and if so, how; or, if it originated with some of his early followers, what was it about Jesus that justified their use of it.

Geza Vermes, the Jewish scholar, subtitles his book[33] *A Historian's Reading of the Gospels*, and in his chapter on 'Jesus the son of God' he attempts to discover what it was about Jesus himself that accounts for the use of this title for him in the Synoptic Gospels (for which, as a historian, he professes preference). He points out that the Old Testament, as Christians call it, offers three types of son of God: 1. angelic or heavenly beings;[34] 2. Israelites or the people of Israel as such;[35] and 3. kings of Israel.[36] In post-biblical Judaism, he adds, 'whereas every Jew was called *son of God*, the title came to be given preferably to the just man, and in a very special sense to the most righteous of all just men, the Messiah son of David'.[37] He dismisses the relevance to Jesus of texts about angelic or heavenly beings (though some New Testament writers were concerned to place Jesus above such beings), and also texts about the Messiah son of David, because he is concerned with the historical Jesus and he was no royal personage (though, once again, as Vermes knows, Jesus was eventually called Messiah and then the title son of God began to expand accordingly). 'All in all,' he writes, 'it would appear that a first century AD Palestinian Jew, hearing the phrase *son of God*, would have thought first of all of an angelic or celestial being, and secondly, when the human condition was clear, of a just and saintly man. The divine sonship of the Messiah was expected to be within a royal context.'[38]

He challenges the authenticity of the only two texts in the Synoptic Gospels which carry a self-ascription of the title by Jesus: Matthew 11.7 and Mark 13.32. We need not delay on the almost impossible question of whether or not Jesus ever did claim the title himself,[39] though on Vermes's own account of its most probable meaning to Jesus and his circle, which we shall soon see, there would be no reason whatever why he should not claim it – except, perhaps, humility. Suffice it to say at this point that in his own particular section on the title 'the Son', which he maintains cannot be derived from the title Son of God, Ferdinand Hahn uses precisely these two texts and explains them in such a way that they can be seen to reflect Jesus' particular awareness of the Fatherhood of God, or what Vermes calls in other words Jesus' 'own consciousness of an immediate and intimate contact with his heavenly Father'.[40]

The so-called Johannine comet in Matthew 11.27 – 'all things are delivered to me by my Father; and no one knows the Son except the Father, and no one knows the Father except the Son and anyone to whom the Son chooses to reveal him' – is interpreted by Hahn to refer, not to any secret *gnosis* about God now revealed by Jesus, but to a choosing and a legitimation of Jesus by the Father, and correspondingly to an acknowledgment of the Father God in the very being and life of Jesus, a life lived in faithful fellowship and utter subordination of will to the God he called 'Abba'. The other text, Mark 13.32 – 'of that day and hour no one knows, not even the angels in heaven, nor the Son, but only the

Father' – expresses the same total filial subordination from the more negative point of view.[41]

Hengel, too, when he has offered a good deal of what he calls 'dogmatic information' about the application of the title Son of God – much of which we have just seen – and when he turns to find 'good historical reasons' for it, also lists first and foremost Jesus' unique filial relationship to God as Father.[42] We do find, then, as the primary historical basis for the application of the title Son of God to Jesus that unique relationship to God as Father (and consequently to all others as sons and daughters) which this man Jesus not only depicted in the words of his parables and his prayer, but which he lived out 'liturgically' in his table-fellowship and more commonly in his life of service to the needs of others.[43] The fact that the New Testament so frequently describes this service to the needs of others in terms of exorcism and miracle-working leads to the main historical ground, in the view of Vermes, for the application of the title Son of God to Jesus, and for the discovery of the original meaning of this title. Vermes is most expansive on the parallels in contemporary or near-contemporary Judaism to the miracle-working *Hasid* who is commended as son by a heavenly voice, such that even the demons (who can overhear) know him as such and fearfully respect him.[44]

All of this, of course, is a very long way from our pre-existent divine figure who becomes man, since it has to do with a man who was known to have lived and died in unique filial relationship with God, and who was believed to have been raised thereafter to God's own presence. Hence our authors, with varying degrees of acceptance of what they find, are anxious to trace the further layers of meaning which in the course of the earliest Christian history this title did undoubtedly accumulate. So Hahn wants to insist that the earliest application of the title Son of God to Jesus of which we can be sure referred to eschatological function. Jesus had died, but he would return as the Son of God. Quite similarly, the title Messiah was also originally used to preach the triumphant return of the crucified one.[45] Vermes, also, when he tries to plot the development of the title, first lists its association with the recognition of Jesus as the Messiah.[46] He is anxious, however, that we should understand that the use of the title in a Messianic sense – for we are now moving towards the use of the title Son of God as a title for the Messiah son of David who was expected still – cannot be assumed unless it actually accompanies the title

Messiah, since he finds no evidence in his sources that Son of God could stand alone and still bear messianic meaning.[47]

We are not here concerned to decide exactly when the title began to be used, whether by or of Jesus, during his life or only after his death. We are concerned rather with the meaning or meanings which it could have had and with the problem of how these could be justified with reference to Jesus. So let us come to what Hahn calls the common view that just as the title Messiah came to be applied to the presently raised (exalted) Jesus, so did the title Son of God.[48] It is well known that texts from the Old Testament which had their original reference to the enthronement of the Davidic king were used in the early resurrection kerygma. So now the title Son of God, which already indicates a uniquely obedient servant of Yahweh,[49] can be used to claim that this one, so shamefully executed, was God's expected anointed one. But this belief that the one who was obedient unto death was now exalted to God's right hand and would rule God's future kingdom is still a long way from belief in a pre-existent divine figure who becomes a man.[50]

The logical path to alleged pre-existence is a tortuous one no matter what selection of authors we make, and its twists and turns are seldom quite similarly described and interpreted, but we can with fair accuracy and sufficient consensus isolate three stages of this path: 1. biblical talk of sending; 2. the pre-existence of the Messiah; 3. texts which refer to other 'intermediary entities'.

1. Both Hengel and Hahn are agreed on what is surely in any case obvious, namely, that talk of God sending someone does not in itself imply any form of pre-existence of that one.[51] Both allow that an idea of pre-existence (or, as Hahn says, of incarnation) would be previously required before 'sending' texts could be used to substantiate and explain the idea of pre-existence.

2. Son of God is a Messianic title in one form of its usage, we have seen, and as such it was applied to Jesus. Now there was talk in Judaism around the time of Jesus about the pre-existence of the Messiah. Vermes explains: 'Another important strand of messianic speculation turning on the verb, "to be revealed", was in great vogue from the latter part of the first century AD onward. Needless to say, the "revelation" of the Messiah demanded a previous concealment either on earth or in heaven.'[52] But he adds immediately the following cautions: 'The surviving sources are concerned only with a kind of notional pre-existence of the

Messiah in so far as his "name", i.e. his essence and nature, preceded the formation of light by God on the first day of creation. . . . In Jewish thought the celestial pre-existence of the Messiah does not affect his humanity.[53] I am not sure if it has ever been shown that this particular type of messianic speculation influenced directly the meaning or use of our title, but if it did, it clearly does not yet yield a pre-existent divine figure who becomes man. It is part and parcel of the revelation model in human imagining by which God, who is not bound by our time, had in mind in eternity or 'before anything was created' the one who was the key to all existence, who would bring all to consummation, and for whom (in whom, through whom) all could therefore be said to be created.

3. These last phrases lead us really well beyond messianic speculation, into the 'intermediaries' of Wisdom literature which undoubtedly appear also in New Testament christology. In a hymn in Colossians (1.13–16), the beloved Son of the Father is called image of the invisible God, first-born of all creatures, and it is said that in him all things were created. At the opening of the Epistle to the Hebrews it is said of the Son that through him God created the world, that he reflects the glory of God and bears the very stamp of his nature. Such language echoes clearly enough what is said of Wisdom in texts such as Proverbs 8.22 ('The Lord created me at the beginning of his work, the first of his acts of old') and the Wisdom of Solomon 7.25–26 (which calls Wisdom a breath of the power of God, a pure emanation of his glory, a reflection of eternal light, an image of God's goodness). Now this Wisdom material makes one thing at least clear, namely, that here is no concept of a pre-existent divine figure, not at least in the sense in which Hengel talks of 'real' rather than 'ideal' or notional pre-existence,[54] or Reginald Fuller, for instance, talks of 'hypostasizing' rather than merely 'personifying',[55] both in obvious reference to a 'figure' distinct from the Father.

It is instructive to notice that Ben Sira gradually identifies 'pre-existent' Wisdom with the Torah (24.23). And as Hengel remarks, it was necessary to assert the unsurpassability and finality of God's revelation in Jesus of Nazareth over against such mediators of creation and determiners of its destiny.[56] Now language which is designed to suggest that Jesus is truly God's wisdom, law or word is no more open to the implications that a 'real'[57] divine figure, distinct from the Father, pre-existed the human existence of Jesus and became man in him than is talk about God hiding his Messiah in heaven before revealing him on earth. In fact the latter talk is much more likely to yield that implication than is the former, but we have seen that it does not yield it. The transference to Jesus of Nazareth of the models taken from Wisdom literature is clearly designed to say that *he* and not, for example, the Torah, is God's wisdom (or God's word) in the concrete, in the flesh, in this world. And the 'good historical reasons', as Hengel would call them, for this transference must simply refer once again to that distinctive relationship to God and to his fellow men which Jesus lived out in his life and consummated in his death and resurrection, and which forms the ground of our hope for the final salvation of all our world.

It is not possible for those who do not wish to write books as long as Schillebeeckx writes to go through all of the New Testament and to analyse all the so-called pre-existence language. In fact, in order to avoid too much unnecessary repetition in modern christology, the reader can be referred to the extensive analysis of New Testament christologies which makes up almost half of Schillebeeckx's *Christ, the Christian Experience in the Modern World*.[58] For our purposes here it will be sufficient to make three further points, drawing on this work of Schillebeeckx, and to end with some summary conclusions.

First, it does no harm to notice briefly three of the main adjectives which the New Testament attaches to the title Son. There is the obvious *agapetos*, beloved, which simply means the reciprocal side of that total commitment of Jesus to the God he called Father.[59] Then there is *prototokos*, first-born, which always seems to carry comparative meaning; that is to say, Jesus is compared to some set of people or things and placed before them or at their head. He is firstborn of many brothers (Rom. 8.9), of all creation (Col. 1.15), of the dead (Col. 1.18; Rev. 1.5). Even Hebrews 1.6, which does not embody the adjective in any comparative phrase, in the context sets the Son before all the angels, who must worship him. And then there is *monogenes*,[60] which the Latin Vulgate, following Jerome, translates *unigenitus*, or only-begotten, and which need not mean that at all. The adjective intends to distinguish one (Son) as unique (amongst others of that genre); it does nothing of itself to suggest that the son in question is the only son. Hence, as Schillebeeckx points out, this characteristically Johannine adjective for the Son offers 'no basis in

Johannine theology for the later scholastic theology of the procession of the Son from the Father within the Trinity *per modum generationis* (by birth)'.[61]

Second, I should say something, however briefly, about Johannine theology, if only because this is commonly regarded as the 'highest' christology of all the New Testament and the one most frequently called in evidence in all subsequent trinitarian theology.

There should be no doubt in anyone's mind about the obvious fact that the subject of John's Gospel is Jesus the Messiah (John 1.17) or, in terms used in the Letters of John, that 'which we have heard, which we have seen with our eyes, which we have looked upon and touched with our hands' (I John 1.1). Jesus Messiah is described in that last text and in the Prologue to the Gospel as the *logos*, the word. Nowhere else, even in Johannine literature, and with the exception of Revelation 19.13,[62] is he so described. Now one does not have to enter into the tortuous argument about the underlying hymn and its place and date of origin before it was transformed into the Prologue to the Fourth Gospel, in order to be allowed to say that there is no problem about reading the application of the title Word to Jesus according to the same model of Jewish Wisdom speculation which we have already seen.[63] This Word, like Wisdom, was with God in the beginning and through it all things were made. Nothing more can be derived from the phrase 'the Word was God' than can be derived from the rest of the Gospel for, after all, whatever its original basis, the hymn in the prologue is now the prologue to the Fourth Gospel and in this form it contains no independent christology. As Schillebeeckx says:

> Throughout this Gospel the evangelist is not interested in the salvation-historical phases of the manifestation of the Logos: over primal chaos, in the world, in 'his own' and finally in Jesus. Yet at the same time it is impossible to ignore these phases. They come together only in the prologue . . . *along with* the historical manifestation of the Logos, Jesus of Nazareth. This particular kind of thinking on a variety of levels is peculiar to the Fourth Gospel. The whole event expressed in the prologue *is* the event of the appearing of Jesus on earth. The Gospel of John speaks of *Jesus of Nazareth* when he appeared on earth.[64]

And the main body of the Gospel itself, where the title Son takes over from the title Word? Schillebeeckx insists that the Fourth Gospel does indeed introduce 'a new feature in the New

Testament'.[65] In the terms of our discussion, there is here something other than the 'notional' pre-existence of eschatological
revelation models. There is the language of descent from the
heavenly spheres (*epourania*) to the earthly spheres (*epigeia*), from
the sphere of God to that of humans. But the subject of this
descent is still Jesus of Nazareth. The model is now the spatial
model, but we shall see that this is the symbolic equivalent of the
temporal model of pre-existence. In any case, where there is talk
of the one who exists in the heavenly spheres and of actual
descent of this 'one from above', the subject is still not a real
'person' or *hypostasis* distinct from Jesus, who only by taking on
flesh or a human nature became Jesus of Nazareth. The subject,
one must repeat, is Jesus whom they had seen and touched, and
the model now used to depict this Jesus as the the definitive
revelation of God's nature and will is one which was also current
at the period in question, as Schillebeeckx amply illustrates.[66] This
means that, resisting the persistent temptation to profess that the
definitive revelation of God and their salvation had come from
any of the 'ideal' or 'real' types of heavenly being of current
religious speculation, the Johannine theologians, like the others
who composed the New Testament, continued the offence and
the folly that the executed Galilean was all this. In other words,
the use of these models by the followers of Jesus of Nazareth was
in every case their most radical transformation.

If we did then go outside that New Testament material which
deals in the titles Son of God or Word, we should no doubt find
the same transformative process at work. For instance the impressive saying of the Johannine Jesus: 'Your Father Abraham
rejoiced that he was to see my day; he saw it and was glad' (John
8.56) reminds us that the Old Testament and its major figures are
witnesses to Jesus – and witnesses 'see' and 'hear' that to which
they give their witness.

Two verses later we find the Johannine Jesus adding the claim:
'before Abraham was, I am,' and this introduces the need of
explaining what the Fourth Evangelist wished to convey when he
made Jesus use the divine 'I AM'. There are probably two sets of
texts to be distinguished in answering this question: those in
which the 'I AM' has an object (I am the Good Shepherd, for
instance), and those in which it stands unqualified (in addition to
John 8.58, perhaps John 18.5–6 and 6.21). The first set of texts is
obviously reminiscent of Old Testament texts in which Yahweh

is described, for instance, as the shepherd of Israel, and the second set recalls even more strongly not only the divine self-ascription of some form of 'I AM' in Exodus 3.14, but probably other echoing texts such as Isaiah 51.12; 43.10, 25. A thorough-going exegesis would probably have to separate these two sets of texts and attempt consecutive assessments of their full christ-ological implications,[67] but it is surely sufficient for our purposes at this point to return to my previous assertion that the subject of whom these identifying or revelatory claims are made in the Fourth Gospel is Jesus the Messiah, the one who walked amongst his fellow Jews and on whose very human lips these extraordinary claims are placed. That they have to do with what later was called the divinity of Jesus (however we may more fully explain that phrase) is obvious; that they must refer to a pre-existent divine figure who later became Jesus is at no stage necessarily implied in their Johannine deployment.

But we may take as our final example and the substance of this third point a text with which we, and Hengel, began this section, a text which does not use the title Son of God at all, but which is seldom absent from discussions of pre-existence: the hymn in Philippians 2.6–11. The subject in question here, as I have already stressed, is Messiah Jesus, who (and then the hymn proceeds),

> Though he was in the form of God (*en morphe theou*)
> did not count equality with God (*to einai isa theo*) a thing to be grasped,
> but emptied himself
> taking the form of a slave,
> being born in the likeness of man, and found in human form
> he humbled himself,
> and became obedient unto death,
> even death on a cross.
> Therefore God has highly exalted him,
> and bestowed on him a name which is above every name,
> that at the name of Jesus every knee should bow
> in heaven and on earth and under the earth,
> and every tongue confess that Jesus Christ is Lord,
> to the glory of God the Father.

Now there is no doubt about the fact that, as Schillebeeckx maintains, this hymn in its present form can be quite adequately and intelligibly intepreted in terms of: 1. Genesis 1.26, where God makes man in his own image and likeness; 2. Psalm 8.4–6, about making man a little less than the *'elohim*; 3. Jewish theology of the king as 'the man' or 'the Adam' and even member, with the angels, of the heavenly court; and 4. the suffering servant material from Deutero-Isaiah. From this background the subject of the hymn, Jesus, though Messiah, did not grasp at the exalted status of the *'elohim*, but was born and 'found' as an ordinary mortal, the slave (as it was then thought) of those angelic powers which envied man and/or ruled the world, and being just this ordinary man, quite empty of that exalted status of the kingly sons of God, he then humbled himself to the very death of a criminal slave on a cross. Therefore, God exalted *Jesus*: no pre-existent divine figure resumed its original status.[68]

The point here is not how exactly these distant writers envisaged the beings and entities they describe as intermediaries between God and human beings either at creation or for final salvation: Wisdom, Logos, Michael-Melchisedek, Enoch, and so on. Whether they realized that they were using imaginative symbols to express belief and hope in God, or whether they thought some of these had individual and 'real' existence in the heavenly spheres, is not of any great importance to us at this point of time.

And the point is not really that if we find each and every model used in New Testament christology already in use in the context of some other religious philosophy or myth, we are destined to see the christology of the followers of Jesus of Nazareth disappear entirely into the incredibly varied fragments of some ancient and extremely complicated syncretism; for we have already insisted that each model taken over was radically transformed towards a new meaning in the process. The real question then is: from where did this new and transforming meaning come and what was it? That is an historical question. It cannot be answered, as Hengel and Hahn and so many others try to answer it, by pointing first to the historical witness of the life of Jesus of Nazareth to a unique lived relationship simultaneously with the God he called Father and with others as God's children, and then searching through the christological models used in the New Testament to find when pre-existence emerges and when, in Hengel's terms, it becomes 'real' rather than 'ideal', or, in Hahn's terms, when it finally implied 'physical sonship', 'sonship of nature rather than function'. The models used, since they are all of non-Christian origin, cannot supply the material which will itself transform them into christologies for Jesus-followers. And when we search back in the tradition to find the incredibly new thing which transforms all previous (and subsequent) models of religious faith, we find the man who, out of his intense relationship with the God he uniquely understood as Father, lived as a servant of his fellows, who, consistent to the last, died the death of a slave, and who was exalted to God's right hand.[69]

What is new, a scandal to the Jews and folly to the Greeks, is the confession, from those whom God empowered to make it, that this crucified Jew was God's anointed ruler of history, his son so uniquely loved that for him he created all that exists. The *basic* meaning of Son of God in the New Testament, then, from which all others are derivative and to which they all therefore point, is the meaning in fact found by all the scholars we have mentioned at the furthest point of their search for 'good historical reasons' for the application of the title to Jesus: the lived relationship of Jesus of Nazareth to the God he called Father.

What then shall we say about this odd concept of pre-existence in the context of such varied scriptural data on the title Son of God? We shall not say that there is no pre-existence language in the New Testament christologies, though the previous pages should give any reasonable reader good cause to suspect that it is by no means as frequent as it is commonly and most uncritically thought to be, even by people of recognized exegetical skills. It is found in particular in those New Testament christologies which make use of the Wisdom symbolism of Hellenistic Judaism, a symbolism which personifies God's wisdom (or word, or spirit), calls it God's image and so on, sees it incarnate, for instance, in the Torah, and declares that in it or through it or for it God created the world. It is found in other contexts also, particularly in texts such as John's 'before Abraham was, I am', and in the imagery of the one from heaven.

That last form of it, being a spatial rather than a temporal image, gives the first clue to its meaning. As Kant once observed, the inevitable forms of all human perception are space and time. As a result, whenever we wish to say something about God we make the most elementary use of the *via negativa* and set God, those acts of God we wish to contemplate, or the 'qualities' of God we wish to mention, outside of space and time where, strictly speaking, we can no longer imagine or conceive of them. Furthermore, when we wish to speak, as it were, from God's side of any person, thing, or event in our perceptible world of time-space in which we believe God to be specifically present and active, we have no option but to speak of God's initiating that relationship, as God does everything, outside of space and time ('before the creation of light', in more concrete and imaginative prose). If God was in Jesus reconciling the world to himself, that relationship to Jesus, that revelatory or functional identity with Jesus, initiated as it must be thought to be by God, is effected outside of space and time. And Jesus, precisely as the one in whom God is present and active, is thus said to originate, to be from God, that is, from above (space), from 'heaven', or from 'before' (time), from before creation. The symbolism of the creative instrumentality of Jesus (as of Wisdom, Torah, and so on) has the additional function of asserting the definitive significance for the whole world and for all of history of what God does in Jesus.

The New Testament, then, even when it does use pre-existence language, does not convey any information about any divine being distinct from the God that Jesus called Father and distinct at first from Jesus the Messiah. On the contrary, all of the New Testament pre-existence language, like all of its varied christological language, is designed to reveal the effective relationship of God to Jesus of Nazareth and through him to the whole world, the reciprocal relationship of Jesus of Nazareth to the God he called Father and through him to the whole world (raised to his right hand as Lord and Saviour of all).

The fact that God's presence and action in Jesus is in the New Testament sometimes presented (rather inevitably) in pre-existence language, of course, makes speculation legitimate; speculation, for instance, about what Moltmann and many others call self-differentiation in God. But we must be careful to give to such theological speculation (much of it trinitarian) no more than the weight which is due to theological speculation, and if we have any remaining respect for what we too often and too glibly profess to be the normative role of Scripture, we simply may not pretend that Scripture gives us any substantial information about a second divine 'person' or *hypostasis* distinct both from God the Father and from the historical Jesus before Jesus was born, or 'before the world was made'.[70] The information it does give us about the time before Jesus was, in the Christian view, in the form of God's history of preparation of the human race and, more specifically, of the Israelite nation for his definitive act in Jesus of Nazareth; and it is therefore to be expected that from the sacred literature of that preparatory stage should come also the models in which

God's presence in the world is claimed for Jesus, including the pre-existence models.

7

The Distinction of the Spirit

Spirit is the third term in the Christian trinitarian formula; third not only in numerical order, but in the importance which traditional attention and interest have accorded it. Though recent trends both in the prayer-life of Christians and in the book-lists of theological publishers now promise better, pneumatology, as the study of the Holy Spirit is rather hesitatingly called, was always the weakest and most neglected part of trinitarian doctrine. The reasons for this are many and various; we shall meet some *en route*, but a detailed enumeration of them should not delay us at this point. Suffice it to say here, without anticipating too much, that apart from the mysterious nature of its subject which the trinitarian formula has in common with many others, one particular difficulty bedevils all attempts to explain it in a simple and straightforward manner. Its terms comprise within the unity of the one formula two quite different, if not contrary, types of problem, and this fact alone lends distance to the prospect of issuing any simple and elegant exposition of the Christian Trinity. In the case of the one called 'the Son' there is no problem about his distinction from the Father, but there is considerable difficulty with any idea of his having existed with God from before the beginning of time.[71] In the case of Spirit, on the contrary, though there is little difficulty with its reference to the eternal and the divine in the relevant pre-Christian sources, grave problems are encountered in any attempt to distinguish Spirit from the God who is named as Father in these sources and in their Christian counterparts. (In fact, in some Christian Scriptures, as we shall soon see, there are problems in distinguishing the Spirit from the one called 'the Son'). Such twin-sets of difficulty, tugging the

66

mind simultaneously in opposite directions, do not make for intelligible and inspiring exposition of the Christian trinitarian formula.

One way of simplifying matters, certainly, is to rid Christian theology of any alleged need to think in terms of a pre-existent divine person who is distinct from both Father and Spirit, who is called 'Son' or 'Word', who took human flesh as Jesus of Nazareth, and who troubled the exegetical waters of the previous section. This is, roughly speaking, the suggestion of Lampe's book *God as Spirit*.[72] We should then be left with the God whom Jesus called Father, with this God as Spirit, and with Jesus. We should suffer no theological loss thereby, Lampe is convinced, since an expanded theology of Spirit would more than compensate for an incarnation christology of questionable pedigree and obsolescent features.[73] For if the long supremacy of this theology of the incarnation of a pre-existent divine person pushed the Spirit to the periphery of God's being and of the Christian life, if it reduced 'the Spirit to a second, and very ill-defined place in God's outreach towards the world',[74] the theology of the indwelling presence of God as Spirit, uniquely in Jesus and continuously in the believing community,[75] could more than adequately replace the usurper of its rightful throne and avoid all the tragic theological and spiritual consequences of the previous reign. In place of the extremely problematic temporary self-emptying of a pre-existent divine Son, we should have the continuous self-emptying of God as Spirit in creation and history. 'In creation there is a continuous *kenosis* of God as Spirit, entering into personal dialogue with his creatures, submitting himself to a relationship in which they may respond either with free co-operation or with rejection and hostility.'[76] In particular, Lampe argues, 'Christian theology has used a variety of models to articulate its understanding of the relationship of Jesus to God, and of God, in and through Jesus, to believers. The model of "Spirit" seems especially suitable for Christology and for interpreting man's whole experience of encounter with God.'[77]

One way, certainly, of solving the divergent problems of theologizing the received trinitarian formula, and one way of redressing its traditional theological imbalance, would be so to assess and to reject as much of that part of it which has attached to the second term, 'the Son'. But since Lampe himself insists that ' "Logos" and "Spirit", if they refer, as they should, to divine creative activity and not to hypostatically subsistent beings, are parallel and interchangeable ways of conceiving of God in his relation to the world',[78] there may be other ways of assessing, or re-assessing, the two elements of the formula with which the present brief scriptural sections are concerned. And it is with this possibility in mind that we look to the Spirit in Scripture.

Yet, if we are ever to see more ecumenical prospects for the understanding of the biblical theologies of Spirit, we must begin with some elementary analysis of the very use of spirit-language; its nature and the more obvious stages in its development. And in order to accomplish this task as quickly as possible in the present context, let us begin with the hypothesis that all the spirit-language in the Bible can be adequately understood in terms (a) of the origin of the word 'spirit', (b) of its more obvious extensions of meaning, and (c) of what Patrick Grant has called 'the condition of humans using words'.[79]

In origin, at the outset of the Judaeo-Christian tradition, the word meant moving air, the wind in the willows or breath from the mouth. Then, since breath is essential to life, by natural extension of meaning and before we talk at all of its religious sense, spirit came to refer to life, measured as it is by the number of our breaths; and thence to refer further either to those particular exertions or achievements of human life which prove crucial to the lives of others – for example, heroism and ecstasy, poetry and social reform, insight and foresight and the courage to speak them forth, wisdom and sacred writing – or to the lives of such individuals as were themselves seen to be crucial to the maintenance and perhaps enhancement of the lives of others, the life, for instance, of the King Messiah.[80]

By the condition of humans using words is meant, first, the fact that those who are somehow enabled to believe that both within and beyond the finite world of their everyday experience an absolute, unlimited being actually exists, realize that they have no special words, concepts, or images which refer exclusively to that being. Consequently, while the present conditions of human existence obtain, spokesmen for religious faith must do one or both of the following: (a) profess to speak, not of God in himself, but rather of his presence and action in certain things, events or people (usually, again, things, events, or people which prove crucial for that same human existence); (b) take those terms which are descriptive of the things, events, or people in which God is believed to be present and active, and use these as terms to denote or to 'name' God. Spirit in origin and natural extension has referred to a whole series of such crucial things, events, and people, and since God was or could be believed to be present or active in these, it could be 'taken' from these and used to denote God.

As a consequence of this condition, of course, language so derived and so applied had, and has, to be used with great caution. Sometimes this caution is felt by the reader in the very manner in which a religious text uses such terminology of God; for instance, in the paradoxical phenomenon of a text which talks of God in the most concrete imaginative terms while solemnly warning the reader that no images of God must ever under any circumstances be fashioned. Often, especially when something like philosophy of religion emerges in a religious culture, in however elementary a form, theories are constructed which explain how terms are to be applied to God with all requisite caution; theories of analogical predication,[81] for example, of the negative way, or of symbolic evocation. All this is to prevent the temptation, to which carelessness bred from familiarity may make men yield, to identify God with that in which he is believed to be present and active (thus reducing divinity or divinizing the creaturely), or to take ways of talking about God as definitions, no less, of the divine nature.

It is probably of some importance to note that when terms drawn from ordinary things are used with such cautious modification to denote the divinity, they retain some modification in all subsequent reference to the very things from which they were at first simply derived. For instance, when the word 'spirit' is taken from wind or insightful courage or the life of some particular individual and, because of the crucial significance of these for human life at large, applied as a term for God ('God is Spirit', John 4.24), it does not thereafter denote these original entities totally or simply once again; it now refers, rather, to something about these original entities which people consider crucial. Three points in particular may be made about this admittedly tortuous use of language which seems to be required by the mysterious nature of the 'object' to which it is now made to refer.

First, whatever modifications of meaning a term like 'spirit' must undergo in order to denote divinity, it must *always* retain its reference to that thing or event or person from which it was first derived, for from it, and from it alone, it gains whatever positive content of meaning it has for its users and all of its evocative power. A cognate point is made by Coleridge about a cognate subject, poetic imagery and symbolism: a symbol, he writes, 'always partakes of the reality which it renders intelligible, and while it enunciates the whole, abides itself as a living part in that unity of which it is the representative'.[82] Hence the spirit in which God was thought to be present and active and which yielded that name for God was once (and can still be) the wind, the breeze that ruffles calm waters and promises taut life and movement to creaking spars and listless sails, the cool wind that heralds rain clouds for parched lands, the storm that levels crops and batters ships and their crews into a watery grave. Or by extension of meaning, spirit can refer to the critical and courageous insight of the prophet or to the life of the anointed one, the Christ, and it will always refer to these for positive content of meaning and evocative power when it is then modified in denotation to refer to God.

Second, and consequently, all terms so derived and so applied must convey quite simultaneously impressions of transcendence and of immanence, of immanence and of transcendence. In other words, immanence and transcendence are inseparable in human religious discourse. As Lampe put it, 'To speak of immanence implies transcendence and vice-versa.'[83] Some authors seem to want to say that 'spirit' when used in religious discourse refers to God as immanent.[84] But since 'spirit', like any other term which is pressed into the service of religious faith, is taken from some thing, event or person and modified to apply to a being which, however much it may be thought to be present and active in these, is not identical with any of them, but rather transcends them all, in its case as much as in any other the immanent and transcendent references are really inseparable.

Thirdly, there is one particular manner of using ordinary language in religious discourse which merits some additional notice, if only because of its frequency amongst biblical uses of the term 'spirit'. In order to prevent impressions of identity between God and whatever it is in which he is thought to be present and active; instead of invoking analogical predication, or the negative way, one could make use of what may be described as the way of the personification of intermediaries. Instead of saying that 'God is spirit' or, for Christians, for instance, that Jesus is 'life-giving spirit' (I Cor. 15.45), one might talk of the spirit of God and the spirit of Jesus, of the former coming on or remaining in the latter, and then 'personify' the term spirit so used by attributing specific actions or attributes to it. This process is, of course, well documented and well known in the literature of Hellenistic Judaism, both sacred (Wisdom of Solomon) and secular (Philo), and though its presence in the developing christology of the New Testament is quite commonly acknowledged, it is not so frequently called in evidence in the exegesis of New Testament spirit material, even though it is quite clear that in the literature just mentioned spirit is associated (if not identified) with wisdom as, for instance, the unique (begotten) one (*monogenes*) of God.[85] It need hardly be said that, corresponding to the advantages of this process of the personification of intermediaries in avoiding over-simplifying identification of God with that in which he is believed to be present or active, there is the disadvantage that an equally misleading impression may be conveyed by careless use of this linguistic process, the impression, namely, that another being, whether semi-divine or fully divine, actually does come between the believer and the one God.

As a concrete illustration of these points one could do worse than to take from the New Testament the application of spirit-language to that very distinctive human activity which is known as prayer; prayer which can sometimes be no more than a deep, unformulated longing that issues only in a groan, which can sometimes be formulated in terms of an envisaged ideal or ideal relationship (Abba!), which is always to some degree a pleading for what is not, and for that reason shows a disconcerting ability to cross any over-neat lines we may wish to draw between the atheists, the agnostics, and the believers.[86] Here the temptation to understand personification language in too literal a sense is particularly easy to follow – however much the image of one divine being praying to or for another may afterwards cause difficulties for those with reasonably retentive memories when they come to stress absolute equality and identity of substance between such beings.

In actual fact, however, this illustration can confirm the hypothesis that spirit-language in the New Testament can be made fully intelligible in terms of the origin of the word, its natural extensions of meaning and the condition of humans using words. It also sets in relief the inseparable union of immanent and transcendent reference in such language, and the indissolubility of its bonds with the empirical. For that deep, groaning, longing[87] can be as powerful and as promising (and, at times, as destructive) as any other manifestation of human life to which the word spirit can naturally be extended. In it, too, then, God can be believed to be present and active. From it, consequently, the term spirit can be taken for purposes of describing the indefinable God. And that linguistic ruse known as the personification of intermediaries can then prevent any simplistic identification of God as spirit with that deep groaning in which God is now believed to be active. The insistence, in this case, on retaining the primacy of the spirit-reference to the deepest experience of human longing can promise rich results later, when religious faith's relationship to hope needs to be stated, or the true dialogue between Christianity and contemporary humanism comes to be initiated, or the character of God as the searching shepherd finally receives from Christians the attention it deserves.

But, for the moment, in order to test our hypothesis more fully, let us turn to the New Testament, or to as much of its spirit material as we can reasonably be expected to survey. Now anyone who looks with a critical eye to the literature on the New Testament uses of 'spirit' must be amazed at the speed with which most authors forget the origin of the term, the obvious extensions of meaning, and what has been called 'the condition of humans using words'. At least many of those who dealt with the other trinitarian term, 'son', were anxious to explain, as we saw, when and how the 'real' pre-existence of a distinct divine figure came to be included in its range of meaning – however successful or unsuccessful their efforts at such explanation may be thought to be. In the case of the term 'spirit', however, we are faced far too often either with simple-minded exegetical 'proofs' that the New Testament understands the term to refer to a distinct divine person or *hypostasis*,[88] or with the apparent assumption that the New Testament can be intepreted without question by use of language which constantly evokes such later trinitarian development. So it is necessary to insist that we have no reason to suppose that the various precedents for New Testament spirit-language ever thought the term 'spirit' to refer to a distinct divine *hypostasis*, and to approach the New Testament with this fact firmly in mind. Only then can we see clearly whether the New Testament spirit-material can be understood within the perimeters of the language models already outlined; whether, on the contrary, some substantial alterations of these models has occurred in the New Testament; and whether, if such alterations have occurred, they are such as to require a trinitarian theology in order to accommodate them properly. First, then, a reminder of some further precedents in Old Testament and inter-testamental uses of spirit-language which made its adoption by New Testament authors something approaching a matter of apologetic necessity: and then a survey of New Testament spirit-material set out in roughly historical sequence.

Apart from the material from Hellenistic Judaism's Wisdom literature already indexed, perhaps the most influential themes for the various New Testament uses of spirit-language were the following: 1. the use of the term for the qualities and achievements of some future messianic figure (Isa. 11.2; 42.1–4); 2. the use of the term 'spirit' to predict a whole community blessed in fidelity to its God (Num. 11.29; Ezek. 36.26–28; 37.1–14; Joel 2.28–29, to which is sometimes added Jer. 31.33); 3. the use of the term to anticipate the eschatological conditions by the Qumran Covenanters;[89] 4. a belief in the cessation of prophecy with Haggai, Malachi and Zechariah which, though it allowed for the application of the term 'spirit' to other activities of the faithful Jewish people, partly resulted also in the use of the term to propose the definitive nature of the Mosaic revelation, now in the Scriptures, and hence forced the followers of Jesus to come to grips simultaneously with Moses, the written Law, and the term spirit used in connection with those, in their efforts to propose, on the contrary, that God's definitive revelation had come only with Jesus of Nazareth.[90] Such precedents made it more than necessary for New Testament authors to present their 'candidate' in terms of spirit. How did they do this, and did they have Jesus' own authority for doing it?

C. K. Barrett wrestled with the extreme paucity of evidence that the historical Jesus ever thought of himself or his work in terms of spirit.[91] Of course, if Jesus never did, this would be odd by comparison with the prominence of the theme later on in some New Testament writing, and not by comparison with other contemporary usage. Spirit was always a replaceable term and seldom so much so as at the time of Jesus. But, Barrett emphasizes, Jesus was certainly a 'pneumatic', an exorcist, a wonder-worker and a prophet, and clearly recognized as such. Barrett uses a variation of the 'messianic secret' theme to explain Jesus' own reticence in availing himself of spirit-language for such obvious instances of its conventional usage: Jesus did not wish to be understood as the kind of messiah who forced assent by miracle and, since that explanation does not cover the rest of his role as prophet, in general he was so creative in the place he gave suffering in his messianic work that spirit-talk would not have helped his cause.[92] There may be much historical truth in this kind of suggestion, provided we recognize that few, if any, of the other messianic titles or terms would have served Jesus better, and in this way once more recognize an equivalence for spirit-terminology.[93]

In any case, there is a synoptic saying which has as much claim as any to be an authentic saying of the historical Jesus – 'if by the Spirit of God I cast out demons, the kingdom of God is amongst you' (Matt. 12.28) – and this single saying would subsume under the category of Spirit the whole existential purpose and achievement of Jesus, the inauguration of the reign of God. Further, as Barrett points out, the synoptic evangelists make up for Jesus' reticence about spirit-talk, such as it was, with their accounts of his baptism, as do Matthew and Luke in their infancy narratives. But before attempting a brief survey, in something like historical order, of this and other New Testament spirit-material, it is well to pause at this point in order to notice the direction which our reflection on this type of material is already beginning to take.

Books like Barrett's really set one wondering about the amount of the spirit-material in the New Testament that may have to be read as christology strictly speaking, a kind of christology that is sometimes alternative to a christology in terms of Word, for instance, and sometimes apparently intended to provide the inner meaning of a christology formulated in terms of, say, Son (as in the nativity and baptism narratives). A christology, after all, is simply an attempt to express the full status and significance of Jesus as God's anointed, and much of the spirit-language in the New Testament may be doing just that, rather than attempting to give any information about yet another 'pre-existent' divine *hypostasis* distinct at once from both Jesus and the Father.

Now it would obviously not be possible to introduce at this point such general considerations about the nature and development of New Testament christology as would be necessary to justify fully this direction which our reflections are beginning to take. So I beg to leave the co-opt from *Jesus, the Man and the Myth* a theme or two which even its critics seem to have left largely intact and which enable us to move forward from Barrett's book.

First, I would wish to see Jesus' exorcisms and wonder-working even more closely integrated with his inauguration of the kingdom of God than C. K. Barrett does. Then the messianic secret theme could be explained less in terms of an allegedly conscious policy of Jesus himself and more in terms of the unexpected, in fact the unwelcome, the almost incredibly demanding nature of the messianic role as he understood it and lived it out. For, second, I am convinced that it was the way in which this man lived and died – what I called the lived conviction of unconditional grace which he consummated by his death – rather than any particular and evasive numinous experiences either to him or to his followers at certain moments during his life or after his death which enabled those 'who could take it' to use of him all that religious language which expressed, at once, belief in God and belief that God was, and continued to be, present and active in Jesus.[94]

If now, along this line of approach, one carries also the explicit memory of the origin and extensions of the word 'spirit' and of the nature of its use in religious discourse; if, in particular, one refuses to read the New Testament material through the spectacles of later trinitarian theologies, much of the spirit-language of the New Testament quite speedily reveals its christological nature.

Spirit, by reason of both origin and obvious extensions, had singled out many things, from moving air to historical forms of wisdom (finally concretized for the Jew in the Law of Moses),[95] as the thing or event in which God was present and active in the world. Now it appeared true to some that the definitive locus of God's presence and action in human history was not any natural force or entity, not any code of law, or cult, or system of truth, but the life and death of an individual man, the person of Jesus who experienced this distinctive life, death and destiny. Spirit, already extended in its meaning to life, and to various significant qualities and achievements of life, could quite obviously extend to this man. Further, as we saw, because a word such as spirit indicates some thing or event in which God is thought to be present and active, it then becomes a word for God. By what we termed the inextricable combination of the immanent and transcendent reference of all language so used, a word such as spirit at one and the same time indicates the thing or the event (or, as now, the one) in whom God is believed to be active, and the God who is active in this one. In actual fact, as M. E. Isaacs has pointed out, the Greek word for spirit, *pneuma*, gained significant religious reference from Jewish influence,[96] and one can notice many ways in which New Testament writers illustrate the increasing exclusiveness of its use as a name for God. In short, to say that Jesus was spirit and, *a priori*, to use spirit language of Jesus with an aim somewhat short of such identity, was just as obvious a way of confessing that God was present and active in Jesus, and of relating Jesus to God as, for instance, to say that Jesus was Lord, Christ, Son of God or to apply to him such language as once was used for wisdom.[97] One can hardly insist too strongly or too frequently on such equivalence, for only by insisting upon it can one properly gauge the extent to which New Testament spirit-material is to be regarded as christology or, more accurately, as a further series of christologies.

For instance, to begin with the earliest New Testament writer, Paul; many students of his genuine letters have commented upon the virtual identity of spirit and lord in his theology.[98] Needless to say, this identity is not confined to the controverted phrase of II Corinthians 3.17, 'the Lord is the Spirit'.[99] It is obvious in the equivalence of Paul's references to Christ in us and the Spirit in us, or to us in the Spirit or us in Christ, and from his attribution of the various characteristics of the Christian's life, the various effects upon the Christian's life, quite indiscriminately to Jesus (who is Lord, Christ, Son of God) or to the Spirit. The body of Jesus' followers in the world is the body of Christ precisely because it is animated by the Spirit. And so on.

J. D. G. Dunn approaches much the same material in a slightly different manner. Jesus, he maintains, who was so uniquely possessed and used by the divine Spirit during his earthly life, became by his resurrection from the dead 'that Spirit which believers experience as the source and power of their new life and new relationship with God',[100] the life-giving Spirit of I Corinthians 15.45. This in turn means that, for Paul, the Spirit has now taken on the character of Christ, or that Jesus has come to be the 'definition' of the Spirit. Dunn works this last conclusion through texts such as I Corinthians 12.3, where the Spirit enables us to confess the Lordship of Jesus; Romans 8.14ff., where the Spirit enables us to pray the filial prayer of Jesus himself; Romans 8.29 and I Corinthians 15.49, which have the Spirit transforming us into the image of Christ; I Corinthians 13 and Galatians 5.22, where virtual character-sketches of Christ's own self-sacrificing love are the 'fruits' or charismata of the Spirit. Such material is then summed up in phrases such as: 'if Christ is now experienced as Spirit, Spirit is now experienced as Christ',[101] or the more enigmatic: 'as the Spirit was the "divinity" of Jesus, so Jesus became the personality of the Spirit'.[102]

Now this way of treating the Pauline material seems to stop somewhere short of asserting virtual identity of different ways of speaking of the activity of God in Jesus; though what it does tell us, it is not easy to say. It appears from the conclusion of his work that Dunn seems to have in mind a sequence of events in which Jesus of Nazareth, whose unique relation to the Spirit as the Son of God continued and developed through his life and death, attained in the unique event of his resurrection the life-giving power of the Spirit, and the Spirit then became recognizably the life-giving power of the crucified and risen Jesus. We are tempted by this kind of language to think, and perhaps intended to think, that the Spirit is already in the New Testament a distinct divine 'person' or *hypostasis* which first possesses Jesus, which Jesus then 'becomes' after his death, and which then correspondingly 'becomes' the life-giving power of the crucified and risen Jesus. And if this is the kind of impression we get, we are bound to ask how we are to make sense of it, or if there is some clearer way of relating what the synoptics say of the Spirit and Jesus to what Paul says about these.

Berkhof also begins by accepting the kind of identity of Spirit and Lord which Hermann argues, but he then seems anxious to introduce a kind of distinction which is as enigmatic in itself as it is obviously constructed with an eye on the later development of trinitarian theology. His suggestion is that Jesus the Christ is Lord in his transcendence, Spirit in the mode of immanence.[103]

However, we have already noted that spirit, like other words used in such religious discourse, implies transcendence as much as immanence; and if the Lordship of Jesus is at all effective in our lives – and if it is not, there is no point in confessing it – then it implies the immanence of the Lord just as much as his transcendence. Such distinctions are quite without substance. The conclusion seems unavoidable that Spirit is used by Paul, just as his favourite titles (Christ, Lord, Son of God) are used, to express God's presence and action in and through Jesus of Nazareth; and the differences between spirit-language in the Gospels and that in Paul neither presupposes nor yields a hypostatic distinction of Lord and Spirit.

This does not mean, of course, that there are no distinctions, or that the language of spirit cannot handle these. There is, for instance, a distinction between God and Jesus, as there is a distinction between God and any thing, event, or person in which people detect the presence and action of God in their world. God is never quite identical with the means of his self-revelation or salvific action; while *in via* at least we do not see God directly, face to face (these are equivalent statements). So a term like spirit, when made into religious discourse by means of analogy, or poetic evocation, or personification of intermediaries, will say that God is in whatever we now extend this term to denote (in this case the life of a particular individual, the person of Jesus), and this is immanence; it will simultaneously say that God is also beyond this one (transcendence), and so that this one is not altogether identical with God. Such distinctions are simply endemic to religious discourse, and really need no separate statement. Hence in the case of Jesus also, in so far as spirit, *pneuma*, had been taken from this alleged instance of divine presence and action which that word named and been made, as then happens, into a name for God, M. E. Isaacs is quite right in stressing that 'it is not the distinction between Christ and the Spirit which warrants comment; it is the connection between Christ and the *pneuma* which we find in the New Testament'.[104] It was indeed not the distinction between God (named, amongst other possibilities, as spirit) and Jesus (the significance of whose life and person attracted the term spirit) which caused trouble for the latter's followers, for that was obvious to everyone; it was their insistence that his life and death, his very personal being or existence, was spirit in the divine rather than the demonic use of that word (Matt. 12.24–28).

There is another distinction which the language of spirit can also handle just as well as the language of son, for instance, or word. It is the distinction between the life which Jesus lived (and still, we believe, lives in his own personal existence) and the life which he enabled others to live in the conviction of unconditional grace, in the self-same faith, as sons, as he was son; some to the extent that they took it as their vocation in life to spread this life by word and inspiring example to the limits of the world and the end of time.[105] If Jesus' life was called spirit as a way of confessing that

God, who by reference to it was also called spirit, was present and active in Jesus, this continuing life of his followers was naturally also called spirit and could only be further specified by calling it 'the spirit of Jesus'.

That last phrase is an example of what has been called the personification of intermediaries, and it implies in the case of Jesus, no more than in the case of God, no 'real' being who comes between us and Jesus. Rather, just as the phrase 'the spirit of God' is designed to imply that that to which we refer is not to be totally identified with God (or even with that in which God is thought to be present and active and to which the word now refers), so the phrase 'the spirit of Jesus' is designed to imply that that to which it refers in the lives of his followers is to be totally identified neither with the person of Jesus nor with those who are to some extent or sometimes his followers. The coupling of the phrases 'the spirit of God' and 'the spirit of Jesus', as well as being a means of specifying the former by addition of the latter, also ensures that the distinctions between God, Jesus, and Jesus' followers are preserved in the very process of confessing that it is indeed the true God who is present and active in Jesus and, through Jesus, in those who are to some degree his followers.

So, those who keep in mind in using or reading spirit-language the origin of the term, its obvious extensions of meaning, and the condition of humans using words, can hardly fail to see that although distinctions between God and Jesus and ourselves are preserved in the very manner in which all are related, no hypostatic distinction between the Lord Jesus and the Spirit has yet emerged. So we must continue our survey into the Gospels to see if a different view of spirit appears and, if so, how it is to be expressed.

In the case of the Synoptic Gospels reference has already been made to the paucity of spirit-language for the life and mission of Jesus, but it was said that some reversal of this state of affairs occurs in crucial scences such as those which depict the baptism and the birth of Jesus.

The holy spirit spirit will come upon you and the power of the most high will overshadow you and therefore that which will be born of you will be called the son of God (Luke 1.35).

To Raymond Brown the 'therefore' in that text 'involves a certain causality'. The coming and the overshadowing *really* beget the child as God's son; there is here no question of mere adoption, no purely figurative sense of begetting as in the application of enthronement imagery in stories of baptism and in resurrection kerygma. On the contrary, for Luke 'divine sonship seems to have been brought about through the virginal conception', and specifically through the coming of the Holy Spirit and the over-shadowing.[106] Yet Brown is very anxious to insist in the course of his exegesis of this section of Luke's nativity story that there is no question of a begetting which is quasi-sexual, as if God takes the place of a male principle in mating with Mary; rather is the Spirit in this text to be understood in relation to the creative Spirit of God that hovered over the primeval waters when earth was void and empty (Gen. 1.2), like Mary's womb. Better still, the real parallels for Luke 1.35 are New Testament christologies in terms of spirit and son, such as are found, for instance, in Paul; just as the proper parallel for the overshadowing is found in the trans-figuration scene where a cloud, signifying the divine presence, overshadows the group and a voice declares the sonship (the parallel of this in turn with the spirit and the voice of the baptism scenes has often been noted).[107]

Interestingly enough it is on Matthew's 'more careless phrasing' that Hahn focusses when, in his effort to trace the steps to the New Testament's alleged teaching about Jesus' sonship of nature (and his pre-existence as son) rather than of function, he sees in this nativity story the suggestion that Jesus is offspring of God as much as, and in much the same sense as, of Mary. Hahn quotes Matthew's phrases in 1.18 and 20: 'with child of the Holy Spirit (*ek pneumatos hagiou*)', and 'that which is conceived in her is of the Holy Spirit', and shows the continuity of this kind of 'careless' phrasing, for example, in the ancient Roman creed which spoke of Jesus being 'born of the Holy Spirit and of the Virgin Mary'.[108] Yet Hahn is also anxious that we should not get the impression of sexual union from any of this, since none of these texts really wishes to convey such an idea, and some quite positively resist it.[109]

We may not now be able to decide exactly what Luke or Matthew thought he was saying in these stories, but the texts themselves leave us with but two basic exegetical options. We can take it that we are being told in these stories of the creation of a human being similar to the creation of the first human being: that is, as it was then thought, without the possibility of human parentage. And this extraordinary emergence of a human being is then seen as the kind of instance of power in the world from which God's existence is suspected and his presence claimed. On this option Jesus would then be son of God in the same sense as, for Luke (3.38), Adam was son of God, a sense which would have little enough relevance to the rest of the New Testament.[110]

Our other option is the one offered by Brown when he says that the real parallels for Luke 1.35 are to be found in other New Testament formulations in christology. In other words, the life of this man had been seen as the locus of spirit, with all the implications for divine presence in it which the religious use of this language conveyed. Correspondingly, when some evangelists decided to add infancy narratives, the presence of spirit in this divine sense was inevitably included at the very origin of the man. The purpose, then, as in all spirit-christologies, is to say that God was present and active in Jesus. It was not the purpose of the narratives to give some odd account of this man's physical origin, though memories of something quite unusual about this too may possibly have survived and provided the occasion for the application of a christology at this point.

On this account of the matter, the infancy narratives fit in well with the accounts of Jesus' baptism. In the baptism scenes also a spirit-christology is combined with a son of God christology, in such a manner in fact as to suggest that the spirit-christology is the inner meaning of, if not the justification for, the son of God christology. However that may be, just as the use of the title 'son of God' for Jesus was, as we saw in the last section, justified by the life he lived, and by his death and destiny, so it was possible to see this life as the locus of spirit, and this conviction is depicted dramatically by having the Spirit of God (the language now is that of the personification of intermediaries) descend upon Jesus (and remain on him), and then have him declared Son of God.

In a brief reflection, *via* the work of C. K. Barrett, on Jesus' own possible references to spirit, we noted the sentiment of Matthew 12.28 which seemed to express in spirit-language all that Jesus was sent to achieve, namely, the kingdom of God. So both the sonship of Jesus and his inauguration of the kingdom of God's unconditioned grace in the world are accounted for in terms of the spirit being on or in him.[111] Now, since Jesus himself is the source (as locus of God's definitive presence and action) of this reign of God, and this reign of God is destined for all who would accept it, Jesus is naturally described as the source of spirit for these favoured ones. In the relevant imagery of this kind of symbolism, to be source of spirit is to breathe spirit. So Jesus is depicted as breathing the Spirit in turn into his followers. Since many of the accounts of Jesus breathing the Spirit are contained in New Testament material concerning the resurrection, in the course of the appearances narratives, for instance, I beg leave to refer to what is said in *Jesus the Man and the Myth* to the effect that depicting Jesus as spirit-breather is a cognate way of saying that he is seated at God's right hand, exalted, or raised. It is another way of claiming, in short, God's definitive presence and action in and through Jesus of Nazareth, so that John, for instance, locates both exaltation and spirit-breathing on Calvary.[112]

What, then, of the spirit in the Fourth Gospel? It is often said that whereas Paul identifies the risen Jesus in so many ways with the life-giving Spirit, Luke and John, the two major theologians of the spirit amongst the evangelists, think of the spirit of which Jesus is the source, which Jesus breathes or sends, predominantly in terms of the prophetic spirit – sending forth apostles and missionaries, keeping them to the truth of Jesus, confounding their enemies. This may provide a hypothesis, but we shall certainly have to verify it in the instance of John's 'other paraclete'. The other paraclete of the Fourth Gospel has always provided the proto-trinitarian exegetes with the solidest ground for their case. But here also a look at the models available to this unique evangelist in the construction of his major spirit-texts can be quite instructive. It is common, of course, to find authors describe in detail the many parallels in the Fourth Gospel between what is said of the spirit and what is said of Jesus, and then drawing the relevant conclusions.[113] But M. E. Isaacs has put together from her own research and that of others a much broader and more revealing set of comparisons.[114] She compares John's sayings about the paraclete, not only to those about Jesus, but to those about the spirit-inspired prophets under the old covenant (with particular reference to Moses, the prophet *par excellence*), and to those about the disciples of Jesus under the New. Hence, like the prophets, the paraclete is sent as God's agent (John 14.26; 15.26); he interprets and teaches (John 16.13), he acts as witness, both for the defence of faithful disciples and for the prosecution of those who will not hear, and (on an Israelite model) he also acts as judge

(John 15.26, 16.7–11), he predicts (John 16.13), and he is rejected
(John 14.17).

The disciples also are sent as agents (John 17.18; 20.21; 13.20),
they teach and witness (John 21.24; cf. John 15.27), they judge
(John 20.23), and though prediction is not ascribed to them in the
Fourth Gospel, they too must suffer rejection (John 15.18; 17.14;
16.1–4). Hence, both the paraclete and the disciples are presented
in the Fourth Gospel in terms of a Jewish understanding of
prophecy. So, as the normally noted parallels between Jesus and
the paraclete would now indicate, is Jesus.

Jesus is, of course, superior to the disciples. That goes without
saying. He is also superior to the prophets of the past; this is made
quite clear in the process of affirming his superiority to Moses
(who witnesses and judges in favour of Jesus – John 5.45f.), the
greatest of these. And if the paraclete were a 'person' or 'hypostasis' sufficiently distinct from the 'person' or 'hypostasis' of or in
Jesus for us to be able to say so, we should have to say that in the
Fourth Gospel Jesus was consistently superior to the paraclete
also. For though Jesus, like the paraclete, is sent by God, he and
not the paraclete is sent with the titles of son and servant; Jesus
glorifies the Father, but the paraclete glorifies Jesus (John 14.16);
the paraclete is the teacher who will guide the disciples into all the
truth, but he teaches what Jesus said, and it is Jesus, not the
paraclete, who *is* the truth (John 14.6); the paraclete witnesses to
Jesus, but Jesus alone witnesses to God (John 3.11, 31f.; 8.14).

But unless we are to indulge in a very specific form of hindsight
– I mean, from the perspective of a later development of trinitarian
theology – it is not at all obvious that we should institute such
comparisons in such a way as to attribute to the writer of the
Fourth Gospel a personal or hypostatic distinction between Christ
Jesus and the spirit-paraclete. Certainly such a move would
involve the Fourth Gospel in many anomalies. For one example,
it would be the same spirit who comes and remains upon Jesus
(John 1.32) who subsequently (as he remains on or with his
disciples – John 14.17) is inferior to him.[115] However difficult it
may be for us now to read the Fourth Gospel without trinitarian
spectacles fashioned in a different century, we must realize that
spirit-paraclete is not really a fourth member in a multiple-
comparison between: 1. Moses and the prophets of old; 2. Jesus;
3. the disciples of Jesus; 4. the spirit-paraclete. Rather is the
multiple comparison between the first three mentioned. And the

point is that Jesus is the one to whom Moses and the prophets of old looked forward and to whom his disciples looked back. In other words, in the spirit-material of the Fourth Gospel, the reader is left in no doubt about the utter supremacy of Jesus as the one in whom God is present and active, but it is *within* the spirit-nspired prophet-model that this utter supremacy is maintained. Spirit, then, as it had by this time become in reference to the prophets, is a way of referring to that manner of acting, witnessing, judging and suffering of theirs in which people believed they saw the presence and action of God. As a consequence, as we saw, they go on to talk of God as spirit, of the spirit of God, of the spirit of God coming on such men. And it is from such an understanding of the imaginative or linguistic model in use here in the Fourth Gospel that the reader can most easily understand the simple point that is being made, namely, that in Jesus, not in Moses or the Mosaic law, God is definitively present and active, and that is the prophetic witness of his true disciples.

What, then, of the two little words 'another paraclete', on which more subsequent theology seems to have been made to rest than on any comparable pair? In view of the comparisons and parallels already referred to, sometimes in detail, it seems best to accept the view that this poetic language is the author's way of stressing the identity of function between the earthly Jesus and the abiding spirit of his disciples, with due qualifications concerning the subservience of the latter to the former, and that 'paraclete' is here a case of the personification of intermediaries and not a separate *hypostasis* at all.[116]

In the case of the disciples of Jesus, then, it could be said that Jesus enabled people ('inspired people') to rise to a love and a faith, and consequently a hope, that they had not known. People lived, to some degree, like Jesus lived. Those who could speak of the source and substance of Jesus' life as the spirit of God, could speak of the spirit of Jesus in their lives as the spirit of God. But they knew that they were still far from the stature of Jesus. The spirit they spoke of as their recreated lives was still to them anticipation or pledge, down-payment or first-fruits[117] of the final perfection which they knew, because of Jesus, was possible in the end. The very same life, the lived conviction of unconditional grace, which was an imitation of Christ, groaned for Christ. It was a prayer for Christ, like Christ's own prayer. And that aspect of the new life, too, was 'spirit'. So that the Spirit and the Bride do pray to the Lord Jesus to 'Come' (Rev. 22.16).

As in the case of the second term of the Christian trinitarian formula, the son, with which we had to do above, there is no possibility here of covering all the New Testament texts on spirit.[118] The baptismal formula in Matthew 28.19, for instance, has naturally been the subject of a very great deal of exegetical and theological commentary, and though almost certainly later than an original baptism in the name of Jesus,[119] it has strong scriptural and patristic implications in the development of what was later to become the classical trinitarian doctrine of the church. Of it C. K. Barrett writes, 'The Holy Spirit has become an object of faith (in a rational sense) as well as an object of experience.'[120] But whether there is yet question of a distinct divine *hypostasis*, or how Matthew could possibly have understood this, it is extremely difficult to say. We should at least not allow our interpretation of this *hapax legomenon* to dictate our understanding of the broader, well-defined pneumatologies of the New Testament, but should rather be guided by these in our interpretation of this particular text. And enough has been said about these pneumatologies in the present section at least to establish the possibility that spirit-language in the New Testament be interpreted according to what I have already called the origin and extensions of the term's meaning and the condition of humans using words. Spirit was used of moving air, and by extension, of whatever in human life was thought to entail the presence and action of the absolute; as such it was used as a synonym for God, or personified as if it were an intermediary between God and the world of human pilgrimage, and so it was said to be in or with men, and in some more than others. As such, like son, it also was used by the followers of Jesus to say that God's definitive presence and action in human history took place in that particular man, in his life, death and destiny.

As in the case of the term son also, what was unique about its use for Jesus was not to be found in the impressions sometimes conveyed of 'another' pre-existent divine figure – the personification language of the Wisdom model which underlay both word (son) and spirit accounts adequately for that – but in the use of the term in such definitive claims for a man who lived the life of a slave in service of others and died as a state criminal on a Roman cross. That men should claim that on such a one the spirit (of)

God *remained* – for the permanent possession of the spirit was an *eschatological* hope of Israel, i.e. it represented the *consummation* of divine action in history – this is where the uniqueness lay, and the scandal for the Jew, and for the Greek the sense of the folly of it all.

In short, most of the spirit-material in the New Testament is christology. It is concerned, that is to say, to give expression to the status and function of Jesus of Nazareth, God's anointed one. It is not in the least concerned to give us any substantial information about a divine 'person' or *hypostasis* distinct both from Jesus the Christ and the God he called Father.

There are, of course, differences between New Testament authors in their handling of this material: there is pluriformity of spirit-christologies in the New Testament as there is pluriformity of New Testament christology in general. Some of this pluriformity was indicated in reference to differences between Paul, John and other evangelists. But the differences that result from decisions to talk of Jesus as recipient and then breather and sender of spirit, or of Jesus himself as life-giving spirit, are all differences which, it should by now be clear, can be accommodated within the various possibilities of this same model of religious language.[121]

There are many distinctions, too, to which this model inevitably gives rise in the very course of its own organic development, like cells dividing and differentiating the functions of an organism: distinctions between God and Jesus and the followers of Jesus; distinctions between the spirit of Jesus and Jesus (for not everything that Jesus was and did and said was 'spirit' in the religious sense); and between the spirit and God (for God is not to be thought wholly identified with that in our world which we name spirit and in which we believe God to be present and active). We must say, of course, of these distinctions, as has already been said about the pre-existence language in the case of the title 'Son', that they give leave to speculate theologically. But, in this case also, we shall have to ask: how much do they really authorize us to say about distinct pre-existent divine beings? Or, if we do wish to talk rather a lot about, let us say, three such distinct divine 'persons' or *hypostaseis*, in any internal order or in none, before we speak of Jesus' life, death and resurrection or apart from this, how much scriptural authority can we really claim for what we say?

There is now an additional factor to be taken into account in all attempts to justify a *trinitarian* theology: if, as appears to be the case, 'spirit' is a way of working out a christology, a way of expressing the divinity of Jesus, which is either equivalent to 'Son' or the reason for and the inner meaning of the application of the latter title, it might well be that binitarian thought is as well supported in the New Testament as is trinitarian. At least we should not be surprised at the substantial presence of binitarian thought in the early Christian centuries.

It is to these centuries we must now proceed to see how early Christian theologians selected from this rich and varied scriptural material in order to fashion their doctrines of binity and trinity, to ask what authority they claimed and actually had for so doing, to find what other influences (other than scriptural) are evident in their work, and so to assess the status of the doctrine they helped to formulate, and its implications for our present formulation of the Christian faith.

PART THREE

The Past

8

Doctrine, Faith and History

It was necessary, when raising the issue of the relationship of trinitarian doctrine to Scripture, to introduce some general reflections on Scripture as a source or support of doctrines. Now, as we are about to open the story of the actual development of trinitarian theologies in the course of the first Christian centuries, it seems equally necessary to reflect, however briefly, upon the nature of doctrine and upon its relationship to history. These are obviously enormous issues in their own right and have rightly attracted an extensive literature. The amount of reflection devoted to them here must then be the minimum required to reveal the present method of treating the development of our doctrine, and to supplement the points already raised in the case of its relationship to Scripture.

The place given in the course of the reflections on the normative nature of Scripture to the founder and his faith might suggest that doctrine, too, should be approached simply as a formulation of religious faith, and since express formulations are normally taken to convey what someone presumes to *know*, our first set of reflections on the nature of doctrine could well consist of some epistemological considerations of the relationship of faith and knowledge. Then, since epistemological considerations tend of their very nature to be general – concerned with the general structures of the human spirit and its general processes – a second set of reflections on doctrine and history (or the relativity of all expressions of what we presume to know) will be necessary, if only to make the former set of considerations reflect the concrete, particular faith which is the only kind that actually exists, and which tries through all the change and *bouleversement* of its

91

relationship to those other particular faiths from which it perhaps emerged or with which it has had to deal, to preserve its identity through the flux of time and the kaleidescopic perspectives of space.

(a) Faith and knowledge

'The natural attitude of mind,' said Husserl, 'is as yet unconcerned with the critique of cognition.'[1] This is true, of course, and there is nothing surprising about it. But when this natural attitude of mind pervades so much academic theology, then academic theology may begin to appear uncritical at a very deep level indeed. For a theology which pretends to be rigorously academic cannot forever satisfy the rigours of its academic vocation by telling us what we know, while postponing indefinitely the answer to the question as to how we know it. Nor can this latter question be answered peremptorily by references to divine act, either to a divine act in history which 'deposited' once upon a time the truth now known, or to a series of divine acts which explain the fact that some individuals seem to have assented to this truth while others do not assent to it. References to such divine acts are not, of course, invalid: indeed at some point of every account of religious faith they become essential. But they do not attempt to analyse from the viewpoint of the human person the manner in which the individual appropriates these alleged truths about God, about cosmic origins, and human destiny. In what manner do I, the conative believer, make such truth my own? This question is not fully answered by reference either to ancient divine intervention or to more recent divine enablement. It seeks, rather, a full description of Kierkegaard's 'appropriation process of the most passionate inwardness'.[2]

Of course the natural attitude of mind has not totally pervaded theology. A book like Van A. Harvey's *The Historian and the Believer*, for example, analyses the different modes, indeed the different 'moralities', which characterize the assent that is given respectively to historical and religious claims. Yet, despite much attention given recently to the epistemology of religious faith,[3] it seems fair to say that the awareness of the need for the critique of cognition still does not sufficiently accompany the unfolding of doctrinal systems. Naturally such shortcomings cannot altogether be made good here, for such an enterprise would presuppose an

approved epistemology of religious faith, but it is still necessary
to offer some preliminary observations, and at the very least to
refrain from engaging in one more exercise of unfolding doctrines
as if no problem of the epistemological status of these doctrines
ever existed or could exist.

As a first general observation one might remark that in any
comparison or contrast between faith and knowledge, faith is the
comprehensive term, in the literal sense of that word, and
knowledge the included term. A second, more specific observation might suggest that it is somewhere at the depth (or height)
of that experience of being in the world which some modern
epistemologists actually call 'primordial faith' that specifically
religious faith occurs. It is, I hope, possible to expand a little on
these two points without any prejudice whatever to any further
claims to the extent that God intervened in revelatory fashion in
the past and acts to enable people in the present. For the past
intervention must have entered human experience at some level,
else we should be quite unable to talk about it, and the present
enablement, unless it be a *creatio ex nihilo*, must enable some
definable structure of the human being to operate in some
describable manner. Otherwise the claims about the original act
and the present enablement are both vacuous.

First, then, 'the essential point,' according to Maurice
Merleau-Ponty, 'is clearly to grasp the project towards the world
which we are.'[4] At a level of our selves which goes normally
unnoticed, and which is correspondingly common to all of us,
educated and uneducated alike, we are, to use a term of modern
phenomenology, intentional through and through. But to see
ourselves in the pristine unity of that project which defines us,
we need to pause and to penetrate beneath the overt intentions
and conscious aims which eat up our waking hours.

> This is why Husserl distinguishes between intentionality of act,
> which is that of our judgments and of those occasions when we
> voluntarily take up a position – the only intentionality discussed in the
> *Critique of Pure Reason* – and operative intentionality (*fungierende
> Intentionalität*), or that which produces the natural and antepredicative
> unity of the world and of our life, being apparent in our desires, our
> evaluations and in the landscape we see, more clearly than in objective
> knowledge, and furnishing the text which our knowledge tries to
> translate into precise language. Our relationship to the world, as it is
> untiringly enunciated within us, is not a thing which can be any further

clarified by analysis; philosophy can only place it once more before our eyes and present it for our ratification.[5]

This basic relationship to the world, this original project of which all specific projects are part, this comprehensive intentionality before any distinctions of artistic or evaluative, theoretic or pragmatic enter in, is called 'faith' or 'primordial faith' by Merleau-Ponty,[6] and it seems as valid a general definition of human faith as may be offered.

One modern route, then, to the proper appreciation of the distinction and the relationship between faith and knowledge begins with the phenomenologists' eidetic reduction, whereby the unity of that primordial projection which we are is sought beneath the reflection upon it which divides in an effort to conquer and issues in what we call knowledge, or, in religious terms, doctrine.

For it is clear that the reflective activity of the mind is by nature analytic, and to a much less successful extent synthetic. It has but two movements, at least at what we call the intellectual level, like systole and diastole of the heart, and it is this which allows those fascinating comparisons with the amazing possibilities of binary systems in the world of what is called, significantly, artificial intelligence. It naturally tends to get the lion's share of attention in epistemology, since epistemology is itself its product. But, being by nature analytic, whether it is directed inward or outward, it inevitably introduces distinctions into natural unities. Looking inward, it can only be its reflective self at all by distinguishing the self from its own acts of consciousness, and then it further distinguishes, at least according to one conventional Western triad, speculative from evaluative and from artistic (pure reason from practical reason and from the aesthetic). Looking outward, it distinguishes the self from surrounding reality, subject from object. Then, apart from the fact that the synthetic activity of the reflective mind never seems quite so successful as the analytic, no synthesis of elements once made distinct can itself ever achieve the status of the foundational unity. It can but point to such unity beyond its own efforts, and consciously seek methods – such as eidetic reduction – by which that unity can be recovered.

The first and general reference of the word faith, then, should be to that foundational unity of the human being's response to surrounding reality ('the world') of which the human being is such an integral part, a response in which theoretical, evaluative and artistic elements are all present but not distinct. This is Merleau-Ponty's 'primordial faith'. Consequently, in his attempt 'clearly to grasp the project towards the world which we are', he describes the phenomenologist's eidetic reduction as 'the determination to bring the world to light as it is before any falling back on ourselves has occurred, it is the ambition to make reflection emulate the unreflective light of consciousness.'[7]

Here are phrases to conjure with indeed: the world as it is before falling, back on ourselves. Simple epistemology seems to open on to larger vistas of innocence and fall, of awakening to the distinctive self and the Kierkegaardian hazards of freedom, of reflection and the Apollonian and the quest for dominance; and the feeling that knowledge, doctrine, product of the reflective mind, herald of its mastery, must be put back in its place. Not that speculative intellect is alone in its penchant for breaking up and breaking from original unity and destroying in its quest for dominance. Practical reason, after all, is the mother of law and stepmother of legalism. And art, as emotion recollected in tranquility, experiences its own moment of reflection and its own anguished quest for a recreated unity. But before giving ourselves to such vistas, with religious themes just about to appear on their horizons, it is well to pause and to notice one sobering fact.

The philosophers whose insights are here laid under tribute have themselves no time for Christianity, and so we must seriously question the propriety of using their work for Christian ends.[8] Husserl, for instance, in a section of his book *Ideas* entitled 'The Transcendence of God Suspended', after he has looked at some grounds for belief in God, writes:

> What concerns us here, after merely touching on the different groupings of such rational grounds for the existence of a 'divine' Being beyond the world, is that this existence should not only transcend the world, but obviously also the 'absolute' Consciousness. It would thus be an *'absolute' in a totally different sense from the Absolute of Consciousness*, as on the other hand it would be a *transcendent in a totally different sense* from the transcendent in the sense of the world. We naturally extend the phenomenological reduction to this 'absolute' and to this 'transcendent'. It should remain disconnected from the field of research still to be created, so far as this is to be a field of pure Consciousness.[9]

To which one can only reply that the word absolute is notorious for the number of senses it can bear; and the fact that God is absolute in a sense of the word other than that used by Husserl for consciousness[10] does nothing to prevent the idea of a God-absolute being found, as Descartes thought it would, or at least in inchoate form, when the phenomenological reduction has bracketed out the problem of the objective reality of all that of which consciousness is conscious. Husserl's decision in the text quoted to disconnect the awareness of God from his field of research is quite unjustified on the critical principles by which he conducts his philosophy, and it reflects a deliberate ignorance of the insistence on immanence in the world with which religious believers consistently balance their profession of God's transcendence *vis-à-vis* the world. In short, and without trying to turn Husserl into another of those elusive anonymous Christians, it must be said that neither Husserl's own method nor the conventional religious view of God and the world can subject even the consciousness of God to the 'epoche', as Husserl here tries to subject it. God's objective reality, if Husserl is to be honest, must remain as much a problem (as Marx and Sartre proved it to be), and yet as much a possibility, as that of the 'world' from which Husserl tries so peremptorily to banish God.

Merleau-Ponty is not quite as peremptorily dismissive of religious belief but, though like many modern philosophers he never in the course of his *Phenomenology of Perception* does Christianity the honour of a sustained analysis of its claims, a pattern is nevertheless discernible in his recurring asides on the question of God. Since, in consequence of considering the human being as 'a project towards the world', he sees the world as something that is continually being 'constituted' by us and never, even in principle, completed he naturally rejects any Transcendent Reason, any divine Logos, any 'subject possessing in absolutely completed form all the knowledge which is adumbrated by our actual knowledge. . . a system of absolutely true thoughts, capable of coordinating all phenomena. . . this absolute object and this divine subject'.[11]

Such a divine consciousness, knowing completely and anticipating already as perfect, finished, what we can only know as for ever being constituted, if it existed, could bear no possible relationship to us or to the world we continually constitute.[12] All that needs to be said at this point is that this particular view of the omniscient (*a priori*) and immutable God, however familiar from so much traditional Christian theology, is also challenged by

Christians, and we shall see something of this challenge when we come to Moltmann. Meanwhile Merleau-Ponty's phenomenology is in itself no more automatically dismissive of any and every idea of God than is Husserl's phenomenology, to which it is so much indebted.

But what we can possibly gather from Merleau-Ponty, more than from Husserl, is the suspicion that the attempt of some of our newer Christian apologists to establish God's existence on the ground of the need for the *a priori* possibility of the truth of our speculative theorizing (or the need for the actual existence and hence the possibility of anticipating the perfection of our partial or partially achieved goals) is highly questionable,[13] and in fact does little more than furnish us with another example of knowledge in the form of theory or speculation, again subsuming the place of that faith within which it should be comprehended and whose 'text' it should really be satisfied to 'translate into precise language'. Here, once again, are thoughts to conjure with: that Logos is not the name of the Supreme God . . . but, once again, it is necessary to pause and, with renewed assurances that we do not wish to turn the following philosopher any more than the former into anonymous Christians, to pursue briefly the second part of the preliminary remarks of this section, concerned this time with specifically religious faith, through some reflections on Heidegger.

Heidegger believed apparently that what he termed ontotheology began with Plato; he is reputed to have executed a kind of 'turn' in the development of his own thought; and he is reported to have said 'that it is the true task of theology, which must be rediscovered, to seek the word which is capable of calling to faith and of preserving in faith'.[14] Some brief concluding reflections on these three admittedly disparate Heideggerian data must suffice for the needs of the present topic.

Ontotheology refers, roughly speaking, to a preference for essence over existence. For the emphasis with essence lies on the form of it which the analytic mind can define and identify. This emphasis in turn eases the way for the reflective mind to indulge its penchant for treating forms which it abstracts by analysis as the truly real things, the penchant for objectifying and reifying its own products, instead of seeing these as ciphers for a more comprehensive and unified reality, or, to use an image from Merleau-Ponty, instead of seeing its task as that of rendering in precise language a more original and authoritative text. Clearly the tendency of modern phenomonology to go in the direction of transcendental subjectivity – to treat as the absolute the *ego-cogito-cogitatum* – can lend support to ontotheology and the excessive dominance of the reflective intellect. The withdrawal of this support, it must be said, is to a greater or lesser extent obvious in most modern phenomenology. In Husserl it takes the form of his distinction, for instance, between intentionality of act and operative intentionality; with Merleau-Ponty it takes the much more substantial and adequate form of his insistence that the subject-object distinction breaks down in the case of the human body and of the central part the body plays in his phenomenology of perception;[15] with Heidegger it leads to the 'turn'.

Without wishing to enter the dubious debate as to whether and when[16] this alleged turn took place in the development of Heidegger's thought, we may at least link this issue with ontotheology by saying that he has certainly moved more and more determinedly in the direction of that 'Being' which erupts into consciousness and language, rather than the direction of consciousness itself and its more reflexive acts. Another way of putting this point, perhaps, is to say that for Heidegger we are *geworfene Entwurf* (thrown project), that, whereas all our emphasis up to now seems to have been placed on the project part of it, on intentionality, on our constituting our 'worlds', the emphasis now is on our 'thrownness', on that in which we inhere and subsist, on the sheer primordial power of being which we tend to forget in the very course of analysing it and cataloguing it in terms of forms and essences.

Heidegger, of course, offers no excuse for writers in English to capitalize 'Being' and then some paragraphs later, hoping the reader will not have noticed, to substitute the word 'God'.[17] On the contrary, for Heidegger we can be described as 'being-unto-death', and in the experience of facing this end of ourselves and our world, in the experience of anguish, as perhaps in other experiences such as those of boredom, joy, and love, we encounter nothingness which is the veil of being.[18] Peering through this veil we see the totality which we call world, we encounter Being, in all its finitude. But this thrown projection, apprehended at this level, can, after Merleau-Ponty, be called faith. It can even be called religious faith because of the depth and comprehensiveness at which it operates, for it structures our most basic existential attitudes to all that is, and it consequently dictates the human quality of every other perception, decision and act. Further, this particular encounter with Being and Nothingness to which Heidegger brings us, and at which he seems to stop, in fact at once veils and reveals deeper enablements or their absence, deeper decisions which may go in quite contrary directions, levels of the human spirit's adventure going still deeper than anything that can be called knowledge, and reaches of human faith at which it seems to turn into pure hope. Does this finite Being we encounter at once veil and reveal a depth or height of Being ultimately unthreatened by nothingness, or does it not?

All we would want to establish in this particular section, however, is the reference of the word 'faith' to that deepest, as yet undifferentiated, and most comprehensive consciousness of our being in the world and of our constitutive projection towards the world. And we would wish to promote the contention that this in itself gives faith priority over that speculative (or pragmatic, or even artistic) elaboration of it, that translation of its text, which is called doctrine (or moral theology, or religious art). This priority must, of course, be realized in the manner in which doctrine or elaborate speculative systems are constantly put at the service of this primordial faith; certainly faith must never seem to be simply assent to the doctrine, for that would reverse the proper priority and leave us under the illicit dominance of the objectified forms of the reflective intelligence. Finally, the contention is, of course, that the proper priority holds for all versions of faith, those associated with the particular religions of the world, but also those associated with atheism (since, as already stated, this contention has to do with epistemology, with the way in which we can perceive the human spirit passive and active at different levels, and not with divine interventions in past revelations or present enablements), for these latter must be reached, if they occur, in quite a different way. And this leads us to our second set of preliminary observations.[19]

(b) Faith and history

Reflection even on a doctrine will be complete only if it succeeds in linking up with the doctrine's history and the extraneous explanation of it, and in putting back the causes and meaning of the doctrine in an existentialist structure. There is, as Heidegger says, a 'genesis of meaning' (*Sinngenesis*), which alone, in the last resort, teaches us what a doctrine 'means'.[20]

We must secure in any worthwhile epistemology the primordial position of human faith, and while remaining suspicious of any automatic moves in modern apologetics that attempt to go directly from human transcendence to divine, we must keep open at the epistemological level the possibility that faith in a God immanent and transcendent should find a place and somehow prove its truth in its own way. But even if we had done all this, we should still be a long way from a full account of the nature and status of doctrine. For epistemology as such deals with the formal structures and processes of human consciousness, with the form and not with the matter or content, though form, in the case of the structures and processes of the human spirit also, can never be without matter or content.

Hence to give a purely epistemological account of religious faith, to set it, as should first be done in describing its human receptivity, against the background of primordial human faith, is still to treat it (together, incidentally, with primordial human faith) as something purely formal, abstract, or general. However, as Schleiermacher insistently pointed out, no such thing as 'religion in general' or a 'natural church' actually exists or has existed, although the phrase 'religious faith', like any other abstraction from the concrete plurality of what actually exists, can be used to designate 'the tendency of the human mind in general to give rise to religious emotions'.[21] Indeed, one might add, no such thing as atheism or agnosticism in general exists either. Whatever must be said in favour of Thrower's thesis on the superiority of absolute over relative atheism, even absolute atheisms are concrete, particular, and conditioned in content by their time and place. Not only are they too forms of faith (as some of the authors in our last section rather clearly illustrate), but they always have specific matter or content, and so, like other forms of faith, history as well as epistemology is required to give an account of them. Hence any new form of human faith, whatever claims might be made for its divine origin or definitive status, must be seen to emerge also, not only from that formal human faith of which epistemology speaks, but from the matter of such faiths as already exist.

It would be a mistake, when dealing with God's revelatory acts in history or God's on-going enablements in the cases of individual human beings, to discuss in the purely formal or abstract terms of some epistemology the creaturely receptivity of such alleged revelations and 'in-breathings' or inspirations, and to do no more. Debates such as that between Barth and Brunner on the actuality or nature of human receptivity to the self-revealing God have a huge air of utter unreality about them precisely because they begin and remain on such an abstract philosophical level.[22] By contrast, if anything at all is obvious from our sections on Son and Spirit, it is that the divine revelation (as his followers believe it to be) that came to them through Jesus and his earliest disciples was received and transmitted by both Jesus himself and his disciples in the existing cultural forms of Hellenistic Judaism. Had it not been so received and transmitted it could hardly have been received at all.

No one, then, disputes so obvious a fact as that the models used, say, in New Testament christologies all pre-existed, although, as we saw, there may be considerable disagreement about the when and the how of the necessary transformation of these models in order to make them fit Jesus of Nazareth. And it would make no sense at all to assume that the unique faith of Jesus of Nazareth as it spread in space and continued in time did not encounter the permanent need for new, hazardous, and often quite hotly disputed embodiments – not, one might add, embodiments in some handy formal 'philosophical' concepts, conveniently left lying around by Greeks and, like thin rubber containers, capable of receiving without reshaping the new Christian religious content. Form simply does not occur without concrete matter, the particular form of which it is.

As epistemology tells us about forms (the form, for instance of primordial human faith), history tells us about the matter or content of which these are the forms (the contents, for instance, which religious dimensions of that primordial human faith had already acquired). And since the matter can only be found where it has already been expressed or explicated, in looking to the origin and development of any new faith we must look to the images and symbols of myth, the concepts of theology, the shapes of practice, which are there for the new faith, in which it embodies itself, from which it can be seen to emerge, by means of the modification of which it secures its own distinctive symbolic, conceptual, liturgical, ethical 'body' in the world.

Hence Christian doctrines also must have their *Sinngenesis* produced by those who would fully understand them; and this inevitably involves full appreciation of the religious faith, or faiths, and at least the theological or doctrinal explications of these, which were already in possession of the post-biblical world that the followers of Jesus of Nazareth sought to conquer. In terms taken from our epistemologists of the previous section, Christians in post-biblical times attempted still to translate into precise language the original text which the life, death and destiny of Jesus of Nazareth, the unique, lived faith of Jesus had furnished for them. But they did so now by using the language into which a different original text – the dominant primordial religious faith of the Graeco-Roman world – was already translated.

So they invited risks and aroused hopes quite similar to those New Testament christologies which used existing religious models. And their resulting achievements, however successful or unsuccessful they may be thought to be, are in any case relativized by the 'translation' they were using. That is to say, if it is now replaced, or in the process of being replaced, by new 'translations' of a new text furnished by primordial human faith, then the doctrines to which it gave rise through its necessary modification, again however successful they may have been at the time, must themselves be replaced. Such historical relativity of doctrine, however, relative not only to the more primordial faith of which it is the expression, but relative also to the terms of the 'translations' of human religious faiths which different times and places offer and which Christians have to accept, if only to modify them, seems difficult to accept.

The natural human desire for the security of the immutable, the reasonable expectation that this should be found amongst the objects of religious faith even if all other endeavours of the human spirit and all other regions of its journeying were to fail to satisfy, has played some odd tricks on theologians and general believers alike. It is an experience common to many Christian churches that as their members, however reluctantly in many cases, accepted what may be called the historical conditioning of first the Old Testament and then the New, these very same members exhibit a surprising degree of resistance to any suggestion that ancient doctrinal formulae, whether sanctioned by councils or developed by impressive patristic traditions, should be considered to be no less conditioned by the by now often obsolete or obsolescent cultural categories of their time and place.

Apart altogether from the manner in which this resistance really gives the lie to otherwise stout confessions of the supremacy of Scripture in Christian life and thought, its main significance is probably to be found in the 'last ditch' mentality which it undoubtedly betrays. So as the long and bitter battle for the properly historical study of Scripture seems almost about to be won, as more and more people see that it can enhance rather than damage their Christian faith, ancient doctrinal formulae are still considered sacrosanct, and any attempt to relativize them, much less to replace them, even when accompanied by the honest intent thus to release the truth of the Christian faith which in their way they preserved for their own time, is still too often met with overt suspicion and hostility. One cannot avoid the impression that so very many of the Fathers, who were themselves only too painfully aware of the risks and the courage required to advance their own creative reformulations of the faith, would look with some misgivings on so many of their modern admirers who use this admiration as a justification of their own refusal, after all this time, to risk moving forward once more.

This is not to say that no voices are heard nowadays to complain about inherited trinitarian doctrine. But one does get the distinct impression on listening for a while to these complaints that they do not go to the heart of the matter. Almost everyone who writes on the Trinity complains, for instance, about the word 'person', how very misleading it can be because of the kind of meaning it has accumulated over the centuries of a struggle for democracy which yielded an age of individualism. Personality came to mean, in Berkhof's words, 'an autonomous and self-conscious power which by its moral strength defends itself against the impersonal powers around'. Hence Berkhof's judgment on the confusing phrase 'the three persons of the Trinity' is that 'it is no use to maintain it any longer, especially since this formula from the very beginning has functioned not as a power of unity but as a source of confusion'.[23]

Rightly suspect of contributing to a tritheistic perception of the Godhead, however unconsciously entertained, the term person has nevertheless been made into something of a scapegoat. Drive this term out of inherited trinitarian theology into the wilderness and all will be well! Such is the implication of the kind of move made by so able and perceptive a theologian as Karl Barth when, having expressed his own reservations about the use of the term 'person' for the Three, he substitutes the terms 'mode or way of being' (*modus entitativus, tropos hyparxeos*) and then continues to enfold the rest of the traditional doctrine.[24] Yet the need for renewal must affect the whole of the doctrine of the Trinity as it has come down to us from patristic times, in all its forms. For it would be naive in the extreme to take Augustine's raillery against the arrogance of the philosophers with which he opens his *De Trinitate* as anything which even remotely approaches an adequate assessment of his debt to them. Similar sentiments expressed by so many of the Fathers have no doubt played their part in persuading historians and patristic scholars alike to underestimate the true extent to which trinitarian speculation is a product of a time and a culture long past. And the need is long overdue to adopt a thoroughly historical approach to the whole issue.

In summary, then, the doctrinal formulations which have fashioned a trinitarian picture of God and which have come down to us substantially from the fourth and fifth centuries AD must be set in relation to the richer and more varied theologies of Scripture; more importantly, they must be set in relationship to the foundational faith of Christians which comes to them from Jesus. It is perhaps the ultimate function of all theology to point as accurately as it may to the living faith of Jesus and continually to deconstruct itself in the process, instead of trying to empty faith into its own theological content and to claim for itself that living assent, that lived-out conviction and commitment which is due solely to Emmanuel, God-with-us. Consequently, as part of their deconstruction and reconstruction, trinitarian theologies must be set in relationship to the pagan religious categories of concept and image, of social model and sacred observance, from which in post-biblical times also their whole expressible content was originally derived by a process of modification, and subsequently developed.

9

Greek Theology

By Greek theology here I mean primarily the religious thought of those ancient non-Christians such as Plato, Aristotle, the Stoa, Plotinus, whose religious quest inspired the educated élite of the ancient Western world and whose theological formulations entirely dominated that world. Ever since an apologist like Justin Martyr in his first *Apology* (written round the middle of the second century AD) complained that the persecutors and detractors of Christianity were simply not acting according to that reason (*Logos*) to which they otherwise paid such persistent lip-service, the influence of their Greek theology upon the development of Christian thought was bound to be much more extensive than that which we should in any case suspect from the normal cultural influences of any time and place upon their writers. The 'booty from the Egyptians' mentality of Justin and his successors saw to that. Like pirates upon the high seas of the ancient world, with full confidence in the divine reason (*Logos*) which they believed had taken flesh in their founder and leader, Justin and his successors simply considered to be their destined property whatever remnants of divine reason they found still captive in the religious thought and imagination of their pagan contemporaries. Not all Christian spokesmen, of course, explicitly adopted this strategy, but most of them did, and even the truculent Tertullian, with his 'what has Athens to do with Jerusalem?', shows far more dependence upon Stoic concepts and Stoic theological formulations than such intemperate outbursts would lead one to expect. The strategy was so successful that the West was quickly won for Christianity.

Now pirates and other adventurers, if they survive at all, have

105

a habit of becoming rich and settling down as establishment figures, guardians of property and therefore of law and order. But it is odd how quickly people become the servants of that which they manage to acquire! And the extent to which Christianity, having won the West, itself became Westernized, has only recently begun to dawn mainly on those engaged in its more recent missionary expansions. Our interest here must, of course, be confined to the theological part of the process, but it is absolutely essential for any correct account of our present subject that we assess as accurately as possible the true and full influence of Greek theology on central Christian formulations concerning the nature of the God of Jesus Christ.

Now, although 'in recent years there has been a welcome increase in the volume and quality of work published in English on later Greek philosophy and a fruitful linking of studies in philosophy and patrology',[25] such studies still remain at such a highly specialized level that they tend to leave the older theological and historical stereotypes still intact. Beguiled, as we hinted already, by so many of the Fathers' own disclaimers about philosophy or the philosophers; misled by the belief that the most potentially destructive heresy which Christianity ever had to face, the Arian heresy, was caused by the dominant philosophical interests of the great heresiarch,[26] and even when prejudices of a particularly Calvinist kind were absent, always reluctant to admit how much the 'queen' owes to the 'servant' sciences, common scholarly opinion has consistently failed to assess fairly and in a balanced fashion the true contribution of pagan Greek theology to developing Christian thought. This is naturally not the place to try to redress the balance in any extensive manner, but it might help our more particular project if we were to pass briefly in review some of the salient features of a theology, a way of talking and thinking about God, which developed and preserved its distinctive nature from Plato, Aristotle and the Stoa (with other lesser tributaries) down to the Middle Ages, and to Aquinas almost as much as to Bonaventure and beyond. It is no longer sufficient, it seems, even in the case of works which restrict their interest to a specific doctrine such as that of the Trinity, to outline the development of the doctrine and, in the course of that outline, to offer cross-references occasionally to similar Greek religious constructs. The full influence of Greek religious thought on developing Christian trinitarian theology can be assessed prop-

erly only by those who take the trouble first to survey in their own
context such Greek theological theses and problems as undoubtedly influenced Christian speculation: the divine ineffability, the
true extent of divine immutability, divine creative activity and its
suggested 'intermediaries', responsive human *eros* and the distinct *hypostaseis* which can be described in its return to the One,
the source of all; all themes of obvious relevance to the developing
Christian doctrine of God.

Plato is the inheritor of previous philosophical themes to the
effect, for instance, that unity must underlie the bewildering
multiplicity of the reality we experience; that the One is God; that,
despite impressions which may be conveyed by the myth-makers
and the poets, God is in no way similar to mortals and that neither
divine revelation nor human ingenuity have yet enabled human
beings to know God in any adequate manner; that, despite the
inevitably problematic nature of any language we may use to
speak of God we may yet be convinced that something rational
(Logos) rules the world and works to bring harmony to its
apparent chaos. It is Plato's view that, despite Parmenides'
argument against the true reality of change, and though we must
hold on to some permanent forms of things, 'Reality or the sum
of things is both at once – all that is unchangeable and all that is in
change' (*Sophist*, 249 C–D).[27] Yet it was the evils associated with
flux and change in the world we know that set Plato too on the
quest for wisdom – and salvation. But more important, no doubt,
than any themes which Plato inherited, or any philosophical
puzzle to be solved, was the powerful inspiration of the deeply
religious life of Socrates and of the death which consummated
Socrates' fidelity to his quest. Aristotle said of Socrates that he
was 'busying himself about ethical matters and neglecting the
world of nature as a whole' (*Met.* 987 3). Socrates' lived conviction
of the superiority of the spiritual over the physical, of soul over
body, the moral and religious conviction in which he lived and
died that goodness mattered beyond death, when taken in conjunction with the notion of a divine mind and its care for the
universe,[28] certainly gave impulse and direction to Plato's quest.

'The notion of Eros, loving desire, is central to the philosophy
of Plato. It appears throughout the dialogues, notably in the
Phaedrus (esp. 249Eff.), but is expounded most fully in the *Sym-
posium*. There it is made clear that eros runs right through the
universe, and affects all forms of being.'[29] Drawn forward by the

loving desire of which Socrates in life and death was the very incarnation to him, Plato, though he often seems about to conclude in his dialogues that human life is laughable, an affair of mere puppets who take themselves as seriously as if they actually ran the show (*Laws* 644D, 803B–C), usually manages to wrestle from his dialogue-form the belief that we do bear moral responsibility for our destiny, and that God, who is 'our keeper' and 'the very best of masters', supremely wise and good, will not allow a good man to come to harm either in life or after death, but will reward the good beyond death with his very presence (see the account of Socrates' death in the *Phaedo*, esp. 62,67).

Not that Plato pretended to know who or what God is. He not only inherited a reverent agnosticism on the subject, a humble sense of the severe limitations of human powers of knowing, but many of the passages he wrote became source texts for the great apophatic theology which is common to pagan Greek and Christian theology in succeeding centuries. He often speaks of God in the personal (indeed 'polytheistic') language of Greek popular religion,[30] but (not unlike God's Word, Wisdom,Torah, in Jewish religious imagination) much that Plato has to say about Forms, particularly the major Forms of the Good and the Beautiful, entities which seem at first more like impersonal principles than personal beings, was taken by his followers and commentators to be about the divinity. For instance, there is a passage in the *Republic* in which he says he cannot really say what the Good is in itself, in which he uses the analogy of the sun and its rays to illustrate his point, and in which he concludes that the 'reality which gives their truth to the objects of knowledge and the power of knowing to the knower, you must say is the idea of the Good, and you must conceive it as being the cause of knowledge and of truth in so far as it is known'. The phrase 'in so far as it is known' is pivotal, for he goes on to insist that we must realize that, as all things owe their very being to it, 'the Good itself is not being, but is beyond being and superior to it in dignity and power' (*Rep.* 506D–509B). This passage was sometimes combined later with the passage on the One from the *Parmenides*: 'It appears that the One neither is one nor is at all . . . It is not named or spoken of, not an object of opinion or of knowlege, not perceived by any creature' (*Parmenides* 141E); and the combination was little less than a programme in successive centuries for the higher flights of mystical thought.[31]

More concrete, perhaps, though no less problematic in their own way, were Plato's scattered suggestions about the God's creative activity in its relationship to the creation. Though the *eros* that drives toward the God was present in all things and the God bore ultimate concern for all, both the evil that seems so endemic to this empirical world, and the natural superiority of soul or mind over matter, suggested some distance between the God and the world of our everyday experience. In the *Timaeus*, where the creation of the world is discussed, there is, for instance, a distinction between the origin of the divine and the origin of the mortal; it is said of the maker: 'of the divine he himself was the maker, but the making of the mortal he committed to his offspring' (*Tim.* 69C). No clear pattern emerges, however, since another passage in the same dialogue describes the creation thus:

> Let me tell you then why the maker made this world of change. He was good, and the good can never have any jealousy of anything. And being free from jealousy, he desired that all things should be as like himself as they could be. This is in the truest sense the origin of creation and of the world. . . God desired that all things should be good and nothing bad, so far as this was attainable. And so finding the whole visible sphere not at rest, but moving in an irregular and disorderly fashion, out of disorder he brought order, considering that this was in every way better than the other. (*Tim.* 29D–30A).

Watson suggests that the phrase, 'so far as was attainable' is explained somewhat in a later passage in the dialogue where the mind or intelligence which is of the maker's comes into contact with some 'necessity' which seems part of matter, and does as much as the latter can be persuaded to allow.[32]

However, even if no clear pattern emerges, enough is suggested by Plato's groping after answers to the problem of existence to support as many systems as his followers care to erect: the God unknown, who creates out of goodness, perhaps creating some things through intermediaries, and, while desiring good for all, meeting the resistance of a certain intransigence in the material world for which it is not responsible.[33] In the end, at the heart of Plato's philosophy, at the centre of this world which was created out of the goodness of the maker, is the loving desire for wisdom[34] or Truth, for the possession of the Good and the vision of the Beautiful, for that which we can hardly name and in this world do not really know. Like Matthew's 'Be ye perfect as your heavenly Father is perfect', the good of human life for Plato is the *homoiosis theo*, becoming like to the God in the measure in which this is possible for humans. And Plato's crowning conviction is that the one whose loving desire for the Good leads to a life of virtue, and to prayer and worship of God, 'is loved by God' (*Laws*, 716).[35]

Already, and before any part of the great expanse and influence of the tradition which Plato founded comes into view, it must be possible to see how attractive this religious vision would prove to be to Christian preachers and apologists, and even to those questors who would finally find in Christianity the true philosophy for which in their lifetime they searched. A scholastic period would soon come to this tradition, of course, for the human spirit cannot stand too much creativity, or the questioning of conventional views and standards which inevitably accompanies all creativity; and scholasticism in any case carries its own advantages, as we must shortly see. But not by any means the least of the attractions of Plato's bequest to history was the dialogue form, the refusal of the closed system, the quest and the openness and the willingness to hold in creative tension themes which, though they seem incompatible, can each promise some progress towards an elusive answer to permanent questions; the strength and the power of all art lies in the delicacy of its probing, as tentative as it is tenacious.[36] Even if it were not encumbent on Christians, out of the very conviction of unconditioned grace by which they are supposed to live,[37] to accept as gift of God to them all that the world and history has to offer, and particularly all human motions towards their God, the aching desire at the heart of this tradition for release from the evils of the world and for the vision of the Good, a desire at once supported by and seeking the conviction that God first loved the world, could not but attract those entrusted with the message that God was in Jesus reconciling the world to himself by his own sacrificial love.

Before we go on to the period known as that of Middle-Platonism, the philosophical period which in fact saw the beginnings of the growth of Christian trinitarian theology, a brief word on the theology of Aristotle and of the Stoa will prove useful, for though the normal stereotypes of these thinkers often unjustly rule them out of serious consideration in contexts such as this – the former being depicted as a prototypical empiricist who gradually turned his back on idealism and the latter as thoroughgoing materialists – their theological influence on the tradition under review was in each case of quite unmistakable significance, and they certainly contributed key elements to that rather eclectic theology which provided the common theological currency in the Graeco-Roman world of the middle-Platonic period, the world which witnessed the birth of Christian theology.

As is often the case with extant religious writings, the texts which undertake to argue to God's existence and nature, though usually varied in approach and often quite elaborate in detail, are in Aristotle not really either the most persuasive or the most enlightening.[38] The 'argument from motion' which Aristotle developed very fully indeed has given critics down the centuries much opportunity to sound superior. But the conviction, or belief, or hope which it barely conceals is that behind all the movement, the growth and decay, the bewildering change and frantic locomotion of this world, must be something which energizes it all. Two things, for present purposes at least, are striking about this belief of Aristotle's. First, when he attempts to explain how his Prime Mover[39] does actually energize this whole moving world, when he deals with the relationship of the world to God, an idea comes to the fore which is suspiciously like the Platonic *eros*. In search of something which does not share the world's condition of perpetual motion, something which can cause all change and movement without being itself changeable or in motion, he advances the idea of that which is an object of *desire* (and thought, of course). Such an object can cause all growth and change and movement simply by being, in its awesome perfection, the object of our contemplation and of the desire that runs through all the world.

Second, and consequently, there is an area of Plato's thought, concerning the immutability of the most real being, which Aristotle tidied up, and though his tidying may have left the state of the question even more unsatisfactory than the rich profusion of Plato's references, it proved quite influential in subsequent development of the tradition. As part of his case for the superiority of soul over body, Plato had talked of soul as self-moving, and he had talked of souls which controlled the world. Again, though he had insisted on the immutability of his Forms – for that which is regulative cannot be as changeable as those things for which it provides the standard – he had wondered: 'Are we really to be so easily convinced that change, life, soul, understanding have no place in that which is perfectly real – that it has neither life nor thought, but stands immutable in solemn aloofness, devoid of intelligence?' (*Sophist* 249A).

So, apart from the untidiness of the many terms in Plato which could be considered as references to the divine (some souls, Forms, the One, the maker or demiurge, as well as the more obvious and more personal references), there was the untidiness of wanting immutability while wondering about life in the immutable. Now 'Aristotle,' as Watson says, 'is insistent that God is a living being, the best living life, who not only has, but is, perpetual life.'[40] And he is equally adamant that there can be no motion (which, as Watson points out, to Aristotle meant growth, alteration, and local motion) in the highest being, the God. His tidying-up, if it may be so described, can be recounted briefly as follows. Mind (*nous*) was, in any case, agreed to be the highest part of soul. So the God is mind, and that spark of *nous* in us is that in us which is most Godlike. Then the activity in which the divine life consists, and which is not motion in any of the senses mentioned above, is simply the thought of this mind, thinking, not anything other than itself (for that would involve dependence and change), but itself. 'Aristotle,' as Watson puts it, 'deliberately emphasizes the unbroken activity of the Divine Mind by repeating the verbal form of the noun – "The Thinking is the Thinking of the Thinking".'[41]

It does sound slightly dreary, even if the God, by definition, is always contemplating the most perfect thing, and it had its own problems for those who wanted the God to be at least aware of the world (Aristotle, naturally, would not have the Forms as the thought of God). But it did transmit a concept of God's life as the eternal and changeless bliss of self-contemplation. And, oddly enough, there is even a sense in which we may hold Aristotle, more than Plato, responsible for that axiomatic conviction of the immutability of God which plays such a prominent part in future theology, Christian as well as pagan.[42]

It is commonplace to wonder how the deep personal spirituality of the *Hymn to Zeus* by Cleanthes, successor to Zeno, the founding father of Stoic philosophy, can be reconciled with the programmatic materialism of the Stoa. But this is now due more, perhaps, to anti-God and anti-mind overtones which the word materialism has picked up in post-Marx and post-Pavlov days than it is to the criticism which the Stoa had to bear in their own era. (Tertullian in his most orthodox works was probably 'materialist' in his theology in something like the Stoic sense.) And few readers of Christian theology can fail to have some sympathy with the Stoic view that 'immaterial spirit' is such an elusive term that more than any other term in the history of theology it provides convenient answers to seemingly intractable problems, as well as providing support to claims for knowledge and truth otherwise significantly unsupported. In any case, the Stoa seemed as determined as Hegel was later to make human beings feel *zu Hause* in the only world we know, to resist the other-worldliness of Plato and Aristotle, and to this end they directed their considerable theological endeavours. It could be a drastic mistake indeed to confine their influence on the future to their moral system, though that is undoubtedly where their influence primarily lies.[43]

In Stoic theology the passive principle in reality is matter, and the active principle is the *Logos* that is within it. A thing of many names – *physis* or nature, *pur technikon* or craftsmanlike fire, Zeus or the Father God, *Logos* or reason, *pneuma* or spirit (but conceived as something like air and fire) – this was the God, the creative, dynamic principle in the world, ever consuming and reshaping the world to its destined perfection, making all that had or would come to be, containing within itself as the supreme principle the seminal principles (*spermatikoi logoi*) in accordance with which all things came to be.

> The *spermatikoi logoi* went easily into Latin as *rationes seminales* and expressed the Christian consciousness of God's control of the world such as we find it in St. Augustine. Whatever about the background and source of St. John's Gospel, the Christian message could easily be represented as the perfection of this branch also of Pagan philosophy, the Stoic. Christ could be presented as the Logos who emerges from God the Father to proclaim his truth in the world – the *logos prophorikos* expressing the *logos endiathetos* (internal reason and reason expressed, according to a common Stoic distinction). And the Logos of course is also *pneuma*, Spirit.[44]

Christian borrowing here was made deceptively easy since in Stoic theory, human beings, as subordinate *spermatikoi logoi*, could participate in the divine *Logos* and thus be sharers in the truth that was both salvific and creative. Indeed the term *Logos* as a principal name for God was a godsend to Christians, in whose founder, according to the Prologue to the Fourth Gospel, the divine *Logos* had become incarnate, and it did more than any other single pagan theological term to justify Justin Martyr's take-over bid for the best of pagan thought, and to set in motion the development of classical Christian theology.[45]

Middle-Platonism is normally taken to refer to a period in the development of the philosophical tradition with which we are dealing which stretches roughly from the first century BC to the beginning of the third century AD, thus spanning the origin of Christianity, with which, needless to say, it scarcely concerned itself at all. Two of the main characters of Middle-Platonism are normally said to be its scholasticism and its 'ecumenism'. Filling a period in which religious and theological issues clearly predominated,[46] Middle-Platonists, though never a cohesive school with a set system of doctrines, nevertheless began to do the things which facilitate the leisurely and detailed perusal of the profligacy of creative thought bequeathed to them: they began to systematize in different ways and to different degrees, to collect major theological texts as *loci*, to comment, criticize, harmonize, and defend, and in this way they began to provide standard ways of dealing with gradually standardized issues; and then they also began to bring together the major contributions of the important theological traditions such as the Platonic, the Aristotelian, the Stoic, and others which I have not had occasion to mention. The characters of scholasticism and ecumenism were to some extent in preparation before the Middle-Platonists, of course, but our main interest in these is less in their historical detail than in the fact that they do give to the time and place of our immediate interest standard modes of religious discourse.

Speusippus, for instance, Plato's nephew and successor as head of the Academy, was already beginning to fashion out of the rich variety of Plato's theological suggestions, it is reliably believed, one of the most persistent themes of later theology: that the One (God), as the principle and source of all that is, divine and mortal, is superior to being and cannot be named even by the names of the Good or the Beautiful. And Xenocrates, Speusippus' successor in turn, is credited with having placed the Platonic Forms as ideas in the mind of God, forming a sort of second level of divine being – the first level being that of the First Principles, the Monad which is Mind or Nous and Dyad (the Dyad in divinity is sometimes later connected with the origin of matter and with rather stronger forms of Platonic dualism than either Plato – probably – or Plotinus would countenance, but such matters do not immediately concern our topic). Later, Atticus, one of the critics of Aristotle on account of the apparent unconcern for our world of the latter's God, appealed to an allegedly Platonic view of Soul, clearly not an irrational (*alogos*) thing, setting the universe in order and in fact moving through all of it as nature (*physis*). 'We are,' Watson comments, 'being presented with the Stoic Logos but now in Platonic dress.'[47]

One would not wish to give the impression of clear lines of development issuing in an agreed scheme, but at the same time one cannot be surprised at the kind of theology one then meets in Middle-Platonists like Numenius and Albinus. Of Numenius Watson writes: 'His first God is at rest, removed from all activity and creation, which is left to his son, the second God.'[48] And he quotes Albinus to the effect that God is called Father, 'because he, as the cause of all things, sets in order the heavenly mind and the soul of the world in accordance with himself and his thoughts. By his own will he has filled all things with himself, as being the cause of its mind. And this, being set in order by the Father, itself sets in order the whole of nature within this world.'[49] And he comments:

> Because of the desire to combine transcendence and providence, this scheme of a First God, and then a second level of being, who or which communicates with a third level, is another recurrent feature of Middle Platonism. We saw the beginnings of such a schema in Speusippus and Xenocrates. Eudorus had his supreme One above the principles of the Monad and the Dyad which are active in the universe. Philo has his own special reasons for insisting on the One supreme God, but with the help of Stoicism brings in the Logos, like the Demiourgos, to be the intermediary with the world. Plutarch too talks of the Supreme God and the intermediary Logos. Moderatus has his First One, but also a system of three Ones. Numenius, Proclus tells us, 'proclaims three gods, calling the first "Father", the second "Creator", and the third "Creation" '. Apuleius too talks of the First God, where the second seems to be Nous or Logos. This development cannot claim to be due to any emergent Christian Trinitarian thinking.[50]

Nor would it ever yield the Christian Trinity. And yet the spread of binitarian schemas, sometimes growing towards trinitarian ones, is unmistakable beneath the variety of thought and terminology. But what is more important for our purpose than these emerging schemata are the common concerns, concepts and even terms which increasingly come to characterize this scholastic and eclectic period in the development of ancient Western religious thought.

Before approaching the development, towards the end of this period, of Christian trinitarian theology itself, and in order to make the sampling in this section seem a little less incomplete, we might look briefly at two major non–Christian figures. One is a Jew who tried to do for Judaism at the time of Jesus and Paul what Christians would soon try to do for Christianity – to cast its claims, that is, not just in the general categories of Hellenistic culture, but in terms familiar to the philosophically educated – Philo of Alexandria.[51] The other is a man who gave the by now eclectic Platonic tradition its final form in Western history – Plotinus, the founder of Neo-Platonism, as more recently it came to be called.

Philo's Jewish faith had of course accustomed him to the idea of one God who could not be seen by mortal eyes, but who had nevertheless created the world, acted, and even appeared within it. And he was accustomed to the language of God's word – the word of God, for instance, by which in Psalm 33.6 the heavens were said to have been made. The first of these ideas seemed eminently translatable into the Greek doctrine of the One or Monad, indeed one 'beyond Monad' for whom no creaturely language whatever availed. Another way of putting this point was to say that God in his essence was utterly unknown to us, but he was known in his *dynameis* (powers) and their *energeiai* (works). The two major *dynameis* Philo named as Creator (*ktistes, demiourgos*) and Lord, for in the works of God's creation and his ruling or providentially lording it over his creation, we can see and know God, though not, once again, in his inner essence.[52] And the term which connotes that level of the divinity which can be known, which is manifested in the *dynameis* and *energeiai*, which expresses God's activity on and in the world of our experience, is *Logos*.[53] Now the use of the *Logos* to express Philo's second idea, about God's immanence, clearly owes a great deal to Stoic theology; indeed, the distinction between the One who is invisible, unknowable, and unnameable and the *Logos* who acts and 'appears' in this world (for instance, to Moses), who is to some extent knowable and visible, was to have a long history in Christian (binitarian and) trinitarian theology, in writers like Irenaeus, Novatian, Tertullian, and many later Fathers.[54] 'The supreme God is too remote to have direct contact with the world,' as Henry Chadwick puts it, 'and it was his Logos who appeared, e.g. at the burning bush. The Logos dwelt especially in Moses, who was thereby virtually deified.'[55] And this *Logos* of Philo, according to

Chadwick, was 'the idea of ideas, the first-begotten Son of the uncreated Father and "second God", the pattern and mediator of the creation, the archetype of human reason, and "the man of God" '.[56] But it is the Stoic origin of this part of Philo's position which is of more immediate interest here, in order to see how obvious a vehicle for Jewish religion (and hereafter, Christian) was this fusion of traditions in Middle-Platonism.

In Philo's words: 'As then the city which was fashioned before-hand within the mind of the architect held no place in the outer world, but had been imprinted on the soul of the craftsman as by a seal, even so the world that consists of the Forms would have no other location than the divine Reason (Logos), which was the author of this physical world' (*On the Creation of the World*, 20). 'There is no mistaking the Stoic influence on the concept in Philo,' Watson writes, 'The Stoic *logos prophorikos* can be interpreted as God's expression of himself in the world. The *logos spermatikos* is the overall seminal principle which rules the world and sees that the world plan is unfolded through the subordinate *logoi spermatikoi* or seminal principles which it contains. By making these equivalent to the Platonic Forms and making them reside in the Logos, which in turn is made equivalent to the Demiourgos or Maker of the *Timaeus*, Philo managed to combine God's providence with his transcendence, because the First God is still unsullied with creation.'[57]

Needless to say, it is perfectly obvious from Philo, if not from the other religious thinkers with whom we have been dealing, that these various distinctions between the God who is beyond being and knowledge, and the God who acts at the level of being and is therefore to some extent knowable (*logos*), does not in the least qualify the basic monotheism. We are not yet in the presence of anything like Lampe's 'double projection', by which the idea of the divine *Logos* is projected on to the distinct historical personality of Jesus, and as a result the distinct personality of Jesus is projected back into the Godhead (and we shall have to decide if that is in fact what occurred).[58] But just as it is declared to be impossible in this tradition for human beings to talk about the One, the God beyond being, the inner essence of God (if even a word such as 'essence' applies), so it is impossible for the human mind to track the emanating powers and works of divinity which are palpable in the world, back to the origin in the unoriginate One and give an accurate, objective account in human language of the 'links' or stages along the way. This point is best expressed in a type of material in the tradition which we have been studying which again becomes standardized during the period of Middle-Platonism. It is the material concerning ways of 'approaching' God: that is, given the agnosticism which is at the very heart of this religious philosophy, how can we know or say anything about God at all? The scholastic answer to this question, which can be found, for instance, in ch. 10 of the *Didaskalikos* of Albinus, is that there are three ways of approach to the First God (*protos theos*): 1. the way of negation (which for positive productivity is equivalent to saying nothing at all): by 'removing' the plane surface and then the line we arrive at the (disappearing) point; 2. the way of ascent, by moving up the grades of goodness or beauty towards that perfection (which will, of course, be beyond good and beauty); 3. the way of analogy from certain things in our world which become palpable to us in their output or effluence, but are often intangible or invisible in themselves, e.g. the streams and river which spring from a hidden well, the rays of the sun, the stem and flower of a hidden root, the offspring from the parent.[59] By such traditional material the dominant religious philosophy of this era is telling us something important about itself. It is telling us that it is not the result of anyone's having been able to observe the One and the whole process by which all things divine and mortal have their source in the One, but that it is nevertheless a way, an approach to God, and that it can only do what it in fact does, that is, describe in stuttering human language, in the pericopes of human thought and imagination, the One God who is beyond being and yet somehow with us; beyond reason, yet somehow making sense of things; beyond good, yet somehow concerned and involved.

Philosophy, after all, was in Plato's phrase 'a training to die'. Difficult though it may be for us to detach the modern image of philosophy and to catch a glimpse of the ancient substance underneath, we can make little progress in our effort to understand the power and attraction of this eclectic Platonism unless we can see something at least of its vocational nature (in the sense in which some Christians speak of a vocation to the religious life). How else can we understand Aristotle's view of the most happy human life, or the near-monastic circumstances of Plotinus and his group, and how could we even begin to understand the death of Socrates? We are undoubtedly dealing with the intellectual élite of the ancient world – for the good and obvious reason that the doctrine with which we are shortly to be concerned was the product of the intellectual élite of the Christian community[60] – but even before we take into account the ascetic and moral stress present fom the beginning in this philosophy (or even the theurgy of later Platonists which at its best resembled the Christian sacramental ideas – at *their* best – on approaches to God through use of material things), and while resisting any tendency to concentrate exclusively on its 'mystical' elements, we are bound to see that the philosopher is one on a 'way', driven or drawn by the divine *eros*. Socrates, philosopher, lover of wisdom *par excellence*, is for Plato the very incarnation of the loving desire for the true and the good, and his death sets the seal upon that hope of eternal life which is its final bequest. Philosophy was nothing less than a way of life and death, a way from the ills and evils of the world we know to the eternal bliss and rest in the God whom in this world we cannot know. We have already commented on the use of the term 'faith', and how apposite it can be for such a religious tradition.[61] It only remains to add here that of course this 'way' to the God would not have been there at all had not the super-abundant goodness of the God first overflowed and eventuated in the creation of all things down to the limits of formless matter.[62] The philosopher, the lover of wisdom in all of us, is thus attempting to return to the source from which all have come. But we begin to anticipate Plotinus, when all we need to say at this point is that philosophy, being a 'way' to God, is itself the groping human attempt to plot that way by following as best it can the tracks of God's creative outflow. It is not, nor can it ever pretend to be, an account of the stages, divine and creaturely, of this outflow by one who has already observed them from God's own point of view.

An interesting observation about *Logos* may be made at this point also, and it will serve as a further introduction to Plotinus. Though Philo calls the *Logos* God's first-begotten Son, the second God, and other names which would suggest a second divine being or even 'person', it is obvious from the complex of his thought that these are but imaginative expressions for that of God which in and through his creative and ruling powers is active in the world and makes sense of it to rational creatures. *Logos* in Philo relates to *ho legon*, One who speaks to us in creation and rule and, of course, for a Jew through Moses and in the Mosaic revelation of the Scriptures.[63] With the meaning of Reason, innate and expressed, *Logos* is even less likely to convey the impression of a distinct individual divinity than are the terms which are normally used for the 'second level' of the Godhead, terms such as Mind (Nous), Creator, Dyad, and so on. And from Plotinus on, as Armstrong and Markus remark, *Logos* comes even more frequently to mean 'a power which represents or expresses a higher principle on a lower plane of being'.[64] Even 'power' may be too substantial a word here, and some such word as 'process' preferable. For what is really at issue once again is the rational faith that the world we know is in structure and destiny a rational event as the expression of the creative goodness of the hidden God.[65]

The outlines of the creative refashioning of this tradition in the third century AD by Plotinus – a man of religious insight as deep and religious experience as high as any in Western history – is already well known. Giving a new intensity to the conviction of this tradition that the destiny of humans was likeness to God, indeed union with God, yet that the One was utterly beyond predication of any kind – 'And yet this "He is" does not apply: the Supreme has no need of Being: even "He is good" does not apply since it indicates Being' (*Enneads* VI, 7.38) – Plotinus described the origin of all things from the One, both unoriginate source of all and ultimate goal, and the way of the return to the One, in terms which were to be axiomatic for all further development of the tradition with which we here have to do, and which proved decisive, furthermore, for the standard mystical treatises of both Christians and pagans thereafter. From the One, again because of the ungrudging expansivenes of its very goodness, comes the Mind or Intellectual Principle (Nous), the image of the One which contemplates the One after its manner and in turn pours forth a lower level of Being which is called Soul, the higher part of which is caught up in the permanent bliss of contemplating the immutable Divine Mind, but the lower part of which is in action in the world of sense and nature, fashioning all that is reasonable, good and beautiful in human behaviour and in the physical realm as a whole. Because we are ensouled, and drawn by this beauty that reaches from the One to the lowest limits of our material existence, we can, by asceticism and virtue, rise to contemplation of the divine Mind and, by the grace of God,[66] come even to that ecstatic union with the One of which the closest bliss of human lovers is but the most distant analogy.

The fact that Plotinus uses the term *hypostasis* for each level of

divinity in its creative emanation – and thus unwittingly anticipated a use of the term for the three-in-one with which the
Cappadocians, perhaps too hastily, are commonly credited with
having finalized the classical doctrine of the Trinity – this fact
should not make us overlook another 'trinity' in Plotinus which,
though not as prominent a feature of his thought as the trinity of
One, Mind, Soul, was in some ways more promising for, and
certainly exercised its own influence upon Christian developments. For in the case of the trinity of One, Mind, Soul, though
Plotinus sometimes suggests a fairly clear-cut distinction between
the divine order where life is immutable and the 'lower order'
where it is not,[67] Soul nevertheless, if only in its lower part, and
if only 'accidentally',[68] suffers motion of the kind that this world
knows. Consequently there are indications that it belongs to the
creaturely sphere of motion, though it no doubt belongs principally to the immutable sphere of truly divine life, and this would
cause problems if this scheme were used in framing a Christian
doctrine of the Trinity, at least after its Holy Spirit had finally
become a fully-fledged member of it, and Christian insistence on
divine immutability had become more absolute even than that of
the Greeks.

But the trinity of Being, Life and Intelligence[69] did in fact,
probably through Plotinus' biographer, Porphyry, influence the
Christian thinker Marius Victorinus, and he, as we must see, is
something of a bridge between Neo-Platonism and the Christian
thought of Augustine and the West. This second 'trinity' arises
largely because Plotinus, who often describes Mind (Nous) as
looking to or at the One from which it emanated, thereby becoming 'pregnant', and thereafter existing as vision identical with
itself since it 'knows what has come to be within it' (*Enneads* VI,
7.35), at times qualifies this account as follows. Is it the case, he
asks, that 'when Intellectual-Principle (Nous) looked towards the
Good it had intellection of that unity as a multiplicity and, itself a
unity, applied its act by breaking into parts what it was too feeble
to know as a whole'? He rejects this suggestion, since this would
in fact imply a looking upon the One utterly devoid of intellection.
And so he qualifies: 'We must think of it not as looking but as
living.' Dependent upon the One and being turned to the One
implies for Nous 'a movement teeming with life' which fills Nous
to saturation. 'Forthwith Intellectual-Principle becomes all things,
knows that fact in virtue of its self-knowing and at once becomes

Intellectual-Principle, filled so as to hold within itself that object of its vision, seeing all by the light of the Giver and bearing that Giver with it' (*Enneads* VI, 7.16).[70] Of the One he later says that: 'It is preserver of what it produced; by it the Intellectual Beings have their intellection and the living their life; it breathes Intellect in, breathes Life in and, where life is impossible, existence' (*Enneads* VI, 7.23). Finally, this surging, teeming life 'breathed' by the One is undetermined, but when as Mind it looks towards the One, it takes form (*Enneads* VI, 7.17). And it is this which allows later Neo-Platonists, such as the author of a surviving fragment of a Commentary on the *Parmenides* of Plato (perhaps Porphyry), to associate Life with procession and Intelligence with reversion.

From section 7 of the Sixth Ennead as a whole one might get the impression that this second 'trinity' with which one is dealing is a trinity of One, Life and Nous. Yet much that is said within the section identifies Being or Entire-Being with Intellectual Principle,[71] and would seem to yield more naturally a trinity of Being, Life and Intelligence, but occurring now on a level of divinity beneath that of the One. It seems that later Neo-Platonists would not quite agree about this.[72] Our interest in the matter stems from the fact that though mainstream Christian trinitarian thought 'located' Trinity at the highest level of divinity, some intriguing Christian writers suggest that Trinity occurs at a level beneath the unknowable One. But this is to anticipate too much.

For present purposes, as a simple propaedeutic to the development of Christian trinitarian thought, it is sufficient to notice this Plotinian trinity of Being (or Existence), Life and Intellectual Principle: the Life streaming super-abundantly from the One, the source of all, and receiving form and structure in and from the divine Mind; so that 'by It (i.e. the One) the Intellectual Beings have their intellection and the living their life; it breathes Intellect in, breathes Life in, and where life is impossible, existence'. We must leave to more specialist works the detailed description of lines of literary influence from Plotinus to Porphyry and thence to Victorinus and Augustine, or from Plotinus to Iamblichus and thence to the Platonists at Athens and to Proclus and the Pseudo-Denys, which would take us into the sixth century and show something of the power and vitality of Neo-Platonism as its great themes moved on towards the Middle Ages. We shall be reduced to borrowing from that particular story the occasional illustratory point.

10

Arius Revisited

I do not wish to repeat in this section the case I argued in the section 'The Definitive Myth: The Defeat of Arius', in *Jesus, the Man and the Myth*, but I take the liberty here to offer a brief summary of that case, hardly more than a table of its contents.

Naturally in a christology the main problem was to see if or how the very faith itself had not changed unrecognizably from that faith in God the Father which Jesus had conveyed during his lifetime in parable, prayer, table-fellowship and healing ministry, to the faith that worshipped Jesus himself to the extent of the Nicene formula which declared that the Son or Word enfleshed in Jesus was 'one in being with the Father', the famous (or infamous) *homoousios*. The way of tackling the problem then was to suggest, first, that it was in fact the saving faith of the historical Jesus, when he was acknowledged as its source in those in whom he inspired it, that required them to say that in him the saviour God was reconciling the world to himself, that God the Spirit was in him, in fact that he was functionally identical with God as Spirit, and so on, and second, that these claims about the exalted Jesus in the New Testament were in fact never really exceeded, not even by the *homoousios* of Nicaea, that there was no development in that sense, although changing cultural patterns brought much change in the manner of expressing this necessary conviction of all true Christians.

Then the Arian view was described mainly in terms of that subordinationism in the theology of the pre-existent Son or Word which is not only possible from many Scripture texts used by the Fathers, but prevalent in the patristic tradition itself from Tatian to Tertullian and particularly in Origen. I then went on to express

123

the failure of Arius as a theologian by saying that he failed to secure for Christians their conviction that in Jesus they encountered the one, true God, and that he thus altered the very nature of the Christian faith as it appeared in the life, death and resurrection of Jesus and in the experience of the followers of Jesus.[73]

I took the Cappadocian formula of one divine *ousia* and three divine *hypostaseis* as perhaps the most successful formula for orthodoxy. Using, after Prestige, an Aristotelian concept of 'primary *ousia*' which the Cappadocians may not actually have had in mind at all,[74] I proceeded to interpret this formula quite brashly in a manner more suited to solving the problem with which I opened this brief summary (the problem of showing that the faith of Jesus was not essentially altered by Nicaea)[75] than to any scholarly attempt to give an historical account of the successes and failures of the Cappadocian theology in its own time and place.

Now the requirements of an historical account differ from those of a systematic treatise, and though I still believe that Arius was wrong for the main reason already stated, and though I still believe also that the formula for orthodoxy which I then offered was in the main defensible, I find it necessary in the present context to go more fully into the details of the common religious traditions which *both* Arius and his opponents inherited *both* from their Christian predecessors and from the dominant Greek pagan religion of the time. This may well lead me to see more reason on the side of the Arians, to detect more flaws in the arguments of the orthodox and, in the end, to the admission that the kind of solution to the problem of expressing 'the divinity of Jesus' which I adopted in *Jesus, the Man and the Myth*, though defensible today, does not in fact coincide fully with any of the solutions offered by the opponents of the Arians in the classical period of trinitarian theologies.

It is best to begin the more detailed historical reconstruction, then, by recalling one of the most determinative motifs directing that long tradition of Greek theology which the last section above so hastily passed in review: the quest for stability in a world of flux, for permanence in a world where everything seems so temporary, for fullness where every development is overshadowed by the ever-present prospect of decline; and the faith, the hope, born of the very promise which this seething, restless world holds out to us, that this stable and permanent perfection is somewhere to be found, even if that 'somewhere' is beyond this world and beyond the common life that this world knows. Since the fact of being composite was recognized, then as now, as a basic cause of instability,[76] this hope was quite naturally thought to point to the non-composite, the unified, the 'simple', the one.[77]

Now it is quite often suggested that this Greek stress upon the utter immutability of God, which practically every Christian writer known to us in this period took enthusiastically to himself[78] and treated thereafter as axiomatic, would of itself tend to render difficult, if not impossible, the development of a Christian doctrine of Trinity with its inevitable complement of inner-divine processions and distinctions.[79] But we have seen the hint in Plato that even the highest Reality can hardly be thought to lack life, and we have seen Aristotle, who was convinced that God was not only a living being, but life itself, attempt to secure this conviction by suggesting a Life, or Act, which did not imply his 'motion'; for his 'motion' involved growth (and hence the possibility of decay), alteration (which could always, of course, be for the worse) and local movement (which was obviously inapplicable in the case of incorporeal beings). And we have seen, particularly though by no means exclusively from Philo, how it was possible to minimize the remoteness of Aristotle's 'Thinking of the Thinking' by first having the exemplar Forms of all things as Ideas in the divine Mind, the Idea of Ideas, and then by conceiving of this as the dynamic *Logos* of the Stoa, containing in its expression the *spermatikoi logoi* by which all things are by the divinity brought into being and brought to their perfection. In this way the utter simplicity, the oneness, and the very highest immutability of God was preserved at the highest, deepest, most invisible level of divinity, while the divine immanence, which involved some complexity, was still thought to preserve its own level of immutability at a lower or second grade. We have also seen how Plotinus, with his three divine *hypostaseis*, insists on the immutability of all three, with the rider that the third level, Soul, suffers motion 'accidentally', that is, by contact of its lower part with mutable things (a suggestion with obvious possibilities for construing in this philosophical atmosphere the relationship of divinity and humanity in Jesus).

The more accurate statement of the position would then appear to be that this Greek theology in fact positively offered the possibility to Christian theologians at least of binitarian and, later, even of trinitarian thought, though only if Christian theologians,

125

as Stead put it, could tolerate a fairly pronounced subordination-ism.[80] Not only did pre-Nicene theologians tolerate subordi-nationism, they lived and breathed it. In fact so massive is the coincidence of this Greek theology, and its essential subordi-nationism, with pre-Nicene Christian theology, that we may well begin to suspect, even at this stage, that the post-Nicene theo-logians who reversed the earlier subordinationism (and adopted in the process a flatter and less nuanced concept of divine immutability than any Greek could countenance) destroyed, by so doing, the mould from which Christian trinitarian theology was formed, and as a result threatened the very survival of trinitarian theology by failing to provide it with an alternative mould of comparable strength and definition.

The first selection of supplementary historical material which may here be offered, then, is simply aimed at illustrating the coincidence of pagan and Christian theology in the development of the latter up to the advent of Arius, and it is offered under two headings: first, the dominance of subordinationism, and second, the prevalence of the binitarian schema. The first heading may be subdivided to yield the constituent themes of: 1. the visible-invisible distinction; 2. distinctions of the word-internal/word-expressed kind; and 3. the use of terms such as 'creation' and the 'will' of God in the origin of the Son.

1. I have already referred above to a convention of early Christian literature of distinguishing the 'invisible' Father from the 'visible' Son or Word. This distinction is highly developed in Tertullian's *Against Praxeas*, chapters 14–16. Taking as his texts such scriptural statements as 'God dwells in light inaccessible', and 'No one can see God and live', he regards this 'invisibility' as the very property of the Father and proceeds to argue, on the grounds that the Bible records many epiphanies of God to human beings who did afterwards live to tell the tale, that it is the Word or Son who appeared both in the epiphanies of the Old Covenant and in the flesh in the New, and that he is therefore the visible divinity. Now this distinction, which we have already seen to be common to many other ancient Christian writers, is much more than a clever ploy which is used against people like Praxeas in order to prove a distinction of divine beings where Praxeas admitted none. The distinction between visible and invisible deity does, of course, achieve that purpose, but it does so because it assumes such disparities of property between Father and Son as

126

can be described by the contraries, invisible-visible. In short, what is happening here (though it will later be questioned by Augustine in his *De Trinitate*, II, 35) is that Scripture texts are simply being used in order to establish and express a basic pagan religious conviction, namely, that the Supreme One, Father and Source of all, is unknowable (in concrete language, invisible), and that divinity becomes knowable (visible) only at a much lower level of itself. The aptness of the analogy of hidden root, spring, or source of light, is also obvious, and this is perhaps the commonest of all shared analogies at this time.

Following perhaps on sentiments attributed to Origen to the effect that the Father transcends the Son as much as the Son transcends creatures,[81] these words from the Arian *Thalia* are simply driving to their extreme logical conclusion this shared insight of pagans and Christians: 'To speak concisely, God (*ho theos*) is invisible to the Son (John 1.18a); for he is to himself what he is – that is unspeakable (*alektos*).'[82] God's essential unknowability, in short, is not one whit diminished after the coming of Jesus. Whatever it is of God that Jesus, his Son, 'declared' to us, the unitive vision of God still remains in God's own gift. God's inner invisibility is inviolate. Hence it is logical to conclude that neither is God as a matter of course visible to the Son. This Arian text shows, at the very least, the possible implications for Christians of adopting so enthusiastically such a characteristic distinction of Greek theology as the difference, and distance, between the Unknowable One and the essentially intelligible Second; yet embrace it enthusiastically they did.

2. As a consequence there is no need either to be surprised by, or to add further patristic references in illustration of, the prevalence in this period of the idea of the *Logos* as the expression of the Divine Mind for and in creation, the implicit and sometimes explicit use of the Stoic internal-reason/expressed-reason schema which the non-Christian theologians had already so well assimilated.[83] Tertullian's trinitarian theology, the most influential of the period, certainly for the Western Church, uses this Stoic schema quite as successfully as did Philo.[84] His theology of the Three is strictly emanationist,[85] and though he is often credited with giving to the West the formula 'one divine substance, three persons',[86] there can be little doubt about the facts that (*a*) he understood divine substance in a sense quite close to the materialist Stoic concept of spirit, and (*b*) that his concept of person

(often where the English translation has 'three persons', the original Latin of Tertullian simply has 'the three') is extremely undeveloped and of little significance when compared to his major way of distinguishing the three. In order to distinguish the three from each other Tertullian really depends upon his concept of the 'economy' by which the created world came to be and through which the divine governance of the world is exercised. This 'economy' was in his view a kind of internal organization of the Godhead in grades or levels which correspond to the kind of pagan emanationist schema with which we are now so familiar, and it, rather than the concept of 'person', served Tertullian to distinguish from each other 'the three'.[87]

It must suffice here to mention one more striking feature of this subordinationist, emanationist model, in view of the features of Arianism which we are about to see. This is the frequency with which it is suggested, or said, that God's Word becomes God's Son only at the incarnation.[88] The general principle is stated by Tertullian as clearly as this: 'He could not be a Father before the Son was, nor judge before there was sin. Now there was a time when for Him there existed neither sin nor the Son' (*Adversus Hermogenem*, 3). Tertullian is not very clear as to when this time comes for the Father to have a Son, but Hippolytus stated it clearly enough when he wrote: 'For neither was the Word, prior to incarnation and when by Himself, yet perfect Son, although he was perfect Word' (*Contra Noetum*, 15). The interesting feature of this theme is that it focusses our attention directly upon the incarnate one, Jesus of Nazareth, in order, not to 'know' God in the sense of comprehending or understanding one who is essentially unknowable, but to realize that God is indeed Father. And this focus on the incarnate one is, as we shall see, once again a prominent feature of the early Arian thinkers.

Of course, the idea of the eternal generation of the Son was also as this time about to make its appearance: its full appearance is sometimes attributed to Origen.[89] The main motive behind the promulgation of this idea, as Maurice Wiles points out, was the effort to secure at all points the by now quite sacrosanct immutability of God.[90] And this sacred concept of immutability could, as Wiles says, prove either too little or too much. It could be satisfied by seeing the Word as *logos endiathetos* (internal reason) not yet uttered until creation, or it could, as it did for Origen, persuade a theologian that other things also must have been created from eternity, if God is not to be thought to have changed by performing some act of generation or creation which 'before' that he had not performed. But since it is the purpose of these pages to illustrate in detail the coincidence of Christian thought with non-Christian theology and to prepare for an understanding of Arius, we may be content with the comment that, in any case, the theme of eternal generation did nothing to qualify the subordinationist view of the Son or Word now prevalent: Origen was perhaps the most thoroughgoing subordinationist of the pre-Nicene period.

3. This last observation leads to a final set of brief comments on the dominance of subordinationism before Nicaea. It is often suggested, and indeed the very most will be made of this by the orthodox Fathers, that whereas generation need involve no element of subordination, any concept or image of origin which indicates the presence of will inevitably involves subordination. To counter this suggestion either by challenging its assumption or by producing a *catena* of texts from pre-Nicene Fathers and Apologists who talk of God's will in bringing forth his Son,[91] is good enough as far as it goes, but it probably misses the real point that should be made here. The point is that in a climate shared by Christian and non-Christian theologians alike, where a central concern was with the simplicity (that is, the immutability) of the One God, and where subordinationist views of those 'levels' of divinity emanating creatively towards the world were the norm for the interpretation of all statements on this subject, a variety of human concepts and images for this whole origination were equally valid (or invalid, depending on whether one is being positive or apophatic at the moment of use) in attempting to describe a process which, like God, ultimately escaped the powers of the human mind. Since it is the theology that justifies the terms, a simple preference for one term over others will not in itself justify a change in the theology.

Finally, a few words on the prevalence of the binitarian schema. The phrase, the prevalence of the binitarian schema, can of course mean many things. If, for instance, it were taken to mean the massive predominance of attention to Father and Son over the number of lines devoted to the Spirit, or if it were to mean the tendency simply to apply to the Spirit concepts and images already worked out for the relationship of the Father and the Son, it would, with a few notable exceptions, describe the whole of trinitarian theology down to our time. So we may take the phrase to mean here a certain confusion or conflation of the 'jobs' or 'persons' of Son and Spirit in pre-Nicene theology which in itself tends to yield a binity rather than a trinity. Once again, the texts are easy to assemble, and they are noted, with varying degrees of discomfort, by all the usual histories of doctrine;[92] although anyone who had paid any attention at all to the dominant spirit-christologies of the New Testament would surely express surprise, not at this feature of pre-Nicene thought, but rather at the seeming ease with which the terms Word or Son came to monopolize the development of christology as time went by. However, the only comment required at this point is again to the effect that this particular feature of pre-Nicene theology both echoes the dominant binitarianism of non-Christian theology and perhaps presages some future problems. That the Spirit, in so far as it is thought to be distinct from the Father, and not, for instance, a name for God, should appear so close to mutable creation as to be considered almost part of it, should surprise no one who is at all aware of the emanationist and subordinationist model which is common to Christian and non-Christian at this time. And the question must again inevitably arise: if a more exalted position is to be given to this Third One,[93] can it be possible any longer to retain this theological model in Christian theology, and if it cannot be retained, with what can it be replaced? But since it is not the place of the Spirit that is in contention with Arius, we may postpone this question for the moment, and come back now, once more, to Arius.

Remember only that the coincidence of Greek and Christian thought so far presented illustrates the common and pervasive influence of Greek theology on developing Christian views. So, first, we shall look at Arius as representative of a common subordinationism and then, in a section on 'The Holy Spirit and Some Classical Trinitarian Theologies', we shall examine the strains involved in making a common and prevalent binitarian model exclusively henceforth trinitarian while at the same time outlawing an inherent subordinationism which had by this time become distinctively Arian.

In a book that manages to make a good deal more sense of Arius than most previous books had made of him, Gregg and Groh write: 'The traditional view of the Arian controversy as a clash between contrary Trinitarian schemes – the one stressing equality of Persons, the other maintaining a graded hierarchy – is not a complete misconception. It is, however, over-simple and basically off-target in that it does not bring us close enough to the truly incendiary issues in the conflict.'[94] They then proceed to argue quite convincingly that these issues, for Arius and his first major supporters, Eusebius of Nicomedia and Asterius, centred upon a particular view of salvation, a soteriology, and a concomitant emphasis in the reading of Scripture. We are thus relieved of the traditional view of Arius as a philosopher, logician, sophist, spinning his theological heresy whole out of a pagan concept of divinity. But what do we now have in its place?

We have, first, 'the special sensitivity which the Arians had for those passages of Scripture that emphasized the suffering and creaturely characteristics to be drawn from the ministry of Jesus on earth'.[95] The early Arians as exegetes – and they have as much claim as any of their rivals to have their theology attributed to, and assessed by reference to, their exegesis – painted their favourite picture of the ignorant, suffering, fearful, and abandoned Christ;[96] but one who was totally subservient to the will and good-pleasure of his Father, who grew in fact in this obedience,[97] until he was given the name and the lordship of the hymn in Philippians. The Arians, however, show no tendency at all to ignore the by now axiomatic pre-existence of this saviour. 'Nowhere does Arius, Eusebius, or Asterius suggest that the Son's beginning was marked by the birth (or baptism) of Jesus of Nazareth. According to them, the one called "Word" and "Son" was created before all ages.'[98] The Word or Son was the very framer of the universe and the only one to be created, or generated, or established, by the Father alone – for all things were made through him. Yet even in his cosmic-creative functions the Son was God's minister, dependent upon the Father. In short, the central relationship of Son to Father which is described in the case of Jesus in the Scriptures is projected back into pre-existence by the Arians. 'Conceived relationally rather than ontologically, and marked by dependence rather than coequality, the "kinship" between the Father and the Son for early Arian thinkers is grounded in the conception of the will of God and the faculty of willing.'[99]

On the negative side, the early Arians absolutely refused the essentialist language which was adopted by their opponents;[100] the language of *ousia* and *physis* (substance or being, and nature), they considered to be 'destructive of core meanings in the record of God's action in the Testaments'.[101] And indeed only those naive enough to think that truth is no more than a matter of securing agreement on verbal formulae will be likely to believe that there was any natural or historical aptitude in the term *homoousios* (one in being or substance or essence) to express what the Athanasian party wanted to say. Without any real counterpart in early Latin theology,[102] it seems to have had its early use largely in Valentinian Gnostic circles; capable of a truly bewildering range of meanings,[103] its use by Origen, however circumspect and tentative, shows that it could of itself accommodate the most determined subordinationism in trinitarian thought.[104]

Apart from what they may have thought to be its incompatibility with the dominant scriptural mode of describing Christ's relationship to his Father, the Arians rejected such terms as *homoousios* and *ek tes ousias* (from the substance) on the grounds that these would imply a sharing by the Son in the exclusive properties of the Father who was *monon agenneton* or *monon anarchon* (sole unoriginate), or else their materialist connotations would impugn the immutability of the Father God.[105] Athanasius, on the other hand, though perhaps recipient rather than instigator of the Nicene decision to pin its theology to the *homoousios*, and though others at that Council, like Eusebius of Caesarea, may not have thought themselves committed by the term to full equality of Father and Son, saw its possibilities to express what Stead describes as the full, unbroken continuation of being, and such asymmetrical relationship as is involved in the physical analogies of water, light, vine, and he probably advances on Eusebius when he takes the term to imply that the Father communicates his whole essence to the Son, though he still wishes somehow to maintain that 'the Father does not surrender, nor does the Son usurp, his distinctive position'.[106] In any case, despite the confusions and hesitations of the decades immediately succeeding the Council of Nicaea, Athanasius did champion the *homoousios* as an apt expression of the full equality of Father and Son in their essential divinity, and the term did then come to connote, in some writers at least, the identity of substance between Father, Son, and later Spirit. We must attempt to assess the success of this orthodox theology, as it came to be regarded, in the next section. But first, and to conclude the present section, it seems necessary to address some critical remarks by the otherwise extremely welcome contribution of Gregg and Groh.

The main reservations about the conclusions of Gregg and Groh are such as would suggest themselves, I believe, to any careful reviewer of the kinds of common precedent which were so briefly described above, and they affect most directly the following positions of these authors: 1. their seeming acceptance of the dichotomous distinction of uncreated and created, and of the place in which this distinction falls, which was of course characteristic of the Athanasian case, but which, as I hope has by now appeared, no simple choice of alternative concept or image for divine origin (essence-emanation or will-creation language) can either automatically or by etymology, history, or logic, of itself support;[107] 2. their consequent use of the distinction of sonship by nature from sonship by adoption, for though the former phrase does depict the Athanasian view (the tie between the *homoousios* and the image of natural generation we shall later inspect more closely), the latter phrase seems quite inadequate to do justice to the divine status of the Arian Son;[108] 3. further, their reluctance to accept Stead's view of Arius's 'one equal to the Son the Superior is able to beget', namely, that 'he has not exercised this privilege',[109] because of their anxiety to place the Son on all fours with all who can be sons of God, scarcely does justice to either the cosmological or the soteriological functions of the Son and Word.

Therefore, if we take this much more compelling account of Arian theology in conjunction with the common theological inheritance bequeathed by Christians and non-Christians alike to both the Arians and their opponents, the manner in which we must direct our further questions is more or less dictated to us. First, it is obvious that a case can be made for Arius's attempt to embody his scriptural and soteriological concerns in the by then solid traditional terms which he too had inherited, even though this meant that he had to come up with a severe form of subordinationism. Second, it is equally obvious that the Christian community, through leaders like Athanasius, was beginning to feel that much more needed to be said in view of the specific nature of Christian soteriology – and it was probably Arius's crystallization of the tradition which began to make other Christians feel so. Hence two temporary conclusions. If we wish to find what is really wrong with Arius we shall have to probe deeper into the inherited terms, and deeper than any simple preferences between different ones amongst these. And we shall have to ask seriously, as already hinted, if the break with the common Greek tradition we have so briefly surveyed, a break represented more by Athanasius than by Arius, did not require the entire replacement of this common Greek tradition by a different conceptual and imaginative theological model – a replacement which, of course, was not actually achieved. In pursuit of these questions let us turn first to some of the most influential Nicene trinitarian theologies.

11

The Holy Spirit and Some Classical Trinitarian Theologies

'The binitarian schema, it is evident, was deeply impressed upon the thought of primitive Christianity,' wrote J. N. D. Kelly in his *Early Christian Creeds*, and he adds immediately, 'so, it would appear, was the Trinitarian.'[110] And of the ante-Nicene writers Maurice Wiles also has said: 'Their thought about God was at least as much binitarian as trinitarian.'[111] In the last section above, the binitarian schema so prominent in these early Christian literary remains was of interest mainly as one of the major illustrations of the close similarity of Christian and non-Christian theology in that era; and not even in this present section are we interested in trying to decide whether this theology was more binitarian than trinitarian, or vice versa. The prevalence of spirit-christologies in the New Testament should have seen to it that we suffer no surprise in meeting a prevalent binitarian schema well entrenched in Christian thought from the outset. So only a very severe form of anachronistic prejudice can prevent us from seeing that the first question which now faces us is, how did a trinitarian schema come to be thought essential, rather than optional?

Now it should be obvious that this question focusses attention very specifically upon the Holy Spirit. Indeed the prospect that the problem of describing and justifying the development of classical *trinitarian* theologies finds its focus in the status of the Holy Spirit should already be obvious from remarks made in a previous section to the effect that, whereas the problem with the Son had to do with his alleged divinity, the problem with the Spirit had to do with its distinct status.[112] But it should be even more obvious, indeed unmistakably so, at this point of our story. For nothing is more obvious than the fact that the Arian controversy, so absolutely pivotal for the formation of the very centre of Christian doctrine, was strictly binitarian before, during, and for quite a considerable time after Nicaea, and that all the major doctrinal moves at that formative stage of the controversy were made with the Father-Son relationship almost exclusively in mind.

Now the focussing of the description and justification of the development of classical trinitarian theologies on the status of the Holy Spirit in turn clarifies our first question and shows it to be in reality a double question. First, a question of fact. Why did trinitarian schemas and theologies come to predominate to the utter exclusion of binitarian alternatives? Second, the more theological question. What images or concepts were formed so as to include the Spirit and thus achieve Trinity while still, of course, preserving monotheism? On the answer to the second question the success of trinitarian theology really stands or falls.

Part of the answer to the first question must be found in the fact that, although trinitarian theologies simply cannot be said to have dominated the thought of this early period, nevertheless the trinitarian schema was well entrenched. One of the authors quoted above, J. N. D. Kelly, puts it like this: 'The Trinitarian ground-plan obtrudes itself throughout, and its presence is all the more striking because more often than not there is nothing in the context to necessitate it. . . If Trinitarian creeds are rare, the Trinitarian pattern which was to dominate all later creeds was already part and parcel of the Christian tradition of doctrine.'[113] And the other author quoted, Maurice Wiles, specifies the threefold forms and structures found in Scripture (for instance, the end of II Corinthians), in semi-credal confessions, in summaries of faith and, most particularly, in the baptismal formula.[114]

It must have been the influence of such trinitarian theologies as were extant, like those of Tertullian and Novation, with their vastly underdeveloped and comparatively minute sections on the Spirit, in addition to the widespread presence of the trinitarian ground-plan, which made it seem obvious to those faced with an attack upon the divinity of the Spirit that the way to defend the Spirit's divinity was to make it a third in the Godhead, and thus to forge trinitarian theologies which would thenceforth become the exclusive norm in theology.

There is a further factor which must also be taken into account. It is surely more than a coincidence that whereas the period of Middle-Platonism is more binitarian than trinitarian in its Greek theology, that period of pagan Greek religious thought known as Neo-Platonism which provides the cultural background to fourth-century Christian theology, is persistently trinitarian. But we shall continue to notice this cultural influence as we proceed to consider in more detail some of the classical Christian theologies of this period. For now we may proceed to our second question, concerning the images and concepts that were used in order to make the Spirit a third co-equal one in the Godhead. And here, of course, the decision to extend the *homoousios* to the Spirit is pivotal, a decision taken by Athanasius and Gregory of Nyssa, though not by Basil the Great.

Naturally, since the *homoousios* was becoming the main theological weapon against the Arians in the second half of the fourth century, its extension to the Holy Spirit would be facilitated to the extent that those who refused co-equal divine status to the Spirit could be described as Arians. Now it seems clear enough that *some* who denied co-equal divine status to the Spirit in the company of the Father and the Son were indeed Arians. The sect of Aetius, for instance, combatted by Basil in his influential *On the Holy Spirit*, were certainly people who endorsed the characteristically subordinationist theses of Arius and his companions, and who simply extended these with stylish logic to the Spirit. For although it is the case with Aetius as with others branded heretics by the great tradition that we can neither trust their opponents to give an adequate account of their case nor repair at this point of time the deliberate damage done by those same opponents to the prospects of survival of their literary remains, we should at least note Basil's report that this particular sect insisted on the doxology 'glory to God the Father *through* the Son and *in* the Holy Spirit' precisely because they saw in the differentiation of the prepositions ('from' was reserved for the Father), which they took to be scriptural, a subnumeration consecutively of Son and Spirit to Father, a clear and again a consecutively subordinate status of each to the preceding one, which amounted in effect to a difference in *ousia* (being or substance) between them.[115] Hence there did emerge Arians, properly called such, who felt the need of a thoroughly trinitarian theology, rather than a binitarian theology, for instance, and who fashioned it according to their own characteristic theological mould.

But if the adjective 'Arian' in the formative decades of the controversy is taken to mean, as it seems historically it must be taken to mean, one who for substantial scriptural and soteriological reasons quite radically subordinates the Son's divinity to that of the Father, then anyone who should agree with Athanasius in attempting to brand with the name 'Arian' the Tropici with which he deals in his *Letters to Serapion*[116] would simply stick one foot in each of two traps, both of which would be much better avoided by anyone who wishes to make any progress through that confusing theological period. First, he or she should be trapped into adopting Athanasius' technique of attempting to damn his opponents by association, just one of the more disreputable techniques used by this redoubtable controversialist which Christian men and women should long since have ceased to emulate. Second, and much more central to our purpose here, he or she should be successfully tricked into making what might prove to be a very premature theological decision indeed, the decision that the only way to serve Christian orthodoxy, then as now, would be to treat the Holy Spirit as yet another distinct divine *hypostasis*, partly by transferring to it cardinal concepts which were specifically worked out to deal with the relationship of Father and Son,[117] and first amongst these, of course, the *homoousios*.

Now whatever the polemical advantages of associating one's opponents with Arians, and as a consequence extending the anti-Arian *homoousios* to the Holy Spirit in order to make the Spirit a third one in the divine being, the theological hazards of such a move should have been more apparent than they seem to have been. Such a judgment of course smacks greatly of hindsight. Still, it is based on observations which seem obvious enough and which may be formulated as follows.

The intrinsically subordinationist pre-Nicene models have distinguished the Spirit from Father and Son (as indeed they had distinguished Son from Father) precisely by subordinating the former to the latter; that is, by placing each successive one in the sequence on a lower level of the divine being or *ousia* as it reached out in creative will and overflow to the world.[118] Now, as the *homoousios* moved closer to connoting identity of being, it destroyed this manner of distinguishing (and with it the Arian option). However, as long as the *homoousios* was confined to the relationship of Father and Son it could (*a*) both be justified and given meaning from its unbroken ties to the image of generation and (*b*) seem, because of those same ties, to leave intact, despite its approach to the connotation of identity of substance, the distinction of parent and offspring which this very image requires. But of course once the *homoousios* is extended to the Holy Spirit, its links to the image of generation are effectively broken, and with these will go also its obvious source of justification and meaning, and even its remaining ability to retain impressions of distinction despite its own progress towards connotations of identity. Hence the whole project of distinguishing *hypostaseis* will be threatened. The break with the explanatory and justificatory link with the image of generation will tend to introduce the kind of equivalence of images of derivation (being born of, created by, established by, and so on) on which Arianism had insisted; and the same break will make the quest of formulae for distinction within the one identical essence even more difficult than it otherwise needs to be, driving the questers either towards considerations of 'properties' of the Three, without being sure now as to how far these should be attached to 'relations of origin', or towards the works or acts of the Three in the world (*ad extra*), without being sure now as to how far any such acts should be thought 'proper' to one or other of the Three.[119]

None of these hazards appeared to trouble those who decided to extend the *homoousios* to the Spirit as a third one in the divine being, but that they were real hazards, and seldom without destructive effect, can easily be illustrated from the trinitarian theologies of those men and their successors. So let us begin with the justificatory and explanatory link that bound the *homoousios* to the image of generation in order to see more clearly how the breaking of that link by the extension of the *homoousios* to the Holy Spirit threatened trinitarian theology in the ways just mentioned.

We have already noted that the orthodox, as they came to be called, seemed to believe that the image of generation did not involve any element of subordination in the one who thus took origin. And it is true from the things we know in our world that though the one generated is at first utterly dependent upon and in every way subordinate to the ones who give it origin, it can grow to equality of status and even to superior status, and it usually does this, as far as the issue of generation is concerned, precisely when it reaches the maturity of becoming parent in turn. But then the writers who use this image of generation for inner divine processes are often either anxious or forced to say how very different divine generation is from creaturely generation, and though this is not one of the facets of the difference they are anxious to highlight, it must then be suspected that being unge-nerate (or unoriginate in every way) is a distinguishing mark of divinity, and being generated a threat to full divine status, whereas it is natural to creatures to be both generated and generators in turn.[120] It must therefore be said that those who declared inner divine generation to cause no subordination in the one generated achieved this theological conclusion concerning equality by their own *fiat* rather than by any natural tendency of the language or imagery used to yield it.[121] But our main interest in the generation image at the moment lies in its use in explaining and justifying the *homoousios*.

Of Athanasius' many defensive accounts of the decision of Nicaea the following is amongst those that most clearly link the *homoousios* with generation; so much so that the latter term is made to provide the justification for the former.

> It was their duty to protect the cardinal truth that Our Lord was really the Son of God, which a deadly heresy had denied. How were they to exclude the evasions to which the Arians had recourse? They pro-ceeded thus: a son, they said, is an offspring, but in order to be such, he must spring from that of which he is the offspring; nor does he so spring, unless he is from what that original *is* – that is, in other words, from its *substance*, as the derivation of the word 'substance' shows. Thus, to be the Son of God, if he is God's offspring or true Son, is to be 'of' or 'one with' God's substance – that is, to be 'consubstantial' (*homoousios*) with him.[122]

Align this logic with the old Greek axiom about the incomposite and immutable God, deploy this axiom in increasingly varied, if not indiscriminate, ways and it will bring one as close to what later commentators call the identity of substance between Father and Son as any theologian who still wished to preserve some distinction between them should perhaps care to come. Since the Father is utterly simple, Athanasius also argued, and does not change as we do from once being son to being later Father, then, in transmitting his substance in the course of generating his Son, he gives absolutely and utterly all that he is; he does not transmit a part of his substance, as happens in the case of things material.[123]

The point has already been noted that the term *homoousios* in itself does not rule out relatively subordinate status amongst those who are said to be of one substance; and though Tertullian's *una substantia* is not really the equivalent of the Greek *homoousios*, of it too it is obvious that it could, and did, accommodate the idea of a divine stuff (to Tertullian, spirit) which was partaken of by, or assigned to, two other 'persons' at increasingly lower 'grades' or levels of divinity. Therefore it becomes clear, as Prestige has stressed,[124] that the more the Athanasian logic moves towards identity of *ousia*, the more the older model for binity or Trinity becomes obsolete, the older model which worked with the ideas of monarchy and economy, the monarchical rule of God in the world through the internal arrangement or economy of increasingly subordinate plenipotentiaries.

The point of centring our considerations on the Holy Spirit should now come even more clearly into focus. For it is perfectly obvious, as it was to Tropici and Arians alike, that if the divinity of the Holy Spirit is to be defended in terms of making it a third, distinct, and co-equal one within the Godhead, then one of the following two implications begin to appear on the horizon: 1. the *homoousios*, because of links closely forged with the image of generation in the literature and never really revised,[125] must not be used of the Holy Spirit; or 2. if one follows Athanasius and insists on using the *homoousios* of the Holy Spirit notwithstanding,[126] then the justificatory and explanatory link with the generation image is in fact broken and, since the 'levels' and 'grades' method of distinguishing the Three is now also irreparably damaged, the task of distinguishing the Holy Spirit becomes problematic: in fact, the problems encountered, because of the same breaking of the link between *homoousios* and generation, will spread even to the distinction between Father and Son.

Take two of the most influential theologies, the one by Gregory of Nyssa in the East in the fourth century, and that of Augustine of Hippo in the West in the fifth. Look at these with some supplementary aid from cognate systems and see how successfully the problems just outlined were met. Simply keep in mind that the *homoousios* can now no longer depend on the generation image and, further, that its effect is to rid theology of that subordinationism in pre-Nicene thought which functioned both to distinguish from each other the Two or Three and to relate the One through the others to the creation. The advantage of keeping this in mind is that it helps one to know what to look for while passing in review the theologies of Gregory and Augustine, for by keeping this in mind one comes to realize that the task of distinguishing three in the Godhead will now fall squarely either on the distinctive properties (*idiotes, idiomata*) of each of the ones within the Godhead or on whatever distinctions can be detected in the manner in which the now co-equals act upon the world.

(a) Gregory of Nyssa

Athanasius, in one of his more transparently honest moments, in his *First Letter to Serapion* (20), asks himself the question, 'But how are these things so . . . how, when it is truly a Triad, the Triad is described as one? or why, when the One is in us, the Triad is said to be in us?' And he answers by appealing to tradition rather than proof, to the faith that has been handed down to him, and to the illustrations of 'the image and the radiance, fountain and river, essence and expression', all in accordance, he believes, with what Scripture teaches, and teaches us we cannot demonstrate. Scripture and tradition we have already interrogated rather intensely, and the results of that interrogation will tell us how far we may agree with Athanasius on the issue of what we must or must not simply believe. The interesting thing about the passage is the relegation of the traditional emanationist imagery to the status of a mere illustration of that which must simply be believed – hitherto, in the older subordinationist model, this imagery was more than illustrative of a faith already established; it was the very analogy of God's presence and action, at once unknown and known, at once transcendent and immanent, in the world.

Changes leading to new trinities are obviously under way, but we must not let a hindsight focussed by too many centuries of unquestioned orthodoxy prevent us from asking for explanation and justification at every point of the proposed changes. Two factors in particular might serve to render us less critically observant. First, the conventional view that the addition of the term *hypostasis* to the *homoousios* finally gave a satisfactory account of the Trinity can easily prevent us from asking what justifies any classical *trinitarian* doctrine in the first place (much as those who over-congratulate Tertullian on his offering us the formula 'one substance, three persons' often excuse themselves thereby from noticing his subordinationism). Second, the conventional view that the Eastern Christians started from the Three (whereas the Latins are reputed to have started from the unity of the divine being) can again trick us into thinking that the desired *trinitarian* result has been achieved before we even look to the logic which is supposed to support it.

First, the conventional account of this doctrinal movement in the fourth century has it that only when the term *ousia* (in *homoousios*) was supplemented by the term *hypostasis* by the Cappadocians and the two were honed and fitted to each other as terms respectively for the One and the Three, did the Christian community possess an adequate instrument for thinking through correctly the central issue of the Christian faith, the very nature of God. The conventional account then continues with subtly coordinated definitions of these two ancient Greek terms, followed perhaps by expressions of regret at the cruder impressions conveyed by the Western term *'persona'* or 'person', particularly in more recent times. Now this account is serviceable enough, and has served me in the past as well as it has served others. And once again, since it may be read in most accessible histories of doctrine, there is no need to repeat it here. But it is necessary to add at least this: formulae which are designed to answer the twin questions 'one what?' and 'three what?' are inevitably constructed of such general terms[127] that they already presuppose precise answers to such questions as 'how is the one distinct from the three?', and 'how is each of the three distinct from the others?' For only if we are already sure that we have one and *three* can we reasonably be required to trouble ourselves to say one what or three what. But, as we continue to see, with the growing distance from the old emanationist, subordinationist model, and its inbuilt answers to just these questions of distinction, the problem of distinction becomes more rather than less acute.

Certainly the finding of a general formula does nothing to remove this problem, or even to alleviate it. And unless we can truly differentiate three distinct 'modes of being' from each other and from one 'something' which is not a mode of being, we shall have no warrant for issuing the formula at all. It is all very well for Prestige to write that as the *homoousios* came to be accepted with the sense of identity of substance of the Three, the older ideas of monarchy and economy were replaced and 'the three Persons no longer lead back to a unity that is primarily found in one Person; they are in a real sense one in themselves'.[128] But you cannot have your cake and eat it; the distinctions between the 'persons' to which the older schema gave identifiable texture and flavour may have disappeared with its substance.

Second, John McIntyre has taken issue with such authors as Prestige and Shapland, who in various ways suggest a secondary place for the unity of divine substance in the 'order of thought' of the Greek Fathers; and it seems obvious that McIntyre is correct in saying that the unity of the divine *ousia* is the primary axiom of these Fathers.[129] Under this axiom, what account can Gregory of Nyssa now give of distinctions?

It is more than strongly suggested by Gregory of Nyssa's trinitarian theology that the one divine nature is distinguished from the three *hypostaseis* precisely by its being utterly incomprehensible. This conclusion does not rest purely on long sections about the utter incomprehensibility of the divine essence such as that which opens his *Answer to Eunomius' Second Book*.[130] It rests also on Gregory's comments on the baptismal formula, where he takes separately from Father, Son, and Spirit, the 'name' there mentioned, indicating that the 'name' (In the 'name' of. . .) refers to the essence, whereas Father, Son, and Spirit apply to the *hypostaseis*. He writes, for instance, 'The uncreated nature alone, which we acknowledge in the Father, and in the Son, and in the Holy Spirit, surpasses all significance of names. For this cause the Word, when he spoke of the name when delivering the faith, did not add what it was – for how could a name be found for that which is above every name – but gave authority that whatever name our intelligence by pious effort be enabled to discover to indicate the transcendent nature, that name should be applied alike to the Father, Son, and Holy Spirit, whether it be "the Good" or "the Incorruptible" . . .'[131] There are, in addition, texts in which Gregory insists 'that the title of Father does not present to us the essence, but only indicates the relation to the Son',[132] and 'we ought not to think that to be unbegotten or to be begotten are identical with the essence . . . because the difference of begotten and unbegotten is apart from the essence,'[133] and even this: 'The orthodox theory allows these words I mean "ungenerate" . . . to be indicative of God's eternity, but not of his being.'[134] So Jesus did not teach us to name the ineffable essence of God, but he did teach us 'to what we ought to look with the eyes of our understanding – that is, the Father, the Son, and the Holy Spirit . . . for each of these titles understood in its natural sense becomes for Christians a rule of truth and a law of piety'.[135]

As there seems to be both a positive and a negative point to this distinction between the divine *ousia* and the three *hypostaseis* – positively it indicates the apophatic and the mystical streak in his theology; negatively it is neccessary to counteract Eunomius' belief that being begotten, for instance, affects the very essence of the divinity of which it is the mode of origin and existence – we shall leave part of its consideration to a brief later section on the mystical approach, and continue at this stage with Gregory's account of the requisite distinctions.

Of this divine essence, then, he writes, 'we regard it as consummately perfect and incomprehensibly excellent, yet as containing clear distinctions within itself which reside in the peculiarities of each of the persons: as possessing invariableness in virtue of its common attribute of uncreatedness, but differentiated by the unique character of each person. This peculiarity contemplated in each sharply and clearly divides one from the other.' Now in line with our insistence that the Spirit provides the test case for any trinitarian theology, we may skip ahead until we arrive at Gregory's description of the 'special and incommunicable property', the 'unique character' which distinguishes the Holy Spirit. Gregory writes:

> His most individual mark and characteristic consists in his not showing either the property of ingeneracy or of being only-begotten. He simply is, without being ingenerate or only-begotten, and this is what constitutes his special character and distinction from the other persons. Linked to the Father by being uncreated, he is disjoined by not being Father. United to the Son by the bond of uncreatedness, and by deriving his being from the supreme God, he is separated by the distinction of not being the Father's only-begotten, and of having been manifested through the Son himself.[136]

The most striking thing about this quotation is surely the contrast between the confidence of its beginning and the lameness of its ending; for the distinguishing properties of the Holy Spirit are described in terms which are either wholly negative or remarkably uninformative.[137] Nor do matters improve very substantially as far as the Spirit is concerned if one were to search through the rest of the writings of the Cappadocian Fathers in quest of further distinguishing properties. It is, of course, common to find Father and Son distinguished by attributing to them the

145

properties of fatherhood and sonship, ingeneracy and generatedness, being unoriginate or originate. But when it comes to the Holy Spirit, it is said to be distinguished by the properties of 'sanctifying power' or 'sanctification', 'being sent', 'proceeding', or alternatively by the properties of its attachment to the Son, for instance, being made known by the Son, apprehended inseparably, with or after the Son.[138] But it is clear enough that the first set of properties here are neither specific enough nor sufficiently exclusive to a Holy Spirit to distinguish it adequately from the other two; and the second set assume rather than help us to see that the Holy Spirit is a distinct *hypostasis* within the divinity and, on that assumption, take over scriptural phrases or suggestions which could then be used to relate this distinct one to the Son.

If at this stage one were to extend one's inspection of Gregory's account of the properties to the cases of Father and Son, one could quickly find ample illustration of the deleterious effects of cutting the link between the *homoousios* and the image of generation which its very extension to the Holy Spirit entailed. One might also notice a tendency to let God's relationship to creation determine more and more the meaning-content of the alleged properties of the *hypostaseis*, accompanied by an implicit admission of equivalence of images of origin in or from the divinity such as Arians appeared to have favoured. And one might even begin to suspect that the older subordinationist model for distinguishing Father, Son, and Spirit was making a subtle back-door entry to help with distinctions which were proving unusually difficult for the replacement model which had just ushered it out of the front door.

Indeed further analytic attention to these impressions could easily show up the interconnections between them. For once the link with the *homoousios* which favoured the generation image is cut, other images of origin in the divinity gain re-entry, and echoes of the older model are inevitable. For the older subordinationist model admitted no distinction of immanent and economic Trinity. In other words, its account of God's relation to creation itself secured the distinctions between the Three.[139] Hence the relation to creation tended to determine the meaning-content of the images of origin even within the divinity, and to confer at least an apophatic equivalence upon them. The newer model, which developed *pari-passu* with the move of the *homoousios* towards the meaning of identity of substance, broke the unity

146

of the older model, tending to look either within God's inner being or within the world of creation (to God's actions there) for the necessary distinctions. As we continue to cast a critical eye, then, on these continuing attempts to secure distinctions without division, we must notice the new equivalence of terms for origin; we must suspect the re-entry of some features of the discarded model; and we must as a consequence come to no quick and easy conclusions about success or failure.

So Gregory of Nyssa is usually quite happy to distinguish the Father as unoriginate (*anarchos*), but he is also aware of the fact that the word origin (*arche*) is one of varied meaning (*polysemos*), and that he cannot altogether exclude the term unoriginate from the description of the Son. His solution to this problem of distinction in *Against Eunomius* I, 33 is to suggest that, though we may call the Son unoriginate as well as the Father, we must call the Father alone, and not the Son, ungenerate (*agennetos*). Now it was because of the ability of the term 'unoriginate' to express the distinction of the Son from things created, that it proved incapable on its own of expressing the distinction of Son from Father. However, in further argument with Eunomius a similar fate seems to befall the term just now preferred in the performance of this essential trinitarian task, the term ungenerate (*agennetos*).

For when Eunomius apparently tried to force this word to express his beloved unlikeness between the One God and the Son, Gregory is quick to argue that from the word ungenerate of itself we learn only of something not having come into being (*to me genesthai*), and this property is common to all three 'persons'.[140] We can well imagine the same fate befalling any pair of contrasting terms connoting origin and absence of origin, and always for the same reason, namely, that these terms derive their most obvious content of theological meaning from the human instinct to contrast God and God's creatures. Hence, if it could be argued that they were unfit to distinguish two or three levels of divinity while keeping these still distinct from the created order, it could equally well be argued that they were even more unfit to distinguish co-equal divine beings from each other, and it is the force of this latter argument that Gregory, more honest in this than most of his later admirers, is conceding.

Having made these concessions, which selective readers of his work, perhaps in search of simpler certainties, ignore, Gregory usually falls back on the names Father and Son and their 'natural' meanings, while complaining (a little vulnerably, I feel) of Eunomius' tendency to prefer other names for these same *hypostaseis*. But of course, if Gregg and Groh are at all correct, this move would clinch Gregory's case not at all. On the contrary, it would re-activate the earlier issues of the Arian debate, and in particular the contention that, if we are to respect *Scripture*, then the terms in which we are to understand the names Father and Son will be predominantly those of will, good-pleasure and obedience.

It is difficult to read through Gregory of Nyssa without noticing his periodic recourse to images and models suspiciously similar to older models which were intrinsically subordinationist, and in the new scheme now developing it is just as difficult to find adequate justification for this recourse. It is true that Gregory shows explicit dissatisfaction with the imagery of sun, rays, illumination, preferring instead to write of three suns, equal as far as their light is concerned, yet one ungenerate, the second an offspring, and the third also having its source in the first. Yet, in the same passage, in structure quite reminiscent of Plato's *Republic* VI, 19, he talks of us knowing the Son only through the Spirit, and finding the Cause Beyond All only through the Son, and then rounding (*anakamptontes*, a metaphor from the race-course) that summit of theology, our mind speeds back from the Father to the Son and then to the Holy Spirit.[141] In his work *On the Holy Spirit Against the Followers of Macedonius*, Gregory is even more insistent that all Power begins from the Father, advances through the Son, and is completed in the Holy Spirit (the prepositions with which Basil had to contend), and, once again, that 'as it is impossible to mount to the Father unless our thoughts are exalted thither through the Son, so it is impossible to say that Jesus is Lord except by the Holy Spirit'.[142] And this leads him to speak of a distinction within the Godhead, not just of *hypostasis*, but of 'order' as well (*kata taxin*), because of an 'order of transmission' in which the Holy Spirit is definitively third. This recalls one of Gregory's ways, temporarily by-passed above, of distinguishing the *hypostaseis* by their properties: one is the cause, another is directly from the first cause, and yet another is by that which is directly from the first cause. And though, we may note here also, Gregory is anxious to insist that this 'order' does not qualify the community or oneness of essence (*to koinon tes ousias, ten henoteta tes physeos*), as he often calls it, of the Three, as if he were still worried about its implications, we are still left wondering about justifying its intrusion in any way in the new scheme of things.[143]

For even if the Scriptures offered us no way of describing the divine Spirit except by treating it as a third and distinct *hypostasis* in the Godhead as the Cappadocians conceive this, they would still not lend their whole and sole support to this rigid order of transmission in which the Spirit has to be third. And indeed references to knowledge ascending through intermediaries to that which is itself unknown, or to power descending by intermediaries to creatures who live on the edge of nothingness, seem to require as their supporting rationale the very model of levels in divinity which is now more the property of the Arians than it is of their homoousiite, equality-questing opponents.

It is difficult to rid oneself altogether of the suspicion that the old emanationist model is emerging periodically still to help a new schema to overcome weaknesses in itself which it cannot itself outgrow. But before I attempt a conclusion to this long analysis, let us see if the distinction between the *hypostaseis* on the new homoousiite (identity of substance) model cannot be established in terms of their works or operations in the world, rather than in terms of inner-divine properties or of inner-divine transmissions alone. After all, the old subordinationist model had to do with how God approached the world and how we in consequence can approach God, and it was upon such considerations that it built its theory of distinct divine *hypostaseis*. Perhaps, then, if we ask the new schema which is now developing if it is possible to distinguish the divine *hypostaseis* according to the action of each in or on our world, we shall see at last both its clear independence of, and its superiority over, the model it seeks to supplant by means of its growing stress on equality and, as a growing consequence, on a common or identical divine essence of the Three. But we soon find that the use of the *opera ad extra* to secure distinctions between the Three is complicated for the homoousiites by their need to use these same *opera*, particularly in the case of the Spirit, to secure the full, equal (and so, identical?) divinity of the Three.

Since those who were finally called orthodox insisted on taking their Arian opponents' position to be a denial, rather than a diminution, of the divinity of the Son and the Spirit, part of their response is usually a 'proof' of the divinity of Son and of Spirit. And in both instances they have two main ways of advancing their argument. They argue from titles and other attributes of Son and Spirit which they find in the Scriptures,[144] but it is their second main way of proceeding that more immediately interests us at this point: their argument that works or activities prove divine status. To the orthodox, of course, in view of their adoption of the *homoousios*, to prove divine status amounted to proving equal divine status and this, in view further of their own hardening of the general Greek dogma of the simplicity and incomposite nature of the One God,[145] must finally make them conclude that a 'common' essence, indeed one and the same identical essence, was that of all Three. Now it is a well-known fact – and it has its own significance – that the full statement of these conclusions was not as automatic or as full in the case of the Spirit as in the case of the Son.[146] Basil's *On the Holy Spirit* neither calls the Spirit God explicitly nor does it use the *homoousios* of the Spirit, though it does say that the Spirit is *homotimos*;[147] worthy of equal honour and glory with Father and Son. Gregory of Nazianzus shows sensitivity to the audacity of predicating equal divine status of a third divine *hypostasis*.[148] And the gradualness with which the *homoousios* came to imply what might be called identity of essence of the Three would be quite beyond the present scope of this work to trace, beyond the indications given when we notice how the old subordinationist model still lived on during the development of the new. Nevertheless, as in the case of the Son, the works or operations of the Spirit were used to 'prove' its divinity, and it is this which interests us here.

A single example of such operation will suffice in the case of the Son, the one taken from the Prologue to the Fourth Gospel and most commonly used: all things were made through him, and without him was made nothing that was made. For the Holy Spirit, Athanasius enumerated such operations as: sanctifying while not being itself sanctified, quickening while not itself partaking of life, anointing and sealing, making men divine, creating and renewing.[149] But the precise point of our interest, it is necessary to remember, is not in the success of these references in proving the divinity of Son and Spirit, for that in their own way the opponents of the Cappadocians accepted, but in the ability of such references to distinguish three *hypostaseis* in the divinity *while leaving the homoousios intact*. And it is at this point that a deep tension is evident in this patristic material, most particularly once again in the case of the Holy Spirit. For if the Fathers often seem anxious to find operations seemingly characteristic of the Holy Spirit which will prove the latter's divinity, they are even more frequently anxious to attribute the same activities to the other persons also, and in this, of course, many of the texts which we already used to show the interchangeability of Son or Word and Spirit come into play.[150] This latter tendency increases until it yields the principle formulated by Gregory of Nyssa in his work *On the Trinity and the Godhead of the Holy Spirit*: 'the oneness of their nature must needs be inferred from the identity of their operations';[151] and indeed it has given to all subsequent trinitarian theology the principle: *opera ad extra sunt indivisa*. Must we then conclude that the very activities which are to prove the deity of the Holy Spirit, since they must be attributed also to Father and Son, threaten the distinct status of the same Holy Spirit?

Not quite; for, as many patristic scholars have observed, the *impasse* is not quite complete. As John McIntyre puts it:

> having observed how insistent the Greek Fathers were upon the notion that there can be no separation of Holy Spirit from Father and Son in all these operations, we might be tempted to think that, in answer to our next question about the nature of the unity of the Divine Operation, they will simply reply that it is monolithic and simplex. On the contrary, we have to say that for them a major characteristic of the Divine Operation *ad extra* is that it is not undifferentiated. The *opera ad extra* are distinguishable but not separable in the sense that the Son or Spirit could act in redemption or sanctification without either of the other two being present.[152]

The formula, then, with the operations as with the *hypostaseis* themselves, seems to be: distinct but not separable. And there is no doubt that, if we could be satisfied on the issue of distinction, we could derive much theological mileage from the inseparability. As McIntyre again puts it, this latter would lead to the doctrine of *emperichoresis*, *circumincessio*, the mutual indwelling in each of the others.

> When we are enlightened by the Spirit, and led by him on that way that leads to Christ and the Father; or when the Spirit initiates us into that salvation which Christ has achieved for us, and so brings us to the fulfilment of God's purpose in creation, the Spirit does not lead us out beyond himself or point away from himself to some Being who is outside him. On the contrary, he unveils the glory and reality of the only-begotten within himself; and so within the Son we are brought to know the love of the Father.[153]

151

Very well, but what account are we to give of the distinctions, for until these are established it is premature to talk about mutual indwelling, and in particular, what account are we to give of the distinctions within cooperative action at the present stage of our inquiry?

This is not an easy question to answer in a short space, but though I am aware that the work of McIntyre and others shows that more than one distinction is offered by these Fathers, and though I accept the correctness of this view, my own reading convinces me also that by far the most consistent distinction invokes precisely that order amongst the Three which was endemic to the older model and which continues to emerge in the new. If the conviction that all operations begin *from* the Father, proceed *through* the Son, and find their completion *in* the Spirit does not quite reach the status of a standard formula, it certainly is the dominant manner of expressing the distinctions within the divine co-operative action.[154] And it is necessary to remember once again that the rationale for this way of conceiving the divine activity was precisely the ancient Greek axiom that though God acted on the world and humans could encounter God, the One God, the God most eminently God, because of his utter transcendence, did not directly act upon the world, but did so through divine intermediaries, and correspondingly, the divine *hypostaseis* which the human spirit encountered in its journey back to God were subordinate levels of the divine reality, and for that very reason more immediately accessible. Once again, in the matter of God's activity as in the matter of divine 'transmissions' or 'processions' and the 'properties' which accrued to the 'persons' from these, we must at least question the propriety of a new schema of things apparently calling upon the aid of a model it meant to make obsolete, in order to secure distinctions within the Godhead which it was itself finding difficulty in providing, without at least offering its own rationale for an 'order' among divine beings which was proving persistently attractive.[155]

In order to see if this predicament of post-Nicene theology is overcome, let us take another trinitarian theologian, author of the most influential trinitarian theology of the Western Church.

(b) Augustine of Hippo

It is difficult indeed to accept Andrew Louth's belief that the starting point for Augustine's influential *De Trinitate* was God's revelation of himself in Scripture and in the church. Without at all prejudging the issue of how well, or ill, Augustine's trinitarian theology represents God's revelation consummated in Jesus of Nazareth and continued in the community of his followers, there seems no doubt at all about the fact that the starting point for this most intricate and magisterial work is the Nicene definition, and more specifically the *homoousios* and its substance language. Twice in the first Book Augustine sets out the thesis which in the remaining fourteen he will explain, defend, and develop. It is the thesis, in its first form, 'that the Trinity is the one, only, and true God, and that one rightly says, believes, and understands that the Father, the Son, and the Holy Spirit are of one and the same substance or essence' (I, 4), and in its second form, 'that the Father, the Son, and the Holy Spirit constitute a divine unity of one and the same substance in an indivisible equality' (I, 7).

There can be no doubt that the Nicene *homoousios* now really does mean identity of substance, one and the same identical substance of the Three, and whatever poor vulnerable case might be made for the contention that a Trinity composed by a strict 'order of transmission' corresponding to an 'order of mission' is first suggested to us by all the scriptural data and need only thereafter be theologized, there can be no doubt at all that the dogma of the identical substance, together with concepts of distinction the origin and content of which it will largely dictate, is itself a theological grid, forged in the heat of bitter and continuous controversy, which, far from being suggested by the Scriptures, needs to be subsequently justified by whatever exegetical moves are in any way possible. We shall not pause here to comment at any length on the fact that we are here witnessing a type of theology which at times comes dangerously close to ignoring, if not reversing, the priorities in the relationships of Scripture to doctrine discussed above, and which becomes more rather than less common as the Christian centuries succeed each other in a lengthening line of time. It is sufficient here to record the impression that as controversy with Arians, alive or dead, drives the *homoousios* all the way to meaning identity of substance, the language of substance assumes a measure of abstraction and logical rigidity (complicated, in the modern mind at least, by its ineradicable materialist overtones) which makes it less and less fit to express the subtle ways of God with the world, much less the relationships of God to his Son Jesus.

Take two more quotations from the *De Trinitate*. In the first Augustine argues that since all things were made by the Son, he himself was not made. This is a familiar premise from which to conclude, as Augustine does, that the Son is of the same substance as the Father; but then he adds: 'since every substance which is not God is a creature, and that which is not a creature is God' (I, 9). So the *homoousios*, in the sense of the one identical substance of the Three, is connected with the most dichotomous distinction between God and creatures in terms of substance. In the second quotation the use of substance to make the edges of this distinction as hard as they can be is carried to the very centre of the being of Jesus Christ, and then into the centre of our being also: 'the humanity in the Son is more another substance in the Son than is the Son in the Father, just as the flesh of my soul is more another substance in respect of my soul, though in one man, than the soul of another man in respect of my soul' (I, 20).

We shall have something to say shortly about the way in which such an attitude must affect one's views on the incarnation. But it is immediately obvious that the task, always an extremely delicate one for all religious discourse, of asserting the wholly otherness of God while yet preserving some affinity with those whom God has created after his own image and likeness, is here jeopardized by encroaching impressions of increasing crudeness: the distinction of divine and creaturely is now that between one kind of substance (stuff, almost) of which there is just one example, and another kind of substance of which there are many (though it is difficult to know what it could mean to include all creation under one substance-category), and the prospect of telling of the relations between them must at least be seriously threatened by this kind of abstraction and rigidity.[157]

Of prior concern, however, is the effect of this increasing conceptual abstraction and logical rigidity upon the account that it is felt must be given of the Three. The Cappadocians wrestled with the problem of distinguishing the *hypostaseis* from each other largely in terms of the relations between them, and even though they encountered apparently insurmountable difficulties in attempting to express clearly and definitively the distinguishing

relationship of the Holy Spirit to the others (or indeed in expressing the Spirit's distinction in any other way), and they met further
difficulties in finding unobjectionable terms for the relationship
of Father and Son, they leave sufficient room for the older
emanationist model, however inconsistently with the main thrust
of their logic, to enable later theology to claim that they had
successfully distinguished the *hypostaseis* in terms of their 'relations of origin' or 'modes of origin' one from another. In Augustine, however, the corrosive effect of the *homoousios* on the
remaining prominence of the older model becomes crucial, and
his account of the distinctions between the Three becomes as
abstract and as rigid as the concept of substance which dictates it.

Wishing to overcome once and for all the Arian objection that
distinctions within the divinity must involve differences within
the divine being or substance, Augustine raises (or lowers) the
orthodox case for distinguishing relationships to a logical rule of
trinitarian discourse. In between substantial predication (which
says something of the substance) and accidental predication
(which predicates accidental qualities, actions, or passions of the
substance), there is relational predication, he argues, and this
states how things relate to each other, rather than what they are
or how they are qualified or behave. Now to say how the Three
are related does not in itself imply either increase or decrease, or
any change whatever in them. Hence relations in God need not
be accidental as they are in creation. Divine immutability becomes
even more absolute than it is in Greek religious thought.

Then, applying this account of relational predication with
which he opens Book V, Augustine goes in search of sets of
relative terms. Ingenerate, unbegotten of course fail once more to
qualify fully, but Father and Son (whatever in Christian discourse
they are to be taken to mean) are clearly correlative. And the
difficulty of finding a relative (hence a distinguishing) term, as by
now we should almost expect, becomes extremely problematic in
the case of the Holy Spirit. Undaunted, of course, and by dint of
what John Burleigh in the theological understatement of that
particular year called 'rather desperate exegesis',[158] Augustine fits
out the Holy Spirit with the distinguishing and relative 'name' of
Gift (relative, one supposes, to Giver). And those who might be
inclined to object that in Scripture the gift of the Spirit refers to
God's relationship to us rather than to any inner-divine relationship can be told that further on (XV, 31) Augustine will, by means

of even more desperate exegesis, try to find scriptural support for defining the Holy Spirit *distinctively* as Love, the love that unites Father and Son (and their mutual Gift?).

Apart, however, from the logical stress and the exegetical strain involved in constructing these rules of theological discourse – the corresponding rule states that predicates which are not correlatives, such as omnipotent, good, and so on, apply to the 'one and the same' divine substance – their most questionable result is that they tend to iron out to the flatness of one general formula all the substantial distinctive properties with which the tradition had so far, however unsuccessfully, tried to flesh out our apprehension of Father, Son and Spirit. Aquinas, with his genius for drawing the lines of tradition together into tight theological formulae, expresses the last state of this development when he declares that distinctions exist in the divine nature where, and only where, there is oppositeness of relations, and then offers the following definition: ' "person" in God signifies a relation subsisting in the divine nature'.[159] The ensuing piece of clever argument in which he shows that, although two 'processions' (of Son and Spirit) must yield four relations, and subsistent relations are 'persons' in God, there are as yet but three 'persons', is an example at once of theological ingenuity and of the dead and rigid abstraction to which this theological development had descended under the weight of its own logic.

Augustine's treatment of divine sendings or 'missions' provides a consequent example of the flattening of perspectives and of the further recession from view of that 'order of transmission' which at once helped to distinguish the Three and was quite inseparable from the 'economy' of creation and salvation. And if we have begun to suspect that the effort to distinguish 'persons' by means of characteristic relative terms is not altogether successful, this treatment of missions offers us an opportunity to see if Augustine can make any better use of the *ad extra* actions of the Godhead than did the Cappadocians.

Augustine's puzzlement at the prospect of explaining how divine agents, Son and Spirit, can be said to be sent anywhere at all, since the divine prerogative of omnipresence is already theirs by nature, is relieved once again by his dichotomous distinction of substances divine (and therefore immutable and invisible) and creaturely (and hence visible and mutable). In the long analysis of mission in Book II of the *De Trinitate* he can therefore say: 'He is said to be sent in so far as he appeared externally in a corporeal creature, who internally in his spiritual nature is always hidden from human eyes.' The one God, Father Son and Spirit indistinguishably, 'makes' 'a mutable and visible creature' by which one of the 'persons' can be visibly manifested – for, as we saw, all attributes connoting what a substance is or how it is qualified or, in this case, behaves, must be applied indistinguishably to the Three-in-One, or rather, to the identical substance of the Three. This account of missions implies, of course, a more extreme and unqualified concept of the simplicity and immutability of the divine being that any Greek would hold, and it does so at the expense of raising some difficult questions, as Augustine himself realized (II, 12). Why is the Father never said to be sent, for instance, since, as Augustine acknowledges, despite all his well-founded agnosticism on the matter of 'who' precisely appears in particular theophanies, the Father is reliably reported to have 'spoken' to or about the Son on more than one scriptural occasion? And was the Son or Word already sent in the Old Testament?

The first of these problems is solved by linking the concept of mission with that of procession. That is to say, one can probably gather, especially from Book IV, 27–28, that the Son can be said to be sent since he proceeds from the Father *and* is manifested in a visible form created for the purpose; whereas, though the Father is in a similar way made audible, he does not proceed and cannot then be said to be sent. This further rule of theological discourse, if it is what I think it to be, is probably one of the last remaining vestiges of the older 'order of transmission', once again making an appearance in an attempt to solve a problem which would otherwise, in the newer scheme of things, be insoluble. For, as efforts to answer the second question above must surely show, the theological model of the one God or the Three-in-one fashioning 'mutable and visible creatures' which will then externally manifest one of them is bound to appear extrinsicist and arbitrary in its mode of conveying the requisite 'information' about things divine, and assertions based upon the model to the effect that the Son, for instance, is properly sent only at the incarnation, are bound to appear to be just that, namely, assertions which the model itself does little or nothing to support.[160] Once again a flat and undifferentiated formula, if rigidly applied in accordance with its own logic, will yield only the sense that the one God 'creates' voices, clouds, fire, or human flesh, to make visible one of the 'persons' and to reveal them thus in their relationships to one another, but no visible means of manifestation has, or could have, any intrinsic relationship to any particular 'person'. *Opera ad extra sunt indivisa* is now so much in possession that it makes all detectable means of distinguishing the 'persons' suspect.

The logical end-result of these tendencies is, of course, a severe devaluation of the incarnation. That this devaluation is no mere figment of a would-be critic's wishful thinking, but an ever-present reality in Augustine's trinitarian theology can easily be seen by anyone who, first, notices that Augustine speaks of the Word being sent to someone when he is *known* by that person (IV, 28), and who, next, becomes aware of the direction of Augustine's preferences amongst the manners in which the human spirit comes to *know* the Word and, thus, the Trinity. This last point requires a brief visit to the much disputed area of the *De Trinitate*, which is devoted to the 'traces of the Trinity', but the influence of this area on subsequent trinitarian theology, particularly of the more popular kind, is in any case too great to allow its difficulties to persuade one to pass it by.

A full and detailed account of Augustine's search through potential 'traces of the Trinity' (*vestigia Trinitatis*) in the world, the flesh, and the human spirit, would take up too much space just now. Some general remarks on the very nature of the enterprise must suffice here, followed by some closer attention to Augustine's preferred 'image' of the Trinity in the human soul, and to the reasons for his preference – for though this matter is generally treated under the title 'traces of the Trinity', Augustine, echoing the account of man's creation in Genesis, talks during his quest of a likeness and, more generally, an image of the Triune God.[161]

In general, then, it must first be said that nothing could be further from Augustine's mind than an exercise in some totally autonomous kind of natural theology which, simply by contemplating the inherent structures of the human spirit, would place under human control such knowledge of the very being of God as would effectively dispel the latter's mystery.[162] For, first, Augustine himself declares the object of the exercise to be to ask, 'by what likeness or comparison with known things can we believe, so that we may also love the God who is not known?' (VIII, 8). Second, whatever ability the human spirit may retain to image forth the being of God is not due to its independent nature or structures, but due solely to God's prior gracious presence to it:

the 'trinity of the mind is not on that account the image of God because the mind remembers itself, understands itself, and loves itself, but because it can also remember, understand, and love him by whom it was made', and it can only love God because from 'the book of that light which is called Truth' God illumines the souls of human kind and conveys to them whatever intimations they may ever have of his guiding and sustaining presence (XIV, 15, 20). And, finally, in a long section of his work which is seldom stressed by theologians who are anxious that the psychological analogies, as they are also sometimes called, should stretch as far as an effective solution to the problem of the Spirit's place in a Trinity,[163] Augustine himself shows in detail how utterly inadequate are those structures and acts of the human spirit to the task of mirroring the divine nature – apart altogether from the additional consideration of the way in which human aberration has already muddled (if not broken) this mirror (XV, 11–18).

Nevertheless, if we pass over the less successful candidates – though the preacher who can think of nothing better on Trinity Sunday than to present the Trinity as a second holy family could benefit from Augustine's dismissal of such a misleading analogy in Book XII – we find that Augustine does prefer, as the best of a bad lot, the trinity of memory (which to Augustine means something like the mind's retentive possession of all its varied content – from impressed forms of truth and justice to the relatively trivial matters to which memory can more popularly refer), understanding (or the mind's conscious contemplation of this content with intent to comprehend it) and will (at once the desire for this knowledge which can set the mind in quest of it, the application to it, and the enjoyment, or love of it in the fullest sense). There is, of course, an obvious enough sense in which these three, though distinct, have an identical content or 'substance' and thus provide some analogy to a Nicene-type Trinity, that is, a homoousiite Trinity; although those who are rightly impressed by Augustine's profound psychological sensitivity in works such as his *Confessions* must be saddened indeed to find such subtle pyschological phenomena as love here described, again undoubtedly under dictation of the needs of the *homoousios*, as a substance (XV, 27).[164] And it is, in any case, to a distinction which Augustine himself makes within the possible content of these mental faculties or acts, and to the reasons for his stated preference within this distinction, that we must here direct our attention.

Augustine draws a distinction between knowledge (*scientia*) and wisdom (*sapientia*). The former consists, in his view, in the rational cognition of things time-bound which we normally have as a result of various observational, mnemonic, and discursive processes; the second consists of a purely intellectual cognition of things eternal which we can possess through contemplation. Now this distinction might be allowed some obscure resting-place in ancient epistemology were it not for the fact that Augustine resolutely confines to the first part of it 'all those things which the Word made flesh did and suffered for us in space and time' (XIII, 24), and then, with explicit references to all that, expresses the clearest preference for that contemplative cognition of things eternal to provide the best image we may have of the Triune God (XIV, 4). The distinction drawn here, the line along which the distinction lies, and the clear preference expressed, really ought to make us pause so that their fullest implications may be savoured, though they are seldom mentioned at all by those who take their trinitarian theology largely from Augustine, and they often receive no more than passing notice in commentaries on his *De Trinitate*.

The human soul or spirit is 'illumined' by God or, to change the metaphor, it has the forms of truth and justice, for instance, imprinted on it by God, and so God is somehow present to the very centre of the human soul, which is therefore (and not because of any independent structure or autonomous features of its own) in God's image (compare IX, 11 with XIV, 4, 6). It is in the triadic structure of memory, understanding and will, when contemplatively operative upon this graced situation of the immortal soul in the mode of *sapientia*, that the truest image of the Trinity available to us while *in via* consists. The image of the Trinity which consists in the triadic structure of memory, understanding and will, but now operative upon 'the faith' (all those things which the Word made flesh did and suffered), and therefore occurring at the level of mere knowledge (*scientia*), is by comparison transient and secondary, not quite fully belonging to the 'inner man'. This quite deliberate effort to second-rate the salvific-revelatory work of Jesus' life and death in this world must surely be more serious for the assessment of Augustine's trinitarian theology than his more uncritical admirers would ever lead one to suspect.[165]

It is true, of course, that Augustine, who likes to scourge the arrogance of the philosophers, correspondingly insists that it is

160

only through faith, through the knowledge we have from Jesus' life with us, that we can come to such distant and imperfect awareness of the divine being as our poor minds can here attain. He insists that it is 'in the Word made flesh, who is Jesus Christ' that we possess both 'the treasures of *sapientia* and *scientia*'. And though he is always clear that 'the Word is beyond space and time, and is co-eternal with the Father and wholly everywhere', and that our judgments about the Word, so far as we can make them, 'belong to *sapientia*', nevertheless, he does insist that it is through faith that we gain such wisdom or, as he puts it, 'through him (i.e., the Word made flesh) we rise to him, we pass through *scientia* to *sapientia*' (XIII, 19, 24). Agreed, but the question does remain, what is the relationship of faith to wisdom, of the historical Jesus to the Word, of the lower image to the higher? This is a very large question of Augustinian exegesis, and all that can be done here is to mention two likely Augustinian answers, both of which can be shown, more particularly in conjunction, to be less than satisfactory.

Apart from the moralizing point that we should be inspired by God's condescension in Jesus to be humble rather than proud in our quest for God, there is, first, the suggestion that the Fall has obscured, if not obliterated, the image of God in the human soul, so that reversal of original sin is necessary for the image to be accessible once more and, second, the suggestion that the purpose of the mission of the Son in the world is to convey the knowledge (information, almost?) of the Word's procession from the Father (IV, 29). But these suggestions are straight-jacketed into Augustine's dichotomous distinction of kinds of substance – divine/ creaturely, spiritual/fleshly – so that the Fall too easily becomes a matter of immersion of the higher substance in the lower, a reversal of the priority of the higher reason over the lower (XII, 13), and our question tends to be answered merely by re-arranging the terms in which it was put. *Our* fall to lower reason and the sensual from the original state of higher reason and its wisdom and divine illuminative presence is simply paralleled by the Word's descent into the flesh, where by actions and passions and other things temporal he recalls us to our original state. And this is little more than a statement of the starting position according to which the image of the Triune God is contained more properly in the soul's attention to its original divine endowment than in its attention to Jesus' life and death. There are, of course, many other ways in which Jesus' work is described by Augustine – as forgiveness of sin, for instance, or reversal of the death-penalty incurred by sin – but none is much more likely to provide a better answer to our question than the one just outlined.

More serious, however, than any dissatisfaction we may feel with one or more answers to the question just posed, is the inevitable implication of the very exercise of making the faith of which Jesus was the source a mode of access to our faulty human understanding of God which is resolutely held inferior to the human soul's more original relationship to God and his Word. This in itself devalues what we Christians call the incarnation, making it at most an adventitious necessity. The point here is not that one must never let it be understood that what Jesus did was to construct, from the human side, the 'essential', 'original', 'right', 'only fully true' relationship between humans and God – for every christology which presumes to be catholic must claim as much, and *Logos*-christologies in particular have been most adept at so doing. But great care must be taken with adjectives like 'original' and verbs like 'restore', for if these succeed in giving the impression either that the relationship in question already in fact existed, or that more direct access to it can be gained from the immortal soul's intrinsic status than can be gained from all that Jesus did and suffered, *then* the incarnational economy is adventitious, *then* a timeless relationship between the God and the 'inner' soul supersedes those relationships to God constructed in time and attributed to God's mighty acts which, however, always take place through mortal agents; the admittedly obscure image of God in wisdom is *then* superior to the obviously obscure image of God which we have from faith, and the Trinity is no longer really a christological doctrine; it is instead a doctrine of God which reveals connections with Jesus of Nazareth as tenuous as those of uncreated substance with created substance in the substance theology of Nicaea and of Augustine.

One final comment before leaving these brief reflections on the *De Trinitate*. I think that one can see in Augustine's preference for the wisdom of the inner man as source of an image of the Triune God a very last vestige of that emanationist model of Greek thought which by, grading reality from the Unknown One to the human spirit, gave to earlier Christian trinities much of the clarity of distinctions which they appeared to possess. Augustine's pilgrim's progress from the 'outer' man, in touch with transient things, to the realm of true *intelligentia* and *sapientia* is in fact just such a 'way back' to the vision and possession of God as this old emanationist model, and it alone, really supports. But if one is right in seeing here a last ghostly appearance of this model, the important point now is not to suggest that it is still attempting to fulfil its familiar post-mortem role of distinguishing *hypostaseis* where such distinctions tend to disappear or to become over-abstract. The important point now is to suspect that in itself the newer Nicene homoousiite model is no more apt than the older subordinationist model to express the Christian conviction that in Jesus of Nazareth, in the life, death, and destiny of the man Jesus, our definitive relationship to God was by God's grace and act established. In order to make this point it is necessary to return again briefly to Arius.

12

Arius, Orthodoxy and Pre-existence

Following the recent work of Gregg and Groh, it should be possible to acknowledge the instinct of the early Arians to be especially sensitive to Scripture's persistent descriptions of the human condition of the Redeemer and to the predominance in Scripture of the language of will, good-pleasure, and obedience in recording the relationship of the Redeemer to the God he himself called Father. It might not be too tendentious to suggest that a great deal of christology in recent times has been rediscovering that same theological sensitivity and that same scriptural predominance. Certainly the more one looks at the texts which Arius and his supporters preferred, the more one is freed once again to ask the difficult questions: was Arius right, then? and, if not, where exactly did he go wrong?

If we are to take into account all that is positively in favour of the early Arian case in the position argued by Gregg and Groh, then we shall have to try to answer these questions by saying: what was wrong was Arius's insistence on transferring back into pre-existence the language which indeed he found all over the Scriptures depicting the relationship between God and our saviour, Jesus. That transference made, of course, it is obvious that the older emanationist model of distinct grades (as Tertullian would say) in divinity, with its inherent subordinationism, was much to Arius's liking and it suited well the theological case he wished to make. It was, in any case, at that time still in possession, essentially undisturbed by any rival scheme.

The combination of such scriptural language as the early Arians, with every apparent right, preferred with that Greek emanationist model which, as I already argued, was the common inheritance

164

of all, did indeed question the nature and status of that divinity which, as Arians continued to insist, was truly present in Jesus. And this in the end, I believe, did at least implicitly reduce Jesus to the kind of bringer of knowledge (information almost) about God and the world which I argued in *Jesus, the Man and the Myth* would alter the very nature, and not just part of the content of the Christian faith. But in view of so much that has been said in the preceeding sections, are we not now bound to ask the question: were things very much better with the orthodox, as they came to be called?

Apart altogether from the fact that the 'substance' language which after Nicaea they came increasingly to champion simply could not claim anything approaching the same scriptural support as the language used by the Arians to depict the relationship between God and his Son Jesus, the orthodox in their opposing arguments have been found consistently wanting on the following grounds. First, they never really shed the older emanationist model to which the Nicene *homoousios* is of its nature, and was with increasing clarification gradually seen to be, inimical. The older model makes various surreptitious re-entries, usually where the newer model erodes the very inner-divine distinctions it is meant to secure, either by turning them into abstract generalities (Augustine), or by so emphasizing its auxiliary dichotomy between divine and creaturely substance that all its names for allegedly inner-divine processes and relationships can be seen at a glance to take their only known connotation from divine-creaturely relationships (Gregory of Nyssa). Even Augustine – especially when he tries to give some content for the human mind to the inner-divine distinctions and relations – finds himself reintroducing the ghost of the older model, if only in its 'return' form. I cannot personally see that the *homoousios* did any more than gradually – as it moved towards the meaning of identity of substance – threaten to destroy an older model, on which its protagonists nevertheless persistently, if surreptitiously, prove themselves dependent whenever they wish to secure their inner-divine distinctions from disappearance. It also outlawed Arians, of course, but at what price?

Now this state of affairs could be accepted on the oft-proclaimed principle that, after all, the dogmatic decisions of the past must be taken to be more successful in what they reject than in what they assert. So the *homoousios* with all its subsequent developments meant to reject the older emanationist model with its inherent subordinationist dangers – and this at least was achieved, even if no positive alternative clearly emerged to take the place of the vanquished schema. Indeed such an account of the matter would be acceptable, but it would be a mistake to think that it could possibly represent an account of what actually happened in the centuries between. As we have seen in the case of our two major thinkers, and as the subsequent history of trinitarian theology would continue to show, the Nicene definition was taken to be a foundation on which to build rather than a 'throw-away' missile directed at an enemy position; and as a foundation it could secure little more than the radical instability of the theological edifices successively erected upon it.

This brings us to the second point on which the orthodox were, and still can be found wanting. In the end of the day – and this becomes painfully clear in Augustine – they were no more successful than were the Arians in securing for Christian theology the central role of all that Jesus said, did and experienced in this world, and of the biblical witness to this. In fact the early Arians at least would seem to have an advantage over the orthodox on this issue, since they did arguably remain closer to the more dominant biblical language of divine will and human obedience.

Therefore, since I have already complained about the Arian tendency to drive back into pre-existence the scriptural descriptions of Jesus' relationship to his Father, we must equally ask about the equally obvious 'retreat into pre-existence' of the orthodox Fathers' alternative, homoousiite theology and say, *en passant*, some further general words about this elusive issue of the distinction of 'real' from 'notional' pre-existence. And since Greek pagan theology is the commonly assumed background of Arian and orthodox alike, we may address these words first to that theology – if only in the hope of getting a better answer to Hengel's question (when does 'notional' pre-existence turn into 'real' pre-existence in christology?) than Hengel himself appeared able to give.

It scarcely needs to be said that some at least of the Greek theologians who talk of binitarian or trinitarian structures within the divine being in either Middle – or Neo-Platonism convey the impression that they refer to permanent and permanently distinct (and in that sense 'real') *hypostaseis* – or whatever other term may be used for the two or three – within the divinity. And to the extent that this impression was conveyed and received, those Christians who used this theology, whether Arian or orthodox, would inevitably take themselves to be talking also about two or three really distinct pre-existent divine beings; pre-existent now in the sense of existing before, during and after (in temporal sense) or above and beyond (in spatial terms) the spatio-temporal world in which all created things live and die, exist and cease to be. No doubt some form of Lampe's 'double projection' was operative both in arriving at and in confirming this view: the known individual personality of Jesus of Nazareth projected back upon a second 'level' of divine being helped in the formation and reception of the impression that this was indeed a distinct 'one' within the divine being, while existing Greek impressions of a distinct divine *hypostasis* called *Nous* or *Logos* helped to recommend the view that such a distinct divine *hypostasis* was incarnate in (projected into) Jesus of Nazareth.

This double projection, to the extent to which it was operative, in combination perhaps with the Christian habit of disowning the influence of 'the philosophers', prevented Christian theologians from availing themselves, even if they had wished to do so, of what might be considered alternative options in conceiving of the status of the members of the Greek binitarian or trinitarian emanationist models, alternative options in deciding about the kind of reality or realities thought to lie behind their terms.

First, there was the image of exodus and return which was endemic to the Greek religious schema. To the extent that this image was temporalized, i.e., to the extent that it suggested that the exodus of the lower levels of divinity had a beginning and would, after a return, be at an end, it would lead to a kind of Sabellianism which was unacceptable to the Christian faith. On the other hand, to the extent that it was not so temporalized, to the extent that it was taken to describe a permanent ladder of descent and ascent for the whole of reality, it simply stressed successive subordination amongst the divine beings involved and thus favoured the Arian view – though there may also have been prospects here of the type that Marcellus of Ancyra wanted to develop but which the harsher climate of polemics-to-the-death finally killed off, as they kill all things delicate and fine.

Second, *within* this master symbol of exodus and return, *because* in one way the whole program of this Greek theology could be described, following the basic Platonic instinct to prefer soul to

167

body and to set mind over matter, as a purely spiritual odyssey, a journey of the soul inward through its own recesses instead of outward to its loss of self in flesh and the physical, a different kind of conception and impression of the reality behind the terms of the emanationist model was not only possible but often actually indicated. In one way it could almost be said that the cosmic image of exodus and return was a projection on to the cosmos outside of the two-way activity and invitation which the Greek religious genius felt within, a projection of the psychic drama on to the whole physical world. However that may be, in this second way of conceiving of them, the terms of the emanationist model would turn out to be a names for the One, forged by the human mind according to the ways in which the One, true Being affected it and could be gradually attained by it, and not in any sense distinct 'beings', real and separable *hypostaseis*, whether permanent or temporary.

One recalls the suggestion, seen particularly in Philo, that such terms as Logos, Pneuma, Creator, Lord referred to powers of the divinity, attributes almost, which from our human experience of the divine in our world we could detect and name: powers, attributes, functions of God, but not distinct persons, beings, or even *hypostaseis*. This is the kind of qualified Greek view of the divine which lies behind the Jewish wisdom literature mentioned in the sections on Son and Spirit and which, if it yielded a binity or trinity at all, would yield one which was as accessible to Jews as it would be to Christians.

One can recall also, in connection with this second way of conceiving of the Greek schema, the Greek accounts of ways of talking about God – particularly the way of analogy and the negative way. The way of analogy, in particular the commonest analogies of root, trunk and fruit, or sun, ray and illumined object, or spring, river and stream, implied, especially when combined with the apophatic way, that such names for God as Nous, Logos, Pneuma, and so on, were just that, names by which we named from its effects upon us the as yet Unknown One, different names, adapted to the finite minds of their human inventors, for the One God. In fact it was sometimes fairly clearly suggested that trinitarian nomenclature was indeed a formula of different names for the one God.

Now this second way of conceiving of the reality behind the binitarian or trinitarian formulae did not really recommend itself to those who became champions of orthodoxy in the post-Nicene era. For them, as for the Arians indeed, the double-projection remained fully in effect. But whereas the Arians, accepting fully the inherent subordinationism of the Greek emanationist model, could avail themselves of such real tolerance for mutability at certain levels of the divine being as that model allowed, and thus do some justice to the scriptural data on a very mutable Jesus of Nazareth, the orthodox, in their retreat into pre-existence, by the very intensity of their defence against the Arians, were destined to leave the historical Jesus even further behind.

Both sides retreated into pre-existence to find the relationship between God and Jesus (and, subsequently, the distinct Spirit); for both, a certain form of Greek theology qualified by the 'double projection' is the origin of 'real' as distinct from 'notional' pre-existence. The Arians thus arrived at a distinct and subordinate, though truly divine being, as the immediate source of our salvation; the orthodox thus managed to insist, on the contrary, that in Jesus the one, true God was reconciling the world to himself, but at the expense of at one and the same time damaging the inner-divine distinctions to which they too were committed and distancing their whole account of the divine Being even more than did the Arians from the life, death and destiny of Jesus of Nazareth. It was orthodoxy at a great price: the Arians saw to that.

Hence at this point of our research it seems necessary to say that the relationship of a 'pre-existent' Word (and Spirit) to the Father had displaced from the centre of Christian theology that relationship of Jesus (and his co-heirs) to the Father with which the Christian Bible is concerned and which is revealed in the life and death of the same Jesus. And, furthermore, that this displacement is, if anything, even more pronounced in orthodox theology than it is in Arian. Nowhere is this more clearly seen than in the practice, which soon becomes a principle of the orthodox defence against Arius, of insisting that texts of Scripture which describe the Saviour as subordinate, created, mutable, subject to passion, and so on, and are to be referred to the flesh of Jesus, to his humanity, and not to the eternal, co-equal and immutable Word which indwells this flesh. Needless to say, Scripture itself gives no warrant at all for such eisegesis; yet the principle, for such it really becomes, quietly takes its place alongside Augustine's dichotomous division of substances into divine substance (now more immutable than any Greek theologian worth mentioning would ever think it to be) and creaturely substance, and it plays its supporting role in the general Christian retreat into pre-existence.

In sum, it should be fairly obvious from the brief preceding survey of some fourth- and fifth-century trinitarian theologies that the proponent of their continuing usefulness would need to give rather careful attention to the following factors at least.

The first factor is all too seldom noticed, probably once again because of our habit of taking at face value the orthodox Fathers' own attitudes and judgments in respect of those who proved their most persistent opponents. Lofty dismissals of the alleged pride of an opponent, or his humble origins, or his suspect schooling, provide the best possible way of covering up the fact, and it is a fact, that most of the positions finally occupied by the orthodox are positions to which they are driven rather than positions they would otherwise have chosen. It would be foolish indeed to believe without question that the end results of the long and discreditable struggles of the fourth century would inevitably coincide with the theological results of peaceful reflection by these same Christian men (who on both sides behaved in the most unchristian manner) on the data of Scripture and on the actual experience of truly Christian living. But true Christian peace, then as now, was the exception rather than the rule, and the saddest heritage of these ancient theological Leviathans is the theological and credal hostility which to this day masquerades as loyalty to Christ. However, it is the theological rather than the moral judgment that is important here, and the theological judgment must be that the more defensive a position is seen to be, the less claim it has to permanence after the particular threat it was meant to meet has declined.

The second factor is more commonly noticed but not always assessed to its full effect: the influence of classical Greek theology upon Christian formulations. It should appear from the preceding material that what have been called, for want perhaps of a better term, the Greek emanationist binitarian and trinitarian schemas, were inherently subordinationist, and yet they did provide the most successful means of distinguishing *hypostaseis* in the God-head for Christian use in the case of the Son, and less frequently in the case of the Spirit. It should consequently be clear that the more the *homoousios* moved closer to the meaning of one identical substance – as under persistent Arian pressure it was bound to do – the more difficult it was to maintain the distinctions between the *hypostaseis* or *personae*. *Opera ad extra* could not really sustain these distinctions, and appeals to an *order* in the divinity in its 'relations of origin', whether these formed part of the description of God's approach to the world or of the soul's search for God, simply recalled, to the extent that they were at all successful, the old doctrine of the *monarchia* with its inevitable subordinationist impressions – for no such strict order could be imposed by means of honest exegesis. These subordinationist impressions could always be stoutly denied – they were, and still are – but stout denial, however loud, is a poor substitute for replacing this schema with another to which such impressions are not quite so natural. The *homoousios*, under pressure, telescoped the *hypostaseis*, thereby damaging irreparably the delicate fabric of the only theological schema which that age really knew how to use.

The final factor is somewhat surprising at first view: for just when one part of the Greek religious dogma (the emanationist-subordinationist part) was being revised, another part of the same dogma (the emphasis on immutability) was, under persistent Arian pressure, receiving more adamant approval than ever before. The Greeks drew the line between divine and non-divine as the line between the immutable and the mutable. They did, however, for obvious reasons try to find a place for life in their understanding of the divine, and this task was made easier by the gently graded schema which depicted a divine Being 'descending' in creative outflow towards the material world, for lower 'levels' of this divine Being could accommodate multiplicity of a kind and even some exposure to movement. Now it is almost as if the Arians and their opponents divided this common dogmatic inheritance between them: the Arians kept its grading and hence emphasized its inherent subordinationism; the orthodox kept its stress on immutability which then hardened (crudified, perhaps), without the balance of the grading element, into a monolithic concept of divine immutability that is with us to this day and that, despite all our efforts to disown it as Greek, is really more Christian than Greek.

Certainly the most influential Christians, Athanasius and more particularly Augustine, hardened the soft Greek line of distinction between immutable and mutable into a dichotomy of two quite contrary kinds of substance, the immutable-creative and the

171

mutable-created, just at the time when they were increasingly telescoping the *hypostaseis*. Thus they simultaneously reduced the life of God more and more to the static abstraction of their own formulae (oppositeness of relations), and severed this life from the life, death and destiny of Jesus of Nazareth which was of course mutable in the extreme. The kenotic effect of this upon the content of the Christian confession of Jesus as Son of God has been indicated already. The orthodox Fathers did in this way secure the contention that it was the one, true God who was operative in Jesus for our salvation – and not, as Arians would imply, a lesser divinity – but still to be counted is the cost of their failure to move far enough, in doing this, from assumptions held in common with the Arians that God's self-differentiation (inevitable from his salvific work in the world) must be described by us in its 'pre-existent' form; for it is surely in their efforts to describe such pre-existent distinctions that the orthodox Fathers' failures can most clearly be seen to lie.

It should be possible to conclude, then, that, given the Greek theological schema which was common in these centuries to both the orthodox and their opponents, the orthodox did as well as they could humanly be expected to do; that they at least prevented the faith from being distorted in the peculiar way in which Arius and his followers threatened to distort it; that we should to that extent have to say that they were right and the Arians were wrong; and that we can today speak the truth they did in this way defend, though now in schemata which they did not envisage and could not have envisaged.

13

Alternative Trinities

Long and bitter polemics always narrow theological vision, and too often it is the narrow vision which is their main bequest to posterity. It is hardly surprising, then, though it is slightly regrettable, that trinitarian theologies deriving from Augustine in the West and the Cappadocians in the East are frequently considered to be the only ones worth considering critically today. Yet there are other trends in trinitarian theology which originate in the same cultural matrix and which in fact avoid some of the pitfalls to which attention has just now been drawn.[166] It is not necessary to suggest that any of these alternative trinities could be transported without further ado into the present century. But it may be of some use to sketch briefly some of their main features, and that for two main reasons. First, it may help to show that the commonly inherited Greek emanationist theology was capable of more subtle and promising use than the main Christian protagonists in the long Arian controversy ever managed to make of it. Second, and consequently, it may be possible to see that the theology of the Spirit, even within the terms of this dominant Greek theology, could have received a much fuller and richer development, such as would bring it much closer to the rich variety of spirit-material in the New Testament. In view of the contention that *trinitarian* theology stands or falls with the doctrine of the Holy Spirit, this is as good an issue as any on which to end the present section.

But let us take as our first example a trend in some ancient trinitarian theologies which relegates the trinitarian distinctions themselves to a second level of the divinity. The source of this intriguing trend in trinitarian theology is to be found in the second kind of Trinity of Being, Life and Intelligence which we already noted from Plotinus, and more particularly in the view, which can be traced through Iamblichus and Proclus to Pseudo-Denys, that this Trinity occurs at the second level of the Godhead and not at the first.[167] It would be possible to trace a part at least of the shadow side of this view in Gregory of Nyssa's specific references to the incomprehensibility of the divine essence,[168] but since the relationships of the *hypostaseis* to each other are far clearer in Gregory than are their relationships to the essence, his contribution to the development under review had better be considered suggestive rather than formative.

The distinction of levels in divinity with the placing of trinitarian distinctions on a second level is formulated in many ways. To Pseudo-Denys, for instance, the attributes of the ineffable and unknowable, permanent (essence) of God are 'incommunicable ultimates', whereas the 'differentiations of the Supreme Godhead' are called emanations and manifestations; so that, whereas the latter can be 'philosophically unravelled and unfolded' in such a manner as to 'guide the holy and unspotted mind to the shining truths of Scripture', the former, concerning the unity of the divine essence, can be apprehended only as mysteries which the mystic attains 'in a manner beyond the activities of our minds'.[169]

In the ninth century the maverick Irishman Johannes Scotus Eriugena (John the Irishman who was born in Ireland), who translated Pseudo-Denys into Latin and knew his Gregory of Nyssa, is even more decisive on this point. God, he insists, is more than unity and trinity, although, in order that we should have material for praise and blessing, we have under the guidance of theology something to say and to think and to understand about God[170] which corresponds to the trinitarian structure of the divine emanation. It is not from the essence, he insists, but from the *substantia* (his Latin translation of the Greek *hypostasis*) of the Father that the Son is born and, through the Son, the Spirit proceeds.[171] There is, in short, a 'level' of divinity, the innermost essence or being of God, which is above the trinity-in-unity of the divine emanation towards its own creation and its consequent manifestation to and in that creation.

Let us look to John of Ruysbroek[172] for an example of the clearest and most consistent statement of this position, and in doing so remember how much part and parcel it is of that classical and cohesive theological schema which united God's transcendence and immanence as it developed from Middle-Platonism to Neo-Platonism. From the utterly incomprehensible One emanates or is born *Nous* or Word and with and in the Word the ideal forms of all that shall exist in the material world.[173] Now, as Ruysbroek puts it, 'all that is in God is God'.[174] So ideal, intellectual being is divine, has affinity with the divine, wherever it is found: in the highest part of the soul, for instance. Hence Ruysbroek continually talks of the continuing birth of the Son from the Father and talks of it taking place 'in the nobility of the (human) spirit'.[175] The higher part of the soul is therefore the natural and most describable 'place' at which God and his human creatures meet. So the quest for God is inward in direction, as always in this tradition, since God comes and acts from within outward. But there is another depth or level to God (and a centre of the soul beyond its higher part) which is in itself neither accessible nor describable at the level of Word, Mind, Intelligence.

Some of Ruysbroek's stronger statements may be collected here for the sake of brevity. 'The Divine Nature eternally works according to the Persons, and is eternally idle and wayless according to the simplicity of Its Essence.'[176] 'In the unfathomable abyss of the Simplicity, all things are wrapped in fruitive bliss, and the abyss itself may not be comprehended, unless by the Essential Unity. To this the Persons, and all that lives in God, must give place.'[177] 'Yet all loving spirits are one fruition and one blessedness with God without distinction; for that beatific state, which is the fruition of God and of all His beloved, is so simple and onefold that therein neither Father nor Son, nor Holy Ghost, is distinct according to the Persons, neither is any creature.'[178]

In short, as we shall see others such as Marius Victorinus suggest, when the divine Being emanates towards the production of the creation in its creative outflow, at that level it becomes differentiated. But in its deepest centre, at its highest level, it is utter simplicity. The creative outgoing, as always in this tradition, dictates the *eros*- driven return. So all that comes from the One, Word, and in that Word all ensouled creatures, must be drawn back again into the utter simplicity, the rest from all creativity and striving, the enjoyment without form, of the One.

It is not necessary here to attempt to go deeper into the mystical theology of John of Ruysbroek, or to call on others such as Meister Eckhart,[179] for all we need are illustrations of a Christian theology of Trinity which, developing the same common Greek heritage, locates the Trinity itself on a second level of divine being. One might ask, of course, what possible advantage could there be in locating the trinitarian distinctions on the second level of divine Being? One possible answer might be that this locates trinitarian distinctions resolutely in God's outreach to the world, it makes Trinity entirely and inescapably 'economic', and though, in the forms in which we have just described it, it could turn out to be Sabellian (or perhaps closer to Marcellus of Ancyra), it may be capable of specifically Christian development. For instance, if God's Fatherhood is understood primarily from his relationship, not to a pre-existent divine person, but to Jesus of Nazareth, then we could have a Trinity which occurs at that level of divine Being and action which is directly involved in our world. And there would still be a genuine 'beyond' for both Jesus and our world. There are also possibilities here for a return to binity, as a revisit to Ruysbroek will shortly show. But this is to anticipate too much of our further argument and to go too far beyond our authors' meaning at this point. So let us look briefly at the second trend which we wish to notice in alternative trinities.

In order to see something of the more creative ways of theologizing about the Holy Spirit which the Neo-Platonic heritage offered, it is well to look to the other line along which Plotinus' thought developed, the line which passes through Porphyry and travels to Augustine *via* the Roman rhetorician who converted to Christianity, Marius Victorinus. The same distinctions of rest and action, inwardness and outward turning, hiddenness and manifestation, occur in Marius Victorinus as occurred in the authors just now passed in review, but it does appear that Marius Victorinus identifies the Father of the trinitarian model with the level of divinity that is at rest (*actio inactuosa*), that is pure power (*potentia*) not yet considered power-in-action, that is life perfectly self-contained, turned in on itself (*in se conversus*); although, strictly speaking, since Father is a relational term, this level of divinity is Father only in relation to the action and movement which goes out from it, the life that flows from it and flows first to the Son,[180] in whom all things come to be in their exemplar forms. So far, then, we seem to have the typical kind of Trinity with which Gregory's 'order of transmission' made us familiar.

But it is at this point that Marius Victorinus begins to sound strange to people who think there has never been more than one orthodox Christian doctrine of the Trinity. For he now suggests that the only-begotten of the Father is really a dyad, or *geminus* (twin).[181] For that power of existence (*esse*) which flows out from the ultimate Source is both life and consciousness (*vivere, intelligere*), and it reaches us as life in the form of Jesus of Nazareth who died in order that we should live, and it reaches us as understanding or wisdom in the twinned form of spirit which enables us to know the way to God through Jesus. But it is important to stress that these are truly twinned forms of the same outflow to us of God's creative and salvific being. There is, then, no place for a strict 'order of transmission' in which the Spirit is third. In fact at one point Marius Victorinus echoes a theme of earlier Syriac theology and talks of the Spirit as the mother of the Word, since knowledge generates (life).[182]

In addition, Marius Victorinus is extremely suspicious of the impressions conveyed by trinitarian formulae commonly in use. 'We ought not,' he declares, 'in fact it is not permissible to say, that there is one substance and there are three persons'.[183] And there is more to his objection here than dissatisfaction with the term *persona*. He is concerned with what can only be called damage to the perceived unity of the divine being by formulae which suggest divisions within it, and thus convey impressions which can later be but imperfectly corrected by protestation. We should so speak as to make it clear that the one divine Being comes to us in the twin forms of life and understanding, and its coming to us in this way is itself its Fatherhood. And it is significant to note that the effort to do so for Marius Victorinus involves the subordinationism of the Greek emanationist model which, in his view, is quite compatible with his use of the Nicene *homoousios*.[184]

But it is his ability to conceive of God as Spirit in ways which do not involve all the difficulties we have already noted in the case of the most influential trinitarian theologies that is of interest at this stage. And for another, though a rather more elaborate (and elusive), example of this we may go once more to John of Ruysbroek. Although I do not intend to attempt anything even vaguely approaching an adequate account of Graeco-Christian mysticism, I hope I may be permitted one general observation which seems to me to be well supported by such works of the various Christian mystics as I have read. Like all who write books, the mystics sometimes show themselves to be more under the influence of the particular shape and form of their very own experience, and at other times more under the influence of the conventional shapes and forms of the received tradition. So at times Ruysbroek will write of the experience of God in terms taken from the set trinitarian theology of his time and place, including the terms of the regrettable *filioque*.[185] Quite frequently, however, at points where his prose achieves a power of conviction and a more poetic quality that seems to come from the very heights of his own experience, the Unity, which is otherwise described in terms of Essence, is named Spirit or, what amounts to the same thing, Love.

Then the impression the reader gets is that the Unity-Spirit-Love *is* that which 'is fruitful in the outgoing activity of the Persons',[186] *is* that which forms the very unity of Father and Son, so that 'the indrawing Unity of God is nought else than the fathomless Love, which lovingly draws inward, in eternal frui-tion, the Father and the Son and all that lives in them'.[187] Now someone might say that such language is due to no more than the common theological ambiguity of the terms Spirit and Love, which can name either the divinity in itself or the 'Third Person'. But, apart from the fact that this ambiguity in itself tells us something about our trinitarian theologies which we do not often wish to hear, it really is too weak an explanation of Ruysbroek. It is, I suggest, impossible to read through Ruysbroek without coming away with the impression that the hidden God who can be called Essence, Unity, Spirit, or Love, overflows in creative quest of the creature, emerging as Father, and as the Son in whom all things are preformed (and in whom the Father knows himself as Father and knows all else), holding all these distinct beings in the unity of its own loving embrace and drawing all back again into its own undivided bliss.

In fact this second trend towards a fuller and richer theology of the Spirit (which in Victorinus reinstates binitarian thinking within trinitarian) can even show at times how the commonly inherited Greek theology could be pushed closer and closer to a truly Christian concept of a questing, passionate and suffering God. One would not want to make too much of this. Marius Victorinus can be as adamant about the immutability of God, Father and Son-Spirit, as the next man, and just as quick to take refuge, when the cross of Jesus comes into view, in the well-worn distinction between the flesh of Jesus and his Spirit.[188] Neverthe-less, at times the possibility of the suffering God does emerge, and at times quite strongly. When Marius Victorinus, like Augustine later, offers the soul (in his case, its existence, life and consciousness) as an analogue to the triune being of God, he is eloquent on the way in which passion and suffering result from the attempts (*usque ad mortem*) to vivify others and make them understand.[189] And many times in his work one gets the impression that his conventional strictures on any talk of passion, suffering, change in God simply run counter to the natural flow of his thought, according to which God's emanation is life and motion and returns to unchanging bliss only through the death of Jesus, God's very life amongst us,[190] and through the probing of the light of the Spirit which is always threatened by the darkness of this world.

But it is in Ruysbroek once again that the theme of God's own need and struggle comes to its most powerful expression. In a deeply moving passage, which simply has to be read in its own context, he declares that 'the Spirit of God hunts our spirit', he talks about the storm of love in which two spirits strive together, the Spirit of God and our spirit, of God being 'touched' when our spirit presses itself into God. And he ends: 'This makes each of the spirits (i.e., God and his creature) yearn for the other in love.'[191]

This is startling stuff, but only by contrast with the rigidly abstract and increasingly contentless accounts of the divine relations into which the more familiar trinitarian theologies were forced. And one can begin to suspect that such a vision as Ruysbroek enjoyed could indeed force open the existing cracks in Greek immutability theology (which he too had inherited) to the extent of admitting God's healing passion in the death of Jesus. But that did not really happen or, to the extent that it did happen, it did not deflect the mainstream development of trinitarian theology, to which we must now return. But before we do so, it does no harm to remark that this second alternative trend in trinitarian theology promises advantages even more substantial than the first.

For it is certainly true that many who read or hear, however reluctantly, the kind of critical survey of the Holy Spirit and classical trinitarian theologies on which we have just been engaged come away with very negative impressions, and find themselves wishing only that the negative critique should be answered and the classical doctrines fully reinstated. This in itself, however, may be a negative reaction, pre-empting the real theological possibilities of the present. For surely the end-result of the second trend in trinitarian theology would be to free pneumatology for the fullest use of the rich and varied spirit-material in the New Testament, and for the recovery of all that was best in the binitarian theologies of the earliest Christian centuries. Holy Spirit, after all, is a name for God, transcendent and immanent, and in the New Testament Holy Spirit is as much at the origin of the sonship of Jesus as it is third in any order of transmission in the economy of God's outreach towards the world. In short, though pneumatology proved to be the Achilles' heel of classical trinitarian theology because of the latter's inability in the end to accommodate it properly, it could also be the bone from which theological archaeologists could reconstruct trinities or binities for today, if it could only be allowed to claim its total scriptural inheritance at last.

14

The Mainstream Development of the Classical Doctrines

In the absence of any ambition to write a history of doctrines of the Trinity, perhaps I may be allowed to skip over various re-emergences of types of Arianism, the emergence of other heretical trends, including quaternities and unitarianism, and extremely interesting cases such as that of Joachim of Fiore, so we may visit only the mainline stations, the most influential receivers and shapers of the classical trinitarian theologies of East and West. And since it is with Western trinitarian theology that we are most familiar on these outer islands of the continent of Europe, we may go straight to the thirteenth century and to Thomas Aquinas, even if we have to double back a little later to pick up some of the Eastern story.

Readers of Aquinas's mini-treatise on the Trinity, in Part One of his *Summa Theologiae*, Questions 27–43, will quickly feel themselves on familiar ground, for Aquinas is systematician *par excellence* of the tradition that had reached him, principally from Augustine. He does not change, add, or subtract, except in the interests of consistency, clarity, or cogency. But perhaps for that very reason the main features of the Augustinian theology, including the most questionable of these, stand out in even greater relief, exuding a kind of confidence, and inviting a degree of criticism, of which Augustine himself might very reasonably fight shy. The treatise now begins with the 'processions' of the divine 'persons' within the eternal divine nature itself, and only at the very end are we told about the 'missions' of divine persons to our world. The divine persons, as we shall see, are defined in terms

181

of relations, and even here Aquinas prefers to stress what he calls the oppositeness of the relations rather than the fact that they are relations of origin.[192] He is quite clear in his insistence that the Trinity cannot be known from the creation – the principle *opera ad extra sunt indivisa* is by now sacrosanct – and he further distances from our world all discussion of real divine relation by stating quite baldly, 'there is no real relation in God to the creature'.[193] Creatures, that is, may experience a real relationship of dependence upon and need of God, but God experiences no such real relationship to his creatures. Consequently when he comes to write of the missions, Aquinas is even clearer than Augustine that the one Godhead as such fashions the creatures (voices, dove, fire, the flesh of the Son?) in which the missions of the persons become visible, but he places before these the invisible missions of the persons to and in the knowledge and love of those rational creatures who stand in the grace of God. Various attributes and actions of the one God which are somehow perceivable to us from his creation can be appropriated to one or other of the persons, and thereby help us to express our belief in the Trinity, but the very use of the term 'appropriation' advertises the fact that nothing in the visible creation or its visible history is proper to one person rather than to the others.

In all these ways the impression is received and constantly strengthened that real relationships, as far as God is concerned, are all within the eternal divine nature. In fact, there seems to be an anticipation of a later social trinity in the manner in which Aquinas insists that God, though sole, is not solitary; not, he hastens to add, because of the company of angels or other creatures outside of God's self, but because of the persons within.[194] In any case, we are a very long way now from the human origins of the doctrine of the Trinity with which we have been dealing in the earlier sections of this work, and that distance is mirrored in a significant way in the distance between the Trinity now presented to us and the created world which we can see and hear groaning all around us. As quickly as people forget the human origins of the religious doctrines they profess, just so quickly do they forget also those human experiences of the creation and its history in which alone the encounters with God take place. Forgetting this they can then, of course, start their doctrinal treatises within the very nature or mind of God, and from this eternal vantage-point relativize all that is seen or heard to occur on this lean earth.

Aquinas assumes, of course, that this self-contained and utterly self-sufficient trinitarian life of God has been revealed to us. But the very manner in which (as we saw in previous sections) the Arian polemicists had driven the orthodox accounts away from the divine economy and deeper and deeper within the divine immanence makes the further account of the way in which that revelation was communicated problematic in the extreme. It might not be unfair to say that, not only is the triune nature of God a matter of knowledge to us – rather than a matter of some more comprehensive human experience of which we have some knowledge – but that it seems almost to be a matter derived from the nature or knowledge and not from some knowledge-content communicated to us. Certainly Augustine's psychological analogies, to give them but one of their names, play a much more substantial role in the trinitarian theology of Aquinas than Augustine himself would ever allow them to do, so that the relationships between knowledge and love, as we know these from the intrinsic structures of the human psyche, become determinative at certain points of the theological argument rather than remain, as one presumes they should, distant and extremely inadequate analogies. Of the many illustrations which we might offer from Aquinas's mini-treatise, let us concentrate on the passage in which he defends the infamous '*filioque*'.

One must begin by saying that Aquinas experiences the by now customary amount of trouble with the search for properties or characteristics which would adequately distinguish a Holy Spirit within the deity. That difficulty at least does not decline with the passage of the centuries. So one finds Aquinas honestly admitting that there are no proper names for the procession which results in the Holy Spirit, for the relationship in which it stands to others, or for its 'person',[195] yet striving manfully to show that Love is a proper name for the Holy Spirit, and that Gift is a personal name for Holy Spirit, when taken personally.[196] This is familiar stuff from Augustine, and becomes no more persuasive with repetition. And it should not be necessary to repeat at this point that failure to find distinctive properties for the Holy Spirit is not really compensated for by success in finding a precise common term to designate the three, for success in honing a term for the three in God which will complement the term for that in God which is one, difficult as that success too is to achieve, of itself does nothing to show that there are three in God in the first place. On the contrary, only when one somehow knows that there are three will it become necessary to answer at some stage the question: three what?

Aquinas does his best to accommodate both the Greeks and the Latins in his answer to that last question. Borrowing from Boethius the definition of person as the individual substance of a rational nature, taking the term substance in that definition to mean subsistence, which in turn he takes to be the best translation of the Greek *hypostasis*, he concentrates on the element of subsistent individuality in the combined traditions, reduces the meaning of the word person, for present purposes at least, to this element, and so declares it not unsuitable to answer the question: three what? However, one must continue to insist, it would be as silly to judge the success of this medieval trinitarian theology on the worth of this redefinition of the term *persona* as it would be to suggest that a modern presentation of trinitarian theology would surely succeed if only one could find a reliable substitute for the modern word 'person'. It should be clear to any careful student of Aquinas that his theology of the Trinity too stands or falls with his treatment of the Holy Spirit, and that his case for the distinct 'personhood' of the Spirit really rests on the passages in which he insists on the *filioque*. For it is in these passages that he really succeeds in showing, to his own satisfaction at least, that the two 'processions' which take place in the inner being of God yield three subsistent relations or persons, no more and no less.[197]

Aquinas's case for the *filioque* seems simple enough in its basic moves.[198] Each inner-divine procession yields two entities-in-relation, two subsistent relations. Hence two processions, that of the Son by means of generation and that of the Spirit by some nameless means of procession, could yield, on this logic, four persons, unless of course two of the persons could be conceived as the unitary source of the other. It is possible to conceive of this, since only oppositeness of relationship distinguishes persons, and 'breather' or 'breathed' do not as such constitute a relational opposition to either Father or Son or even as between Father and Son. Then when it comes to answering the question as to which pair is to be the joint source from which the other proceeds – and here is the major evocation of the human psychological model – Aquinas asserts the principle that love always of necessity comes after conception by the intellect, or understanding. So Father and Son (his conceived word) are together joint breather of the breathed Holy Spirit, and thus the relational opposition of breather and breathed yields three, and not four or two, 'persons'.

The issue of the *filioque* arises inevitably in the effort to describe how Aquinas arrives at a distinct Holy Spirit, and hence at a Trinity rather than a binity or a quaternity. It is certainly not my intention at this point to raise the enormous political as well as theological issue of the *filioque* in its own right, and so on that issue, and if only to ensure that we do return as quickly as possible to our mainline interest, the following few remarks will suffice.

The tragic need of human beings to make war rather than love contributes far more importance to the long and bitter debate about the *filioque* between the East and the West than could any light which that debate would ever throw on the deeper problems of classical trinitarian theologies, and the present laudable efforts at reconciliation between the churches of the East and those of the West[199] are likely to do more for much needed Christian unity than they could ever do for the prospects of a viable trinitarian theology for today.[200] The manner in which the *filioque* gained a late entrance into the Western version of the Nicene-Constantinopolitan Creed, the objections from the East, the apparent intransigence (not to say worse) of the Romans at the Councils of Lyons (1274) and Florence (1439), the much more recent and tentative offers of some Western church bodies to drop the offending term from the creed, all this may be read in the history books, and most of it makes doleful reading. But more doleful still perhaps is the manner in which the *filioque* provided a kind of rallying point for the more diffuse and bitter differences of belief and practice which then served to divide further, rather than mutually to enrich, the warring parties of the East and the West. Somewhat reminiscent of the story of the man who sneezed on a headland on the south coast of Ireland just as the *Lusitania* exploded and sank and got the distinct, if fleeting impression that his sneeze had caused the whole disaster, Vladimir Lossky blames the *filioque* for a subordination and depersonalizing of the Spirit *vis-à-vis* Jesus Christ, a severe downgrading of the Spirit's work in the incarnation, life and resurrection of Jesus and in the recreation of human life, a reintroduction of Sabellian tendencies, and an emphasis on objective reason (Logos) and consequently on the structures and formulae of the past which had as its result an elevation of the institutional church at the expense of the Spirit, as well as the inevitable reaction of the anti-Christian humanism of the modern period.[201] At the same time the controversy tempted some of the Greek theologians so to oversimplify their own tradition of classical trinitarian thought as to pretend that their fourth-century Fathers already found in procession (*ekporeusis*) as a name for a mode of origin a sufficient means of distinguishing the Spirit (which it quite obviously is not), or even that these early Fathers operated with a clear distinction between immanent and economic in their trinitarian theologies, such that one could allow, in their name, a *filioque* in the latter which need have no place in the former. Controversy seldom does any good at all to any part or aspect of doctrine which it happens to touch.

At a conference held at Bonn in the years 1874/5, the Old Catholics, as they came to be called, and Greek Orthodox theologians forged an agreement on this controversial topic round some theses of John of Damascus, and this agreement, looked at without prejudice, can be seen to have not only the seeds of future reconciliation, but elements of agreement between the warring traditions which had in fact existed from the beginnings of classical trinitarian theologies, and which the anxious polemicists on both sides were either unable or unwilling to see. According to John of Damascus the Holy Spirit proceeds from the Father as from the principle (*arche*), the cause (*aitia*), and the source (*pege*) of divinity. The Holy Spirit is not said to proceed from the Son, since there is but one principle and cause from which all that is in the Godhead proceeds. Yet we do call the Holy Spirit the Spirit of the Son, and so it is proper to say that the Holy Spirit proceeds from the Father through the Son.[202] Now it has been pointed out that even in the discussion of his so-called psychological analogies from which the *filioque* position is supposed to have originally derived, Augustine himself insists that the Holy Spirit proceeds *principaliter* from the Father, and that *principaliter* here must be taken to mean, not merely 'chiefly', but 'as from the unique principle'.[203] Only those who are anxious to contrast the views of Anselm and Aquinas with this earlier Augustinian possibility could fail to notice that Aquinas quite explicitly accepts and defends the procession of the Holy Spirit 'through the Son' and, far from seeing these as incompatible, treats the *filioque* and the *per filium* in successive articles.[204] What must be said about the *filioque* then, as far as this long and tiresome controversy is concerned, is simply this: when taken in a sense exclusive of the complementary *per filium*, it has just as little claim to the support of Scripture or tradition as has the even more explicitly exclusivist 'from the Father alone' (*ek monou tou Patros*); and neither could in any case do justice to the rich variety of Spirit material in the New Testament, in which Spirit can also name God and serve to account for the origin of the Son.

But what is to be said of the *filioque* in the context of our present interest, the context in which we would argue it should be more properly considered, the context of the very effort to establish Trinity rather than binity or quaternity? First, perhaps, that it is interesting that the *filioque* should continue to keep company with the *per filium*, almost as if to remind us, however faintly, that the task of distinguishing three can never quite succeed without some reference to the order of the old emanationist model to which the very concept of procession really belongs.[205] And, second, that the *filioque* is no more successful in securing the distinction of the Holy Spirit than are any of the other methods we have seen; it only seems to succeed to the extent that alleged structures of the human psyche are given a determinative role in trinitarian theology which they should never in fact be given and which Augustine at the end of his *De Trinitate* did everything in his power to prevent. So, from the point of view of trinitarian theology, the noise and smoke of the *filioque* battle (and even the pacific murmurs of the *filioque* treaties) do little more than help hide the fact that an adequate *trinitarian* theology still needs to be developed, if such a theology can be developed. More particularly, these battles and the ensuing peace conferences prevent us from noticing how much our trinitarian theologies, especially in the West, are dependent upon views of the *nature* of knowledge and love rather than the *content* of any knowledge allegedly conveyed to us by divine revelation. Aquinas may have managed, to his own satisfaction at least, to combine Father and Son into one term of a relational opposition to Holy Spirit, thus avoiding the quaternity with which his own logic constantly threatens him,[206] but the ensuing image of the Holy Spirit as the *love* which unites the Father and the Son (consequent, in this kind of philosophical psychology, upon the knowledge which the Father generates as his Word) does nothing whatever to secure a distinct 'personhood' for the Holy Spirit which would be in any way equivalent to the distinct personhood which can quite easily be attributed to Jesus the Christ and to the God he called Father. Brave assertions to the effect that although love in humans is a mere attribute or act, in God it is a person, are no more than forms of that very foolhardiness which does not hesitate to abuse language itself, the most obvious means of communication available to those who really have something intelligible to communicate.

It would be difficult indeed to overestimate the influence of this psychological model of Trinity in the West, both on the popular mind and in the reflections of professional theologians. More than any other model it has managed to convey the impression that we do in fact have a Trinity, and that we know with a fair degree of accuracy what it is. Yet the imagery of a person, its knowledge, and its love, on which this model is based is, as Augustine well knew, misleading on almost every point of its analogy with the kind of Trinity which the Nicene *homoousion* required as it approached the meaning of identity of substance. For, to give an illustration of this point different from the ones Augustine chose, in the human circumstances from which this imagery is drawn, one's knowledge is the knowledge through which one knows what is other than oneself, and only through knowing this knows oneself, and one's love consequently is the love of what one knows to be other than oneself, and only through that is it love of self. Hence the imagery involves a kind of going out of oneself and a return. In the case of love in particular, if it is to be anything other than the most self-destructive of forces, it must return to the self only by the most determined detour through the most unselfish love of another.

So this imagery, by its natural powers of evocation, if undeterred by more artificial polemical considerations, would make us think first of God, then of his knowledge of the world – though in this case his creative, original and originating knowledge, his creative word or wisdom – and his love for this world, a love which is at once desire for the world and creatively active within it. And then we should almost inevitably be reminded once again of that pagan Greek emanationist Triad of the One, the divine Nous or Intelligence, and that moving or impulsive principle called Soul.[207] Telescope this imagery, on the other hand, within the immanent essence of the divinity itself, and the result is likely to be a God even more self-enclosed than Aristotle's God, a Thinking of Thinking and a simultaneous Loving of it all. One really can not have it both ways by insisting that it is only by knowing his own Word that God knows the world, for that too is part and parcel of the peculiarly Greek conviction of the divine transcendence, and it specifically entails a kind of 'composition' at the level of Nous which inevitably places the latter on a second, lower level of divinity than that occupied by the One.[208]

This conclusion could really have been anticipated from the beginning of any straightforward account of Aquinas's theology of the Trinity. For, we may repeat, as far as Aquinas is concerned, those relations which are fully real to God are the inner-divine relations and 'there is no real relation in God to the creature'. Complete now, and crystallized in such a sentence, is the tendency of the *homoousion* (identity of substance)-type-Trinity to oust the older emanationist-subordinationist-'economic' Trinity, while signally failing to perform the functions which the older ones, within its limitations, performed. And the further consequences are even clearer now than they were with Augustine. The Father-Son relationship recedes within eternal immanence where, of course, it can only be described in the most abstract logical terms of the oppositeness of relational pairs; at which level of abstraction the Holy Spirit can by sheer logical ingenuity also be accommodated. The relationship of Word to Jesus is consequently rarified to the abstraction of hypostatic union between 'natures', the relationship of Spirit to Jesus rather consequential, if not contractual. The Father-Son relationship, the saving presence of God the Spirit as Jesus, the substance of our faith and the ground of our hope, is deprived of all the concrete content which the life, death and destiny of Jesus of Nazareth alone can give it, and that concrete content has then to be found somewhere else in the theological corpus: under 'Miracles', perhaps, or under 'Satisfaction Theories of Redemption'?

Knowledge of the trinitarian being of God, then, seems to come, not from our world or from anything that is or happens within it (including Augustine's 'all that the Word made flesh did and suffered'), but from some words of Scripture or of Jesus the key to the meaning of which, however, is something like the knowledge of knowledge (and of love). It almost seems as if the most determined effort to ignore what has happened in our world and our history as the only source of our knowledge of God in the end results in the elevation of one alleged structure of the human psyche into a model of the inner divine being of God. Rahner, amongst others, complains that at some stage in the history of Christian theology the treatise on the one God became detached from the treatise on the Trinity. He traces this to an accident, an unexplained change by Aquinas, in the arrangement character- istic still of the Sentences of Peter Lombard,[209] and regrets its occurrence on the perfectly good grounds that Christians should begin and end by talking about the God who is Father of the Son they know and source of the Spirit. But if the Triune God is as poorly related to the world as this developing traditional account of our doctrine would suggest, then there may be more than an historical accident involved in the decision to talk first of the one God who does at least create and sustain us. The doctrine of the Trinity is perfectly capable of relegating itself to later sections of a Christian system by the increasing irrelevance of its own abstractions.[210]

During the Protestant Reformation of the sixteenth century many central areas of Christian belief and practice came into dispute, but the doctrine of the Trinity was not amongst them. That is not to say that there were not trinitarian 'heresies' in the sixteenth century also: Calvin complains against a certain Serve- tus, on the one side, who apparently maintained that a trinitarian 'person' was no more than 'a visible manifestation of the glory of God' and, on the other side, against one Valentine Gentile whose Trinity appears to have consisted of Essence, Son and Spirit. But, however well or ill we may think Calvin himself accommodated one essence and three 'persons' without arriving at a quaternity, the doctrine of the Trinity was not as such a bone of contention between the Reformers and the Romans. The most that can be said is that Calvin did in fact make a different selection in emphasis than did Aquinas from the commonly inherited and quite varied material of patristic provenance, and to this we might pay some brief attention in order to illustrate further the mainstream devel- opment of classical doctrines of the Trinity. The characteristic contribution of Luther we may pick up later under Moltmann's treatment of Luther's phrase, 'the crucified God'.

Calvin, it has already been remarked, insists very strongly that Christian talk about the one, true God should begin and end with explicit talk about the Triune God, for otherwise they will find themselves talking about idols, and only the bare and empty name of God will flit about in their heads, to the exclusion of the true God.[211] Nevertheless, it is not from the developing doctrine of the divinity of the Redeemer, Jesus Christ, that Calvin derives the further development of the doctrine of the Trinity. On the contrary, the knowledge of God as Trinity belongs with the knowledge of God the Creator.[212] That is not to say, of course, that the practice of some so-called natural theology would now place us in possession of the doctrine of the Trinity. Calvin, operating as he does with a late Augustinian theory of the Fall and Original Sin, could never permit such an implication. Indeed it is difficult to know exactly what Calvin thought of the vagaries of our human knowledge of the Triunity of God. He appears to have believed that if Adam had not sinned, we should have been able to know from God's self-revelation in creation the true, that is, the triune nature of God, though we might not have precisely the kind of trinitarian doctrine which we now possess. But the sin of Adam somehow negated the revelation of God in creation in such a way that, even though with the aid of the 'spectacles' of Scripture we can today see much of the revelation of God in creation, we cannot see as much as we would be able to see if Adam had maintained his integrity, *si integer stetisset Adam*. In particular, to take the one example that matters to us here, even with the spectacles of Scripture, we cannot now see revealed in creation the triune nature of God; only *in* the Scriptures, and not by use of the Scriptures as spectacles to help us look elsewhere, can we now come upon God as Trinity.[213]

There are two implications from this, one positive and one negative. Positively, this means that according to Calvin the doctrine of the Trinity is scriptural in the most exclusive sense, and so he proceeds to derive the doctrine, to 'prove' and to illustrate it, from texts assembled from Old and New Testaments alike. Negatively, it means that the doctrine neither depends upon nor develops from the christology of the New Testament: it concerns, rather, the pre-existent Word or Wisdom of God which only upon incarnation in Jesus of Nazareth occupies the office of Mediator.[214] In this manner, then, is maintained the distance with which we have now become familiar between the doctrine of the Trinity and 'all that the Word made flesh did and suffered'.

As far as concerns his own selective emphasis within inherited material, Calvin reminds one sometimes more of Gregory of Nyssa (and sometimes more of Philo) than of Augustine. If one coupled together, as one could also do with Gregory of Nyssa, those texts in which Calvin – often against the *superbia* of the philosophers, without which few trinitarian theologians could sound as superior as they do – insists upon the utter incomprehensibility of the divine essence, his concomitant insistence that it is the work, power, or activity of God (God's *energeia*?) and not God's essence that is revealed, with his firm proposal that it is the *hypostasis* of the Father that is made known by the Son, one would have to wonder once again what is the relationship of the divine essence to the divine *hypostaseis* or 'persons'. One realizes that none of these theologians wishes to arrive at a quaternity, and one hesitates to count Calvin, or even Gregory, amongst those theologians who seemed to place the Trinity itself on a second level of the divine Being.

Aquinas, following one major suggestion of Augustine's, defines personal distinctions within the Godhead, and hence 'persons', in terms of opposite relations, and so it is not the logic of including the divine essence in his system that threatens it with implications of quaternity. On the strict logic of relational opposition, only those which are relationally opposed are distinct from each other; all else in the divinity is identical. And since the essence is not in relational opposition to any of the subsistent relations, it can simply be declared identical with each in turn: 'in God relation and essence do not differ from each other, but are one and the same'.[215] Calvin, however, is not satisfied with the simple logic of relational opposition in order to distinguish 'persons' (and quite rightly so). He wants an additional means of distinguishing 'persons' and, above all, he wants to retain in trinitarian theology the one thing which strict relational logic is incapable of yielding, namely, a strict 'order' amongst the three 'persons'.

Hence Calvin defines person as a 'subsistence' in God's essence, and when it comes to saying what distinguishes these from one another he shuts out the siren voices of the opposite relations and refers instead to 'an incommunicable quality'. This is safe, if not very informative; the idea of distinguishing one from the others by simply calling it incommunicable goes back at least as far as Richard of St. Victor – though in Aquinas it is hidden away in the answer to an objection[216] – but it avoids having to say what exactly the incommunicable quality is, and so it simply evades the problem which, in the case of the Holy Spirit in particular, had consistently troubled the tradition. If one assumes Trinity, it should not be necessary to repeat, one can assume that some incommunicable quality distinguishes each from the other two, but an assumption is not an established case. By Calvin's time, however, the assumption of Trinity is so massively present that one hardly needs to trouble onself too much about the details. And Calvin in fact, on closer inspection, proves to be suffering from the same confusion about the distinguishing characteristics of the 'persons' as we saw in Gregory of Nyssa, for instance, when the breakaway of the *homoousion* from the imagery of generation – itself necessitated, as I said, by the extension of the *homoousion* to the Holy Spirit – relativized even the opposed or relational terms father and son. So Calvin, in words at times reminiscent of Gregory, insists that when we have the relationship of the Father to the Son in mind, then the Father is the 'beginning' (*arche anarchos*); but when we speak simply of the Son without regard to the Father, then it would be proper to say that he is the sole beginning and 'of himself'. In fact, when we mention Father and Son together, or Spirit with one of them, the very word 'God' applies then particularly to the Father, whereas when the word is used without particular reference to any of the 'persons', it designates all three.

In spite of this confusion of personal characteristics and terms of reference – though Calvin himself would almost lead one to think that it was somehow *because* of personal characteristics of being the beginning, the source and so on – Calvin insists upon what he calls 'a reasoned order' of the 'persons' which, however, in no way threatens the unity (identity?) of the essence or the ensuing total equality of the 'persons'.

What can be said of all this? Simply, I think, that Calvin's compact systematization of those traditional options which he selected highlights the problems connected with them in a manner roughly parallel to the way in which Aquinas's systematization highlights the problems connected with his selected options. Calvin's view is that the doctrine of the Trinity is scriptural in the sense that it is derived from the selection and combination of set texts. We are already aware of some of the problems connected with this approach, and may yet become aware of more. The way in which the doctrine, in Calvin also, is detached from all that the Word made flesh did and suffered should be familiar to us by now, though its familiarity should never allow us to accept it without question. For the rest, Calvin's particular selection of traditional material, owing more to the kind of theology which we saw in Gregory of Nyssa than it does to the kind which Aquinas selected from Augustine, shows once again how difficult it is to relate the divine essence to the three 'persons'. In particular, it illustrates once more the difficulties which, we have already noticed, derive from the twin moves of extending the *homoousion* to the Holy Spirit, while moving its meaning to that of identity of *ousia*. For, to repeat, the inclusion of the Holy Spirit as a third within the divine being relativizes the term Father, for instance, for the first One, and sets the theologian in search of less distinctive characteristics such as 'principle', 'cause' and so on; while the *homoousion* as meaning identity of substance 'telescopes' the distinctions within the immanence of the divine being and disallows those grades or levels in the divine being which were part and parcel of the older emanationist, 'economic', subordinationist theology, and on which distinction *and* order amongst the three (or two) were *simultaneously* secure. On the premises which Calvin selects from the common tradition, there is simply no good reason for his 'reasoned order', and the distinctions between the three 'persons' are as shaky as ever.

Some comment has already been made upon the relative neglect of the doctrine of the Trinity in recent theology, yet it would exceed our purposes here to attempt a comprehensive survey of the trinitarian theology that has recently emerged. However, a number of trends in that theology – three in particular – should prove to be of interest to any who have followed the analysis of the development of classical trinitarian theologies up to this point. The first trend is towards the recognition of the fact that the development of classical trinitarian theologies has quite unjustifiably restricted the fullness of the treatment that is undoubtedly due, and indeed long overdue, to the Holy Spirit in Christian thought and practice. The second takes the form of expressions of varying degrees of dissatisfaction with the manner in which the divine 'persons' are connected with their palpable manifestations in our world – is it, for instance, an arbitrary matter or an accidental affair that it is the second 'person' who became incarnate in the flesh of Jesus of Nazareth? This is sometimes expressed in terms of dissatisfaction with the way in which the immanent Trinity and the economic Trinity are related to each other. There are problems with this latter way of putting the matter which have been noted briefly already, and which may call for some concluding comment later, but for the moment let us pass to the third of the trends in question. This is a trend to suspect, quite roundly, that the development of classical trinitarian theologies which we have described as mainstream development has not in fact as yet yielded a real Trinity, though it does carry with it most of the material necessary for the construction of a theology of the real Trinity, and examples of that construction are now on offer. There are other trends, of course, in the contemporary theology of the Trinity, but none, I believe, which hold out as much prospect for renewal as these; some, I think, though of undoubted validity and limited worth in their own right – for example, the common critique of the term 'person' in the trinitarian formula and the renewed attention to the *filioque* controversy – can easily serve to distract from the far more substantial review of which trinitarian theology is now so blatantly in need. We shall have paid to contemporary trinitarian theology, then, the dues to which it is entitled if we offer a brief outline of these three trends and use them as pointers to a fuller theological future.

Prominent amongst the authors who complain about the very restricted treatment of the Spirit are some whose work has already been laid under tribute in the section above on 'The Distinction of the Spirit': authors such as Hendry, Berkhof, and of course Lampe. To these might be added examples of recent authors who have written specifically on the Holy Spirit and whose expertise lies mainly in the biblical field. C. F. D. Moule, for example, allows, on the one hand, that personal language used of the Spirit in the Bible 'only shows that "Spirit" is a word for a personal God's personal activity'; that the term 'spirit', like 'word', 'wisdom', 'finger' or 'hand', is 'only one of several terms denoting divine action or divine intention or (especially) divine immanence',[217] and, on the other hand, that 'threefoldness is, perhaps, less vital to a Christian conception of God than the eternal twofoldness of Father and Son'.[218] Yet he wishes to secure some ground for the traditional affirmation of threefoldness, and he does this by making a valiant attempt to draw an 'absolute distinction between incarnation and inspiration';[219] not, one would have thought, a very much easier task than that of distinguishing Word and Spirit in the first place, and certainly not one for which Lampe, for instance, would have much exegetical sympathy. Michael Ramsey, whose book on *Holy Spirit* tries to recover much of the neglected scriptural richness of his subject, also senses the apparent dilemma that he seems thereby to be moving away from a threefoldness which he nevertheless wishes still to assert. So, by page 119, he manages to capitalize his previously lower-case divine spirit and, as far as the careful reader can detect, he derives this subtle implication from two kinds of premise: first, the rather weak analogy of the alleged threefoldness of all personal self-realization; and second, the assertion that 'spirit' refers, not to the mere impact of Jesus on his followers, but to that which from within Christian lives makes response to Jesus and to God possible. From this last assertion in particular he draws the questionable conclusion that 'Christians were encountering not only their own relation to God but the relation of God to God'.[220]

So, with the very significant exception of Lampe, all of the authors mentioned, and some others who might be mentioned, want to complain about the treatment of the Holy Spirit in traditional trinitarian theology; want to recover particularly from the Scriptures the richer material which this treatment had so consistently neglected; *and yet want a trinitarian doctrine not significantly different from those which the mainstream traditional development has provided.*[221] So does this first trend seem, on reflection, very like a theological revolution with much justice on its side which lost its nerve at the half-way stage. Failing to show how trinitarian theology would be possible, much less what trinitarian theology would look like, if the richness of scriptural material on the Spirit were truly re-introduced to it, pursuants of this trend usually take the shortest cut back to one of the more familiar trinitarian models, and leave it at that. The task laid before trinitarian theology by all that is positive in their work, therefore, still remains to be completed, and the promised theological harvest still remains largely to be reaped.

The selectivity of this concluding survey is, like all selectivity, vulnerable in any case, but perhaps it will be less vulnerable, at least to certain objections of bias, if we take as illustrations of our second and third trends the works of Rahner, Barth, and Moltmann, with some other writers thrown in for good measure. Rahner, certainly, though he does not appear to be very clear about the origin of the distinction between the immanent and the economic Trinity,[222] is very unhappy with it. He writes: 'No adequate distinction can be made between the doctrine of the Trinity and the doctrine of the economy of salvation,'[223] and takes as the basic thesis of his work on the Trinity the statement that 'the "economic" Trinity is the "immanent" Trinity and the "immanent" Trinity is the "economic" Trinity'.[224] He feels very strongly that if all that has happened in what we Christians are

wont to call salvation history is as detached from the individuali-
ties or the distinct 'personalities' of the Three as the principle *opera
ad extra sunt indivisa* and the ensuing theory of appropriations
would have us believe, then we should be left with no real option
but to admit that the revelation of the trinitarian being of God was
a purely verbal matter, that we should have no way of knowing
of the trinitarian being of God other than some preserved words
of Jesus or of some inspired writers, that the doctrine of the Trinity
would consequently have no substantial basis in the broader,
more varied, and more concrete experience of the grace of God in
Jesus by which we are saved. 'Since that which *happens* in salvation
history might have happened through each other person, since it
is but the neutral vehicle of a merely verbal revelation, not the
revelation of some intra-trinitarian occurrence, it tells us nothing
about intra-trinitarian life.'[225]

Now I believe that such dissatisfaction is more than amply
justified, but the success of Rahner's efforts to remedy the fault to
which it points is not at all as obvious. In aid of his contention that
we actually experience the trinitarian being of God in the actual
history of our salvation (or, that the inner, immanent trinitarian
being of God is just what we experience in the economy of
salvation), Rahner offers, basically, an argument to prove that it
must be so, and an explanation to show how it is so. His argument
can be summarized as follows: if the human nature in which the
Word of God is incarnate has no closer intrinsic relationship to
the Word than any other nature which, like it, is simply created
by the one God, then it will be a mere instrument for whatever the
Word wishes to communicate, but it will not itself express the
Word; as Rahner puts it, 'in this hypothesis we cannot say the
Logos has stepped outside his intra-divine inaccessibility and
shown *himself* . . . we could not say: He who *sees* me, sees *me*.'[226]
The human nature which the Word assumes must, then, in itself
express the Word, and not do so merely as the Word's megaphone.
So that, if 'what Jesus is and does as man reveals the Logos
himself; it is the reality of the Logos as our salvation in our midst.
Then we can assert, in the full meaning of the words: here the
Logos with God and the Logos with us, the immanent and the
economic Logos, are strictly the same.'[227]

Rahner's explanation as to how what must be so can be takes
the form of a rather large thesis which he has argued in his
writings on christology in general and incarnation in particular.

Briefly, we should not assume that we simply know what human nature is, so that when we say that the divine Word assumed human nature we know very well, from the point of view of the human nature at least, or from our prior knowledge of human nature, just what that means. On the contrary, we only know what human nature truly and really is from the (full and definitive?) expression of the Word of God in the humanity of Jesus of Nazareth. Hence from this point of view also it must be true to say that we do really and truly encounter the very Word of God in the history of Jesus and of the concrete salvation which Jesus brings; that salvation history, which has 'all that Jesus is and does' at its centre, is not a screen behind which the Word of God is hidden in the very act of revealing itself.

Here again, as in the first trend from contemporary trinitarian theology, we have a general position very convincingly argued which, I believe, we can only applaud. Except that, once more, we may find that we are given pause by the very writers who so insistently advance the new position, and are tempted to think that they themselves have failed to carry their arguments through to their logical conclusions, and have thus failed to reap the fullness of the rich theological harvest promised. It is not easy to beat Rahner out into the open from the thickets of his favourite Heideggerese, but those who have the patience and persistence to do so may find that he tends to fly off in the wrong direction again (namely, back into a hidden pre-existence), and that it is necessary to fire at least a warning shot or two across his beak, if only to get him back on to his original course.

For, as far as Rahner's *argument* above is concerned, it can hardly fail to strike the attentive reader that an argument which is suspiciously similar in structure is used later to show that the Father must express or utter himself in a *divine* being (the pre-existent Word) and not in a creaturely entity.[228] The key concept in the whole of Rahner's trinitarian theology is the concept of God's self-communication. And in both uses of the argument to which we must now attend, the emphasis is very insistently upon the term 'self'. Now in the case of the Father, the insistence that it is *himself* that he communicates is combined with the infinite distance which separates divine and creaturely substance to prove that nothing created could be the expression of the Father's *self*. If something creaturely could, indeed must, express the Word, then, we would either have to conclude that the Word was not divine (or at least not as divine as the Father – good Greek reasoning), or we would have to admit that in the case of the Word we had in fact misused the logic of the argument. The suspicion that the second alternative here is the one to choose in interpreting Rahner is increased if we combine with this argument about the Father's self-communication a passage in which Rahner argues for a real pre-existent distinction between Father and Word.[229] If there were no fully constituted pre-existent Word, then the humanity of Jesus, the human being called Jesus, could of course in respect of its divine origin say 'Father', but 'it' (to use Rahner's own revealing term) could not with respect to its fellow humans express itself as the *Son* of the Father.

The strength or weakness of that further piece of logic is not now the issue. What is important is the implication that it is the pre-existent Word or Son, and not the creaturely, historical human entity, that can express itself as Son to our common humanity and our common history. And that implication seriously damages, surely, Rahner's original contention that it is 'what Jesus is and does as man' that expresses the Word, the Son, that is indeed the reality of the Word or Son as our salvation in our history, in our midst. Running right through Rahner's trinitarian theology, in fact, in spite of his stated preference for the phrase 'distinct manner of existing' over the word 'person' (with its modern connotations) in order to name the Three, is his persistence in using personal psychological terms such as self-communicating, receiving, giving, mutually loving, of the Three, independently of any reference to what Jesus is and does, or to the rest of us who are led by the Spirit of Jesus. He simply assumes that our faith, Scripture, and tradition, all three, carry to us a knowledge of three distinct divine beings who are as yet one God, and though he shows himself more aware than was Aquinas of the limitations of the psychological analogy (while making even more substantial use of it in his argument than even Aquinas did), he nevertheless helps himself to its terms to the extent of constantly giving the impression that there really are three persons up there communicating and loving much as persons do in our experience, as the condition of the possibility of the communication that we know takes place between the Father, Jesus, and the rest of us.

In the end I think it would not be unfair to say that Rahner's valiant attempt to arrive at a true identity of immanent and economic trinities gets no further than some success in providing a kind of fairly precise parallel in the inner life of God to what goes on between the Father, Jesus, and Jesus' followers in the world. And a parallel is not an identity; it is in fact as near as makes no difference to being the contrary of identity. And the life of God in himself still goes on behind the scenes. That, one must hasten to add, is not in itself a questionable admission to make. But when one insists on operating with a distinction between immanent and economic, if only with the intent of negating it, and when one succeeds in negating it only to the point of providing parallels, however precise, between the life of God 'in himself' and the life of God 'with us', then the suspicion must arise that one is importing into the divine being the descriptive structures of human experience – in this present context, some structures of the human spirit.

'God corresponds to himself' is the slogan here, of course. But, to the extent that that statement is not just a clumsy attempt at tautology, or a piece of nonsense, or both, it appears to be based on the same assumption of a distinction between 'immanent' and 'economic' trinities which then wishes to unite them by either showing or merely insisting that they must exactly parallel each other. The key concept in this kind of thesis, of course, is the concept of God's self-communication. But is this really to be taken as a literal and adequate term for God's saving activity in our world? If it is, then of course we can say that what can be known of God through what Jesus is and does must correspond exactly to the inner structures of God's inner self. And then salvation is so noetic an affair. Even love is thought of as the spiritual counterpart to knowledge, if not the love of the knowledge itself, rather than love 'made real in act'. And we are still very close again to some classical Greek ideas of salvation.

On the other hand, it just might be the real purpose of a doctrine of the Trinity, though one which some such doctrine still has to achieve, simply to describe the ways of God with us, to express as much of God's being as these ways reveal, and no more, to *leave* the rest a mystery (rather than, having described it in suspiciously human terms, *then* insist that it is a mystery), and so to leave a real future for us, and perhaps also for God. It is this tantalizing possibility which Rahner's opening concentration on the economic Trinity opens up for us, and then gradually closes out from our view.

Rahner, of course, offers us the possibility of taking quite a different perspective upon his trinitarian theology, in some correspondence with the ambiguity of the trinitarian term 'person'. Suppose that we were to concentrate on the rather impersonal term for the Three, 'distinct manners of subsisting', and in addition to this take to heart his footnote: 'within the Trinity there is no reciprocal "Thou". The Son is the Father's self-utterance which should not in its turn be conceived as "uttering", and the Spirit is the "gift" which does not give in its turn.'[230] Suppose that we were then to substitute 'mode or way of being' for 'distinct manner of subsisting' (though Rahner himself would object mildly to this particular substitution), and self-revelation for self-communication of God; we should in fact then arrive at a trinitarian theology virtually the same as that of Barth.[231]

From Barth we gain the same impression that God, unqualified, refers first to the Father of our Lord Jesus Christ; we see the same emphasis on the sovereign, lordly freedom of this God to reveal or not to reveal himself, for in himself he is utterly incomprehensible (indeed for Barth, God's essence is to be found in his lordship and not in any abstruse philosophical attributes); we see this lordly, sovereign freedom emphasized to the point in fact where it leaves God just as free in his self-revelation in his Son as he was to reveal himself in the first place – so that he is in a sense veiled in his very revelation, he is the 'God who in assuming form in the Son always does not assume form'; and, finally, we find the same insistence that it is (therefore) God himself, now in his third mode of being, who alone can draw men and women to this veiled revelation in the Son and thus become in our history the actual Lord of concrete individuals.

There is no need to comment at any length on this trinitarian theology. Some attention has already been paid to the way in which it relates trinitarian doctrine to Scripture, and the very slight scriptural basis for confining the Spirit to the role of enabler of 'subjective' appropriation of the revelation has already been mentioned. Suffice it then to add that Barth pursues the logic of this more impersonal trinitarian terminology with a consistency which eludes Rahner but which makes the discovery of any Trinity, 'immanent' or 'economic', equally and correspondingly problematic. For Barth has no ambition to try to show that an 'economic' Trinity is an 'immanent' Trinity, and to modify correspondingly the principle *opera ad extra sunt indivisa*, and the theory of appropriations. On the contrary, Barth will only say that the scriptural testimony to the event of divine self-revelation allows us to say that there is some threefold self-differentiation in God, that the same Scriptures offer us the distinguishing terms Father, Son, and Spirit, as well as differentiating language such as Revealer, Revelation, Revealedness or Creator, Reconciler, Redeemer, or holiness, mercy and goodness. 'There is an analogy,' he then writes, 'between the terms Father, Son and Spirit along with the other formulations of this triad in revelation on the one side, and on the other side the three divine modes of being which consist in the different relations of origin and in which we have come to know the truly incomprehensible eternal distinctions in God.'[232]

This, as one might expect from Barth, is an analogy of faith, not an analogy of being. That is to say, only the way in which Scripture testifies to the event of divine self-revelation allows us to know of self-differentiation in God, and only the triadic language of differentiation which Scripture actually offers us allows us to talk of this self-differentiation. But we cannot be said thereby to know the inner-divine distinctions (as we could if they corresponded to some structures of the created reality which we do know – analogy of being), and we certainly should not conflate these with 'persons' or their attributes such as the three scriptural names might suggest, or with the differentiated acts of such triads as creator, reconciler, redeemer, and so on: 'the distinctions in God himself cannot rest in these distinctions'.[233] In short, we know *that* there is triadic self-differentiation in God, and we have scriptural terms and scripturally-endorsed appropriation-language in which to speak of and even to comprehend these strictly incomprehensible distinctions according to our measure, but we do not know *what* these inner-divine distinctions are.

It is at this point that some writers begin to suspect that we have in fact no real Trinity at all. It has disappeared in one direction into the ineffable mystery of the divine being and, in the other direction, into the insubstantial realm of authorized linguistic formulae. And it is at this point, therefore, that the third trend in the contemporary theology of the Trinity emerges. If Moltmann is now taken as the example of this third trend, it is not because he is thought to have invented or discovered the so-called social doctrine of the Trinity or, better perhaps, the doctrine of a social Trinity. Not only are there others who have written in this vein before him,[234] not only is the impression of a company of divine persons constantly conveyed by all trinitarian language both ancient and modern, as Rahner's work has just now illustrated, but Moltmann himself would be the first to argue that the doctrine of a social Trinity is the full and real truth towards which trinitarian theology has always been striving but which it has unfortunately tended to obscure mainly by what he calls a Trinity of Supreme Substance, on the one hand, and a Trinity of Absolute Subject, on the other.[235] Therefore, precisely because Moltmann has so recently and so decisively set aside both the Trinity of Supreme Substance and the Trinity of Absolute Subject, because he has subsumed under this combination of titles so much of what has constituted in fact the mainline development of classical trinitarian doctrines, we may take him as the prime example of the third trend, and take his theology of a social Trinity as the prime example of the real Trinity which must now at last be made to stand up.

Moltmann describes what he means by trinity of substance and trinity of subject by painting on a very large historical canvas and with very broad strokes indeed, and so it would be quite invidious to attribute each of these trinities to particular names in the history of trinitarian theology or in its contemporary conduct – although Barth's seems an obvious enough name to attach to a Trinity of Absolute Subject. Suffice it to say that, as far as Moltmann is concerned, the Trinity of Supreme Substance gives such a central and influential place to cosmological speculation about God as the supreme *ousia* that it, first, relegates the treatment of the Trinity to a distant and very minor place after the treatise on the One God and, second and as a consequence, 'leads unintentionally but inescapably to the disintegration of the doctrine of the Trinity in abstract monotheism'.[236] The Trinity of Absolute Subject, on the other hand, though it does at first sight secure the personality of God, does this by so concentrating that personhood in the Oneness of God that the Three are reduced to the neuter modes of being, and the result once again, unintentionally but just as inescapably, is a similar loss of the doctrine of the Trinity to monotheism. It should be permissible to accept these criticisms here without further comment, partly because an adequate amount of critical commentary has already accompanied our survey of the development of classical doctrines, partly because it is more interesting to ask Moltmann about the real Trinity which must now replace these failed attempts at its presentation.

I think it is fair to say that Moltmann's case for a social Trinity is made up of two separable strands of thought, and that the fact that they are separable, or at least the fact that they are not shown to be inseparable, reveals the weakness of his case. Nevertheless, it is worthwhile to present the strands separately, for one of them on its own has a strength and a promise which the other one signally lacks. So let us take first the strong and promising strand in his trinitarian theology. It is the theme of the suffering God, a theme prominent in his other writings, especially in *The Crucified God*,[237] certainly *his* most impressive contribution to contemporary theology, and possibly *the* most promising theme in contemporary theology.

The contrast which Moltmann draws between the apathetic deity of the Greeks and the God of the Christians may not be the best way to introduce his theme, for as we have had occasion to notice, some classical Christian deities, produced under the force of Arian polemics, were considerably more immovable than any deity which the Greeks had ever envisaged. And Moltmann, in any case, does occasionally appeal to us not to dismiss too hastily the overflowing goodness of Platonic emanationist theology. Hence it is better to set off with Moltmann through Old and New Testaments, through Jewish and Christian authors, in quest of the passionate God who triumphs precisely in the suffering which he must endure as a result of his passionate love for others. That quest leads him through Abraham Heschel's theology of the divine pathos, through early rabbinic doctrine of God's self-humiliation in service of Israel, through relatively neglected Christian authors such as Berdyaev and Unamuno, the insistence by the former that God's very commitment to freedom inevitably involves him in love and suffering with his Other (Man), and the more off-beat suggestions of the latter that even God is limited in a way by his own creation and must himself atone for having created man, and with man evil and suffering. But the quest culminates, of course, with Moltmann's moving and masterly analysis, repeated once more in his book on the Trinity, of the passion of God at the death of his Son, Jesus, on Calvary. This crucified God is the Christian God, beside whom Christians at least may worship none other.

To expand upon this theme at this point might only take from the power of Moltmann's own exposition of it, and might even take from the honour that is due to Moltmann for his service to modern theology in so determinedly bringing it once again to the fore. More use can certainly be made of it in the final assessment of the prospects for trinitarian theology today. At the moment it is sufficient to note that Moltmann concludes his section on 'The Passion of God' with the insistence that God's passionate involvement with the world implies a self-differentiation in God himself. So, with this result duly allowed, we may pass to the second strand in Moltmann's argument for a social Trinity.

I can only say that it seems to me that the second strand in Moltmann's argument is made up almost entirely of assumptions. First, he assumes that Christian theology must have a Trinity. That assumption is, of course, by no means unique to Moltmann. It seems to have been in possession at least since the fourth century, though how exactly it came to be the common assumption is far from easy to say. We do not need, at this point at least, to question the assumption; but it certainly is necessary to the integrity of any theological exercise to know when one is dealing with an assumption and not with an established case. Otherwise, to give an example of one of the more serious possibilities, one may begin to mistake human academic creations for divine revelation itself, or at least for such necessary and essential expressions of that revelation that the distinction between them and revelation must be difficult to perceive and to maintain. Second, it seems to me that he really assumes the social nature of the Trinity: in other words, that he really assumes that the Scriptures, for instance, present us with a society of three divine persons who are persons in a sense clearly analogous to the way in which the human persons in our experience form and are formed by their social groupings. 'The New Testament,' he writes, 'talks about God by proclaiming in narrative the relationships of the Father, the Son and the Spirit, which are relationships of fellowship and are open to the world.'[238] In searching through Moltmann for evidence for this position we must discount his criticism, however successful we may think it, of the alternative types of trinity of substance and trinity of subject, for their demise would not necessarily give birth to his alternative. Nor, in virtue of all that has been said above in the sections about the pre-existence of the Son and the distinction of the Spirit, is it really possible to accept a great deal of Moltmann's rather hasty exegesis of texts concerning Son and Spirit. And the assumption that if we are ever to have a 'real' Trinity it must consist of a social grouping of three real persons in some way really analogous to the social groupings of people we know is still an assumption, however obvious it might seem to some people to be. Finally, the advantages of such a social Trinity for practical preaching and behaviour *vis-à-vis* the oppressed of the earth, a consideration which weighs very heavily with Moltmann, will only persuade us to look for evidence that such a Trinity in fact exists, and only if we assume that Christian commitment to the lot of the oppressed could not be fully sustained upon other theological grounds.

Having said all that, one must then admit, quite without hesitation, that if Moltmann's assumptions are allowed, then the trinitarian theology which he produces is just as good as any other trinitarian theology recently produced or still extant, and in fact has certain advantages over other more familiar trinitarian theologies. Its solutions to familiar difficulties are at least no worse than theirs. As an example of its advantages one might cite the greater flexibility which it allows in dealing with the rich and varied scriptural material on Father, Son and Spirit. For if we do conceive of Father, Son and Spirit as three really distinct subjects-in-relation, we automatically gain much more freedom for the sequences in which we can consider them to form and influence each other; we are no longer tied to the strict sequence already twice repeated in this paragraph, which derives either from the rigidity of the emanation model of divine being or from the rather wooden revelation model with its Revealer, Revelation, Revealedness. Instead we can have the sequence Father – Spirit – Son to deal with the coming of Jesus, his mission and his resurrection; the sequence Father – Son – Spirit to deal with Jesus' post resurrection sending of the Spirit; and the sequence Spirit – Son – Father to deal with eschatological consummation, to give but some simplified examples.[239]

And as far as Moltmann's formula for the unity-in-trinity is concerned, it is not obviously weaker than the problematic 'essence' by which theologians formerly tried to unite the three without seeming to constitute a fourth. Moltmann's explanation of the unity of his 'three divine subjects'[240] which, he explicitly states, lies in their fellowship, is as follows: the analogy for the divine unity-in-trinity is not at this stage of the argument the self-differentiation of the individual person (and it is certainly not found in the impersonal homogeneity of substance), but rather the way in which we know from our experience in this world that being-in-society and being personal or being a person are simply two aspects of one and the same thing. One does not grow to personhood outside of society, and society strictly speaking is made up of persons. In an analogous manner the Three are a society (one) and they are yet (distinct) persons by one and the same process. The traditional term for this process, the term by which Moltmann can claim most traditional backing for his social Trinity, is the term *perichoresis*, a term which conveyed the mutual indwelling of the persons, their mutual involvement in and with each other, again on the analogy of the manner in which I lose myself in another in order to truly find myself and in and with the other create or act upon a third.

> In their perichoresis and because of it, the trinitarian persons are not to be understood as three individuals who only subsequently enter into relationship with one another (which is the customary reproach, under the name of 'tritheism') . . . Interpreted perichoretically, the trinitarian persons form their own unity by themselves in the circulation of the divine life.[241]

Whatever else may be said about Moltmann, he certainly makes people face up to the fullest implications of talking about three persons in one God. For my part, I feel that having said that his theology of the Trinity seems as good as any other, nothing more is required than some concluding comment upon the manner in which Moltmann uses the crucifixion of Jesus to derive a trinitarian view of God's own being, for this at once brings us back to Moltmann's most important theological insight and prepares us for a final assessment of the prospects of trinitarian theology today.

'Anyone who actually talks of the Trinity,' Moltmann had already said in *The Crucified God*, 'talks of the cross of Jesus, and does not speculate in heavenly riddles.'[242] And in the section of his book on the Trinity entitled 'The Surrender of the Son', he repeats and develops a good deal of the material from the earlier book to the effect that when the Father gives up the Son to death, the Father forsakes the Son in order to become the forsaken Father. There then comes about an inner conformity of all will between this loving surrender of the Father (in a way a loving surrender of his very fatherhood, of himself) and the loving surrender of the Son. And it is here, as usual, that the Holy Spirit comes in. He fuses together this very inner conformity of love and will between Father and Son in their very separation.

So far, so good. But the more one notices that Moltmann constantly uses scriptural language about Calvary which seems to be talking about Jesus of Nazareth, the God he called Father, and the Spirit in which the offering was made and which was then breathed into a dying world, the more one wonders about Moltmann's apparent assumption that here is being described a kind of pre-existent drama which takes place in God himself before, or as, it takes place betwen God and Jesus of Nazareth. 'Before the world was,' writes Moltmann, 'the sacrifice was already in God.'[243]

One can see in Moltmann the same kind of thrust as one sees in Rahner, for instance, towards such a theology of the Trinity as will show it to relate to that concrete experience of God which in turn is made possible by God's own revelatory and salvific activity within our world; the same kind of impatience with those who draw distinctions between immanent and economic trinities, if only later to declare them somehow identical; for Moltmann does not want to work with an immanent and an economic trinity; for him there is but the Trinity and the economy of salvation. And yet the closest he seems to be able to come to the realization of these theological desires is the kind of parallelism which we found also in Rahner between persons and activities in God and divine persons and their activities in the world. And the very success of this paralleling process makes one wonder about the need for the first, pre-existent member of the parallel. Is it really the case that one cannot have Moltmann's major insight that the cross of Jesus is the most radical critique of all human ideas about God and the one, true index to the being and action of God, without the duplication involved in having also a kind of pre-existent Calvary taking place between three divine persons in some (non-temporal) sense 'before the world'?

Indeed if one takes the view of the first trend offered above, to the effect that it tried to release from traditional trinitarian strictures a richer and more complex role for the Spirit, and if one agrees that this richer and more complex role will comprise the Spirit's own 'incarnation' in the coming, the mission, and the continuing work of Jesus, as well as being breathed and sent by Jesus in order to bring people to Jesus and to the Father, then one may begin to see a common strand of interest joining all three major trends in modern trinitarian theology, and a major clue perhaps to its further development. It all does seem to be trying to make of the doctrine of the Trinity a description of the ways of God with men and, as such and only as such, a description of the only experience of the one being of God which, in this world at least, we can have. If we had the wisdom to see, and the courage to admit, that the immanent trinity of traditional theology is but the last theological ditch to which Arians drove Nicenes, and that the economic trinity of the same traditional theology is but the last dying remnant of earlier pre-Nicene trinities still guarding the exposed flanks of the newer *homoousite* formations, could we then perhaps find an economic trinitarian (or binitarian) theology for today, such as so many modern theologians seem to be looking for?

PART FOUR

The Future

15

As it Was in the Beginning

There is something in us that attracts us strongly to the search for roots. The extent to which television and publishing companies and other commercial interests have exploited interest in clan roots and family trees bears its own kind of witness to this fact. And the search for sources, sources of light and heat, of energy to sustain life, is even more crudely obvious still. In all this busy questing, though at one extreme it may seem merely recreational and at the other extreme look too often as if it were about to lead to war, something of the answer to the questions of our identity, where we have come from, how long and how we have survived, and how we may go on, is at stake. And it is more than obvious that if we drive such questing deep enough, it tends to turn into metaphysical, even religious questions, concerned with the deepest origins of our existence. It should come as no surprise, then, that in a variety of religious cultures – Greek, for instance, as well as Christian – the images of hidden root, branch and fruit, of spring or source, river and stream, of sun, ray, and energizing warmth and illumination, should provide the most persistent analogy for the primordial ground of our being in its simultaneous transcendence and immanence, distance and involvement with us, hiddeness and historical unveiling.

Of all the terms and images we use for the hidden depths that hold the secrets of our identity and the ciphers for our future, the term 'beginning' (*arche, principium*) is perhaps the most potentially misleading, and it might not be too great an over-simplification to suggest that much of the disagreement and confusion which occurs in trinitarian theology can be traced to the variety of meaning of which the phrase 'in the beginning' (*en arche, in principio*) is patient. For on the very briefest account of the matter, the phrase can bear either a predominantly temporal or a predominantly existential meaning, but its obvious suitability to the story-telling mode (one cannot easily begin a story with 'in the root', or 'in the source', and 'in the spring' would be taken to refer to a recurring season) would surely see to it that its temporal meaning was usually the most likely to be received. 'In the beginning was the Word, and the Word was with God, and the Word was God . . . and the Word became flesh and dwelt amongst us.' The persistence of the past tense throughout this brief quotation comes from the story-telling mode of communication in which it is cast, and enables the temporal meaning of the term 'beginning' to predominate. 'In him we live and move and have our being.' All the verbs here are in the present tense, and so the existential meaning is more directly suggested: he (the *arche, pege, aitia*) 'in' whom we exist precedes us as source of our existence, though it would make no sense, at least as far as he is concerned, to say that he precedes us temporally.

Now ask yourself the question: would it make any difference to the truth which the first quotation above means to convey if all its verbs were put in the present tense, rather than in the past, and the temporal meaning of the term 'beginning' were thus relegated to utter unimportance? 'In the beginning is the Word, and the Word is with God, and the Word is God . . . and the Word is made flesh and dwells amongst us.' Whatever else may be said about this exercise, it must surely be admitted that it opens up to view vast christological vistas, and that by contrast the impression of a string of past facts conveyed by the prevalance of the past tense of the story-telling mode seems simply to leave us with the question: very well, but what is the bearing of all that on my present existence? There are answers to this question of course, but the very asking of it means that we have taken the terms of the story-telling mode quite literally, so that the content of the story then forms a kind of prelude to the important things we want to say to this time, rather than a summary statement of the whole nature and significance of Jesus, yesterday, today, and tomorrow.

Read John's prologue again in the present tense (with the – very significant – exception of the bit about John the Baptizer which of course must be read in the past tense). Then centre your reflections on the verse which surely represents the inverted pinnacle of the piece, 'the Word is made flesh and dwells amongst us'. Is not

214

Jesus of Nazareth the Word enfleshed? He is with God and with us, and all the New Testament material about the resurrection of Jesus and more particularly about his appearances, that is to say, his real presence, his being with us again or still *in the eucharistic setting*,[1] comes flooding back to the mind. He is God as God's Word, through whom everything is made by God, and as such he is the light of everyone-who-comes-into-the-world, and the source of life for all. There is here a comprehensive christology and the question of its present relevance is already answered in its own terms.

Here, however, the exercise of changing the tenses in John's prologue is suggested simply as a means of illustrating the variety of impressions which can be conveyed by these common analogies of beginning, source, root, sun, spring, which so naturally symbolize the human quest for origins. At the very simplest account of it, this variety consists in the difference between temporal (or spatial) and existential interpretation, and it is of interest at all only because of the suspicion that much of the disagreement and confusion which occurs in trinitarian theology seems somehow to be bound up with it. Now instead of plunging straight into this variety, with the ensuing prospects of confusion, it might be wise to take the phrase 'in the beginning' in a much simpler sense still, to go back to the beginning of the topics which have so far made up the substance of this book, and to look over these topics again in search, this time, of straws in the wind.

The strident claims of modern humanism formed the perhaps unpromising opening of our work, and since this work is entitled *The Christian experience of God as Trinity*, that very feature alone might tend to arouse, and to justify to an extent, Christian suspicion of a type which is already common enough in some quarters, to the effect that philosophy is encroaching on the domain of Christian doctrine, or more generally that the Christian faith is once again about to compromise itself for the sake of pandering to the secularist spirit of the present age. It should of course be obvious from the way in which both modern secular humanism and the most characteristic Christian answers to it were handled that no such compromise or encroachment was even contemplated. The more prominent Christian answers to modern secular humanism were challenged precisely on the grounds that they started from such general structures of human experience as its self-transcendence in order to argue, or plead, for belief in some general concept of God, while they still left open the possibility that the kind of trinitarian theology which we have all inherited might be a hindrance rather than a help in presenting our Christian message to those who are engaged in the pursuit of alternative goals for humanity.

The problem with such an approach is the problem with all so-called natural theology – and that fact cannot be disguised by beginning with 'experience' these days instead of beginning with some features of 'nature', whether human nature or nature in general – but it is a problem which is seldom properly understood or precisely stated. For all too often natural theology is set over against revealed theology, accused of Pelagianism – just another example of the use of a man's name by those who know nothing about him to complain about others whom they have taken little trouble to understand – and dismissed for otherwise unspecified reasons. The same kind of complaint is then made for the same reasons against the use of human experience as the starting point in the quest for God. But the real problem with natural theology, as for its more modern experiential surrogate, is not at all connected with its alleged neglect of divine revelation; the real problem with what normally passes for natural theology, the traditional arguments for God's existence with their concluding Prime Movers, Necessary Beings, First Causes, Supreme Values, and Cosmic Orderers, the real problem with the newer arguments or pleas from more pressing analyses of the structures of human experience with their concluding Grounds of Being, Transcendental Horizons of our human experience of transcendence, or the final Transference Object at the end of Becker's *The Denial of Death*,[2] is not that they rule out revelation, which they seldom if ever do, but that they are so concerned with what is abstract and general rather than with the concrete and actually existing.

There is no natural theology known to me which does not proceed upon the basis of God's prior approach to the world. The only solid reason for calling it natural theology at all is that it is the kind of approach which stresses the very existence and nature of all finite being as God's primordial act *ad extra*, God's most original approach. There is no distinction between nature and grace because all the world is God's grace or gift; there is no distinction between revelation and reason because everything of which we have knowledge, including whatever poor knowledge we may have of God, is known to us in so far as God unveiled it to us. If there are Christians – and there are – who wish to deny that we can know God from the revelation of the things that are made, then they must be clear that they must support this denial, not on non-existent distinctions between reason and revelation, nature and grace, but on their particular views of sin. And I strongly suspect that if they did support their hostility to natural theology in this way, the ensuing view of human sin and its intrinsic effectiveness upon the nature and success of God's dealings with humans would prove to be no more than a kind of inverted Pelagianism – if I may join them for a moment in abusing the name of that great Irishman.

The kind of critique epitomized in Barthian thought of what is called natural theology, and of its more contemporary surrogate, simply misses the real problem; the real problem consists in the fact that these approaches, in both premises and conclusions, are so general and abstract in nature that they fail to come to grips with any of the actual, concrete systems of belief by which people actually live and for which they are sometimes prepared to die. A comparison with pure mathematics may be instructive. One might discourse on the nature of mathematics, on the principles and methods of that science. One might engage in heuristic or demonstrative mathematical processes which could apply to a five-dimensional universe rather than to ours, or to a five-dimensional universe just as much as to ours; but it is not until applied mathematics or mathematical physics brings these processes to bear upon the concrete contour of our actual universe and in fact derives their direction from that contract that the discipline of mathematics can enable us to deal effectively with the actual physical reality with which our destiny is bound. The former processes give the mind some assurance that it can operate mathematically, probably because it evolved from a universe which appears to behave according to mathematical principles, but nothing of any true existential significance emerges before the latter processes take place.

Similarly, the rational arguments or pleas which begin from the general structures of nature or experience and conclude with some general concept of a god which is then declared to exist or not to exist, or possibly to exist or not to exist, assure the human spirit that it can operate at the level of religious truth or falsehood, probably because it evolved from a universe which has heights or depths to it that only truly religious sentiments can touch. But they do not of themselves yield an operable form of religious faith, nor indeed do they yield any operable forms of atheism either.

For atheism (and perhaps agnosticism also) suffers much the same hazards as religious faith suffers. It as often appears in primarily literary and superficial forms, in somewhat the same way as one can sometimes be given the impression that its doctrinal expressions are the most important form of theistic faith. And quite often also, with atheism as with various forms of theistic faith, people can for a variety of social and personal reasons proclaim themselves adherents, and even honestly think themselves adherents, but only because the existential question to which all forms of faith respond has never really yet come home to them.

The fact of the matter seems to be that authentic atheism, the atheism that is the real state of real persons' spirits, and not just a pretence, however innocently held, is entitled to the adjective 'religious' just as much as are the various forms of theistic faith. For such an atheism occurs at the same or a similar depth of the human spirit; it reaches for the same or similar depths of the universe which we experience; it results in a similarly comprehensive view of the whole, binds one to a similarly comprehensive attitude to all that one may do and must suffer in life, and requires of one a similar commitment even to the point where matters of life and death are at issue. I personally feel that much the same can be said about authentic agnosticism, the kind that names a deep and anguished quest for perpetually elusive assurance (and not the kind that represents once again a posture or a fashion or a personal pretence, however innocent), although in this case the nature of the commitment even unto the death (of others or, preferably, of oneself) is more difficult to detail.[3]

Consequently, authentic atheism always occurs also in concrete forms, and this is real atheism as distinct from that abstract account of atheism which, like similarly abstract accounts of theistic belief often known as natural theology, are abstracted from the concrete forms which actually exist and do more to reveal the formal structures of the human spirit and its formal ability to operate in certain ways than they do to actually describe any of the actual forms of atheism to which actual people profess their varying degrees of allegiance.

The kind of critique with which Marx faced Feuerbach is therefore of more general relevance than it might seem at first sight. For though Feuerbach was sufficiently aware of the basic similarities between atheism and theism to which we have just now paid some attention, it is the Marxist and not the Feuerbachian form that has gripped and changed whole human societies. Feuerbach knew, and said, that the radical and total humanism which he recommended was just as religious as the traditional faith whose essence he believed it to be and from which he wished it finally to emerge; he believed that what today was called atheism would tomorrow be called religion. But – and this was the point of Marx's critique of Feuerbach – he arrived at his new religious atheism, his religious atheistic humanism, from such an abstract account of the general structures of human nature that the resulting picture corresponded to no actual grouping of human beings and as a consequence had no power to change any.

If one were asked to point to other real or concrete forms of atheism on the modern scene, apart from Marxism, one could point to the manner in which atheistic existentialism, at least in the hands of its most consistently atheistic exponent, Jean-Paul Sartre, took concrete form in drama and the novel, and how the philosophical works, too, always aimed at actual existence rather than abstract essence and thus sought at once to describe and affect the concrete contours of the real world. And one could possibly trace much actual influence of this kind of philosophy, or actual correspondence to this kind of philosophy, in the lives of actual individuals and groups. Nevertheless, the more obvious candidate for the answer to our present question is undoubtedly that consumerist form of capitalism which Marx so relentlessly criticizes and to which he saw contemporary forms of Christianity to be more subservient than we are normally prepared to allow. It would serve well the neatness of our presentation if this contemporary consumerism were the philosophy of life actually presented and advocated by the third of the forms of humanism visited at the beginning of this book, the general humanism of Humanist Associations of which writers like A. J. Ayer are card-carrying members. But it was admitted then, and must be repeated now, that linguistic philosophers in general are not quite as forthcoming as the others on the details of the comprehensive vision and goal of human life. For this very reason, and if we except for the moment some later Christian awakenings, the task of resisting the definitive incarnation of the god Mammon has been left largely to the Marxists.

219

But we must not pursue these particular issues further in this context. Enough has been said, I hope, to show something of the consistency and perhaps of the correctness of the treatment of modern forms of humanism and of their Christian correspondents at the beginning of this book and to point the way forward to a concluding statement. For in face of much contemporary phenomenology it was necessary to contend that religious discourse is as valid as any other; that it cannot be discriminated against, much less already ruled out, at the very basic and elementary level of general epistemology. At the same time the suspicion had to be put very strongly that those contemporary apologists for Christianity who tried to meet the modern humanist case by arguing from general structures of human experience were at once failing truly to meet their opponents and properly to represent the concrete historical power of the Christian faith. The god which they derived from the general structures of human experience in the world was still too like the god of abstract (so-called 'natural') theology, and too little like the real God to which the doctrine of the Trinity at its best might yet perhaps point. I must say 'perhaps' here, for there is undeniable force in Moltmann's complaint that the two forms of traditional trinitarian doctrine which he rightly identifies as its principal forms too easily allow the concrete 'trinitarian' God to collapse into an undifferentiated monotheism, and yet I see reason to doubt that Moltmann's substitution of a truly social doctrine of the Trinity really succeeds where the others failed. So the question *is* acute: what is the Christian experience of God which can meet atheistic humanist alternatives at the same religious depth and – here is the real rub – with a similar existential concreteness; and does any doctrine of Trinity, ancient, modern, or yet to be devised, truly point to such an experience?

As we attempt to move closer to an answer to this question, then we can surely agree that all people live by faith, that this characteristically human faith always has truly religious or 'binding' depth and comprehensiveness (even when it is called atheism), and that it always takes concrete and practical form (that it is primarily *praxis* and more derivatively *theoria*). In a way, to say this is no more than to revert to more ancient usage of the term 'atheist', in which it referred, not to one who could be presumed to believe in no 'god' at all, but to one who believed in and worshipped a god other than the god of the user of the term, the one who worshipped a god which was in the user's view a false god. Now once agreement is reached on this point, *if* agreement is reached on this point, and however this agreement may be expressed, the next crucial question to emerge, at least for the theologian or philosopher, concerns the relationship of doctrine or theory to power or praxis. For it must be very obvious from the most superficial perusal of human affairs that theories, however idealistic and attractive, and doctrines, however clear in their content and persuasive in their presentation, have little power of themselves to change for better or for worse the course of human history. It is just when the vision is clearly described that the question of the source of the power to make it real becomes particularly acute. The question of the relationship of doctrine to praxis, theory to power, has already surfaced at a number of points in this work, so that a brief summary and some provisional conclusions should be sufficient for our progress at this juncture.

Some modern phenomenologists have written about that 'project towards the world which we are', that 'primordial faith' which is as yet an indiscriminate mixture of the cognitive, the evaluative and the practical, and they have talked of this furnishing to us the basic text which our more reflective, analytic and synthetic or imaginative consciousness reads and then formulates in the conventional ways. Perhaps because much of the phenomenology in question still operates at the level of general epistemology and correspondingly deals with general structures of the human embodied spirit, it does not yet sufficiently emphasize the fact that, probably since the very origin of the species, the project towards the world which any particular society of human beings was or is, is already quite concrete and individual in its actual form. However, the point surely is that the first relationship in which theory or story, doctrine or myth stands is the relationship of pointer to the project, the particular project toward the world which at any time or place we, any of us, are, and this project is itself a combination of a particular praxis and the power to pursue it. To read the basic text of our primordial faith, the basic text furnished to us by that project toward the world which we are, is to fashion a language which is, as all language tends to be, a fascinating mixture of the general and the particular, a way of at one and the same time locating things on the proper rungs of the ladder of significance, value and practical priority, and of naming the particular things (or persons, or places, or times) themselves.

221

This point corresponds to some extent to the point already made about the relationship of what is sometimes called natural theology and the particular religious beliefs by which people live: the basic text of our primordial faith furnishes us with general concepts and images which tell of the deep and comprehensive and indeed definitive significance and value of certain persons, things, times or places, while that concrete form which in reality it must always take furnishes us with precise descriptions of the actual persons, things, times or places to which our beliefs are actually pinned. To detach the former from the latter may be legitimate for certain purposes of intellectual abstraction and analysis, but the former, if left in its detached state, will tell us about certain abstract human possibilities, and tell us nothing as yet about the concrete, actual faiths by which real people actually live.

The first function of doctrine, then, is the demonstrative function, but in the literal meaning of the word in which to demonstrate means to point out. By means of evocative description, analysis and synthesis, it seeks to draw people's attention to the power and the praxis which is the substance of the religious position in question. One should not perhaps keep on referring to the power and the praxis as if these were two separable things, like some household appliance and the already distinct electrical power which may or may not be fed into it to make it work. At the religious depth of human existence the power takes its form from the praxis, so that it differs from other forms just as the forms of praxis which make it effective in the world differ from each other. The power of self-sacrificing love is already as different from the power of legal coercion as is the praxis in which each is embodied. So the first function of doctrine, to name its more abstract and conceptual form, or myth, to name its more imaginative form,[4] is to point to a concrete form of praxis or power in the world which people believe or, better, experience to be so binding or compelling in its nature, so comprehensive in its influence, and of such ultimate promise, that it attracts to itself the various absolutes of which human concept and imagery are capable.

At times, of course, it does seem as if doctrine in particular, instead of exercising its demonstrative role, threatens to become some kind of substitute for the power or praxis of which it should simply be the herald and general servant. Orthodoxy sometimes overtakes orthopraxis; words, be they scriptural or more generally

didactic, tend to supplant the Word. Then one gets these fascinating comparisons between infallible books and infallible popes,[5]
although, since infallibility is by nature a personal attribute, one
knows very well that the alleged infallibility of the book is really
being claimed for the one by whom the claim is made, if only on
the grounds that this one tacitly assumes that he is true to the
book. Hence, even though verbal formulation seems here to be a
substitute for some very fundamental power and praxis, on closer
examination it will be found to be pointing to a very particular
kind of power and praxis. For a dominant emphasis on orthodoxy
always contains implicitly, and sometimes explicitly, the premise
that one is brought to fulfilment, made whole or saved by decree.
I have lost count of the number of times I have heard members of
the Roman Catholic episcopate defend their offices and the
present prerogatives thereof on grounds of the need for orthodoxy, and on these alone. I am thus invited to conclude that my
salvation depends on assenting to the right things which they
say, since these are the right things that God said, and that my
salvation therefore depends particularly on them – both of which
conclusions I know pefectly well to be false. But even Christian
bodies which tolerate no such *magisterium* on earth too often
merely succeed in conveying the impression that salvation is still
a matter of assent to verbal formula which point in much the same
way to a dictatorial power, but one which now resides exclusively
in the heavens. I use the term 'dictatorial power' here quite
literally to describe a powerful person who dictates formulae, be
they doctrinal or judicial, by which one's destiny is determined,
and which determines one's praxis also as primarily one of assent
or acceptance, and I do so merely to establish the fact that the
demonstrative role of doctrine, its function of pointing to or
pointing out something, is primary, even when the doctrine or its
usage itself attempts to obfuscate or even to deny this.

If the first function of doctrine is demonstrative, its second
function is discriminatory. This second function corresponds to
the ability of the human mind to abstract the general from the
particulars, so that the characteristic differences between the
particular instances can be seen. (In older text-books of psychology the definition of intelligence which underlay the practice of
intelligence-testing regarded intelligence as the ability to notice
differences and similarities.) The general ability to arrive at
abstract universals (and the correspondingly abstract symbols

which are distinctive of human language) is already given with that general structure of human consciousness known as its reflective capacity, its power of bending back upon itself in action, its self-consciousness; but that general ability can hardly arrive at any practical result or any concrete content until it has more than one individual instance to work upon. And this is as true of those concrete forms of power-in-praxis which are sufficiently deep and comprehensive to deserve the adjective 'religious' as it is of any other objects of human reflection. It is when one religion emerges from another by a process of gradual self-differentiation, or encounters another through its wandering devotees, that the distinction between the general level of concept and term and their more particular and concrete content begins to emerge and, incidentally, the manner in which the discriminatory role of doctrine supports its demonstrative role becomes clear. The concept or term 'god' as a name for the power that is palpable in a particular form of praxis can in fact function as a general concept or term, and can tell us something about the general ability of the human spirit, as a result of being exposed to such concrete power, to operate at the religious level, but it can scarcely do even this in any effective manner until one is exposed to another usage of the concept or term to point to a power experienced in a different type of praxis; and then, simultaneously, one feels the need to fill one's own term 'god' with more distinctive content, more discriminating content, precisely in order to enable it to demonstrate more accurately the power-in-praxis which one all along named 'god'.

What is true of the term 'god', is true also of course of other terms, concepts, or images for power which is palpable in praxis: the term 'word' for instance, as a term for something which can illuminate, direct and motivate; or the image of the parent, father or mother, as an image for anything which gives and supports life. One learns quickly enough that all such terms for the deepest and most decisive powers which can be encountered in the practical experience of human beings, just like more abstract terms for absolute origin or goals, can apply to more than one kind of concrete encounter, and that they are therefore of general relevance and simultaneously in need of concrete content if they are ever to relate to the individual forms which alone really exist.

The pressing example of all this in the present context is Christianity, which gradually emerged by a process of self-differ-

224

entiation from its Jewish matrix and which practically from the outset of its individual career encountered the dominant religious movements of the deeply Hellenized Roman empire. Of course the Judaism from which Christianity first gradually differentiated itself was itself already extensively Hellenized, so that the actualities of the case are more complicated than our over-neat schema of a new religion emerging from one older one only to encounter different ones still would suggest. Nevertheless, since we now need only some summary thoughts that might lead to a general conclusion, our purpose will be sufficiently served if we observe in turn some features of Christianity's emergence from Judaism and of its encounter with Greek pagan religion which may illustrate the general view we have just now taken of the demonstrative and discriminating roles of doctrine.

Philo of Alexandria, the Jewish theologian who was part-contemporary of Jesus and Paul, wrote a *Life of Moses*.[6] It would, I believe, be impossible for anyone to give that work a careful reading and yet fail to see that Moses, for Philo, is the Word incarnate, who is called 'God' in set terms, and who after a life in which he exercised in an unsurpassable manner the functions of king, lawgiver, priest and prophet, had his material being transformed into a spiritual one so that at his death he was raised, exalted and ascended into heaven, and no tomb, but only a monument to him remained, though even this 'no man has ever seen'. There are significant differences, no doubt, which help to distinguish this Life from, let us say, the Johannine Life of Jesus. But these differences should not be allowed to obscure the basic similarity of the general structures of the religious discourse involved. On the contrary, if these differences are carefully attended to, they will show how religious categories which the human mind always tends to reduce to the generalities of its own basic possibilities inevitably take on (different) concrete content when they are used to point in a discriminating manner to the most impressive powers in praxis[7] which are or have been known to exist. This is just another way of putting the point made above in the section on 'The Problem of the Pre-existence of the Son', that what is distinctive about a title such as Word of God when applied to Jesus is not anything that can be detected in the title itself but precisely *its application to Jesus* or, in terms of this present context, the concrete content it gathers precisely from its new demonstrative, discriminatory role.

225

Logos (Word) in Philo refers to that of God which is powerful in the world, to God's *dynameis* as Creator and King, and it is operative in the 'works' of these divine powers. Now although Moses, like Jesus in the New Testament, is never said to be the creator *tout simple*, he is explicitly described as lord of the creaturely elements, like God, and for this reason given the name 'God'; furthermore the Law, which is the inner meaning and goal of the creation, takes the form of the person of Moses.[8] It is difficult indeed to avoid the impression that Moses is the *Logos* incarnate. Yet the differences between Philo's Moses and John's Jesus are instructive. It is probably significant that the Law is said to become psyche in the very person of Moses (*empsychos*), whereas the Word is said to become flesh in the case of Jesus; and it is probably also significant that when Moses' being is transformed at his death into a more spiritual mode, he is said to become *nous* (mind) rather than spiritual body. These differences may of course be attributable simply to the extent of Greek religious influence on Philo's mind, for the Greeks did have less time for the body than they had for psyche in general and quasi-divine *nous* in particular. (And even if this were the case, the differences would be instructive in their own way, but more by references to the Greek religious idiom than to the more strictly Jewish.) And yet on a more strictly Jewish interpretation of what Philo has to say about the incarnation of the *Logos* in Moses, the differences with the application of the same model to Jesus would be instructive. For it is, after all, the miraculous power of God to command the elements, on the one hand, and the Law, on the other, that take human personal form in Moses, and both of these seem to need psyche more than body. So that when one says that the Word became flesh in Jesus one is not simply referring to a formulated Law which he left us, or to the stories of his miracles; one is seeing God's power and works in the very weakness of flesh itself. But more of that later.

The point here is simply to illustrate as briefly as possible the discriminatory function of doctrine, and of other forms of the predominantly verbal expressions of a particular religious faith, to show how this complements the basic demonstrative function, and to draw some of the more obvious implications from this twinned functioning of all religious doctrine. So it is not only the doctrinal formula of God's Word taking concrete form in the world that is already familiar from Judaism; formulae concerning

God's spirit and God's sons, to choose but those which most intimately relate to Christian trinitarian doctrines, are already part and parcel of the Jewish way of pointing to God's power in the world and to the particular kinds of praxis in which it is palpable. And the immediate implication of insisting on the primacy of the demonstrative-discriminatory function of doctrinal (and even scriptural) expressions is to make doctrines derivative from and dependent upon the concrete forms of religious praxis in the world, so that the verbal expressions themselves are not thought to be the direct results of the divine power operative in the world. We thus distance ourselves from propositional views of revelation, from such conceptual or imaginative views of revelation as issue intentionally in verbal formulae, from Jesus the Christ, for instance, as the mouthpiece for the transmission of already formulated divine truths, concepts or images. This does not mean that theology can never conceive of God's acting on human efforts to utter the truth about God's acts: it is simply significant that our theological tradition refers to this as inspiration rather than revelation, and in this way acknowledges the fact to which I wish to point here, namely, that it is in certain forms of praxis that we believe the power that is divine to be unveiled, whereas the search for concepts, words and images in which to represent this is one of the first of human services to its presence in the world, though one which is sometimes thought to be aided by an extension of that very same divine power (or spirit) to which it attempts unerringly to point and to invite.

It seems fairly clear that if one were to take the opposite view of the relationship of doctrine to praxis; if one were to believe that the presence of the divine power in the world – symbolically referred to as the unveiling of God – was primarily in the form of verbal expression, one would have as little difficulty in showing Trinity to be a Jewish doctrine as in showing it to be a Christian one.[9] At least one should have as little difficulty in selecting three 'titles' from the variety offered in the Old Testament, as Christians call it – Father, Word, Spirit, Wisdom, etc. – as one would have in selecting three, and only three from a quite similar variety offered in the New; then, on a similar plea that one would have to conclude to some 'self-differentiation' in God, driving just these three back into divine 'pre-existence' and insisting that a trinitarian doctrine, and it alone, was orthodox. It would be a different Trinity from the Christian one, of course. But what would be different about it? Surely not just the success with which it could distinguish three, and only three *hypostaseis* in the godhead, for such theological ingenuity is by no means monopolized by Christians. And surely not the mere historical fact, if it is a fact, that Jesus *said* that he and not Moses or any others was the (definitive?) incarnation of the Word. No, it is Jesus himself, Jesus, as we have been saying, in his life, death and destiny, that makes the difference. And that brings us back again to the demonstrative-discriminatory function of doctrine and to its derivative status *vis-à-vis* praxis.

To attempt to illustrate these twin functions further by distinguishing Christianity in detail from its Jewish matrix would be impossible for me, and in any case quite imprudent in itself. That is to say, even if I had such knowledge of the detail and variety of the Jewish faith to be able to issue a complete account of its differences from an equally varied Christian faith – which I very evidently do not have – it would be wrong to embark on such an exercise. For the discriminatory function of doctrine must always be kept in its place, that is, in permanent subservience to the demonstrative function. Once loosed from that prior function and pursued for its own sake, the discriminatory exercise tends merely to support the false view that religious faiths can be shown by analysis and ensuing argument to be right or wrong, or better and worse. A substantially independent exercise of the discriminatory function too easily feeds into the kind of polemic that brings all religious faith into disrepute. On the contrary, a sustained attempt to describe, to point out the concrete power-in-praxis from which each one or each group of us derives the courage to be, together with the subsidiary attempt to say in what specific direction this develops what is there before us (either in the straight temporal sense of 'before us', or in the spatial sense of that which we find as we move out into different cultural milieux), such an attempt does most to suggest what is common or may be shared while seeing simultaneously to the unique spirit and the individual riches of what we each have to offer. For – and this last point may be made before going on to say something about the religion which Christianity encountered when it moved out from its Palestinian home – it is in praxis and not in theory that the verification of religious claims takes place, and the issue of which form of religious faith is the truest and most perfect is decided.

That last point expresses no more, and no less, that the

conviction that it is the witness of people's lives, the ways in which they actually relate to other people and things, the things that they do and the ways in which as a result they fare, that prove to the rest of us the truth or falsehood, the goodness or evil, of the faiths by which they live, that attract or repel us. And whether or not a particular faith be from the one, true God, whether or not it be the definitive act in our history of the only real God, whether it will ultimately save us or simply contribute to our final destruction, or merely make us less well-off than we might otherwise be, only history can decide that, and only the end of history can decide it definitively, whatever or whenever that may be for each one of us. This does mean, however, that doctrine, that reflective attention to the concrete faith by which we live, has in addition to its demonstrative and discriminatory functions, a third function which may be called its critical function; although this third function is as much an appendage to the discriminatory function as the discriminatory is to the demonstrative. For an important part of the task of detecting the precise direction in which a new faith is diverging from, or attempting to draw, another faith is an effort to notice the new ways in which lives are being shaped, together with an attempt to assess the measure of added happiness or added misery which this new shape of life delivers or at least seems to promise. And this leads us back again to the primacy of praxis. Certainly, if no significant change of life were in evidence, the contention that a new faith had really entered upon the stage of human history would be seriously vulnerable, and if the change were not clearly for the better, the claim of the new faith to lead us forward rather than backward would surely be vacuous.

Whatever else may be said for or against this concentric configuration of the functions of doctrine in terms of demonstration, discrimination, and critique, surely this much may be said for it: that, on the negative side, it provides a welcome diversion from these futile attempts to compare and even to evaluate different faiths according to their doctrines or theories, as if the proof of the pudding were in the recipe, or the essence of the faith were in its doctrine. On the positive side, it directs the theologian's attention from first to last, from the demonstrative through the discriminatory and the critical, to the practical and concrete living-out of his own faith in its own social groupings and to the actual manner in which this affects themselves and others. One is then less likely to hear claims for the superiority of Christianity over Judaism or Marxism, though one might occasionally have reason to point out that a real Christian somewhere had provided an example of truly Christian love for a Jew and in this way shown up the distinctive nature of Christianity, or that another Christian had somewhere else proved in practice that relations of grace are even more promising than any relations of production which we have as yet experienced or even as yet envisaged.

It should be no surprise, then, at least in retrospect, to find that the most basic denotation of the re-applied Jewish term Son of God was Jesus' lived filial relationship in his life, death and destiny to the God he called Father; that the Word was neither a propositional or conceptual revelation of which the human Jesus was merely the megaphone, nor yet some personal divine being distinct from the Father and, before Jesus was born, distinct from Jesus also (for no such divine person is either subject or object of the New Testament stories and reminiscences), but a term for that of God which was powerful and effective in its own distinctive way precisely as Jesus of Nazareth; that spirit-language is a most concrete if complex manner of speaking about God in such entirely local and temporal ways as might be expected of Paul's transcendent and yet immanent life-giving spirit. Nor should it come as any surprise that in the case of the broad tradition of Greek pagan thought the emphasis should be found to lie, not on any set of abstract philosophical terms of elastic substance left lying around for newer Christian shapes, but on the organic and assimilative growth of a powerful Greek religious praxis which the Christian faith would have to conquer in its own distinctive way or to which, if only by means of a dictated reaction, it would eventually succumb.

It would be as impossible for the present writer to give an adequate account of the detail and variety of the Greek religious tradition which accompanied the first formative centuries of the life and thought of Christianity as it would be to give an account of Judaism; and it would in any case be equally imprudent to attempt to do so with the intention of showing the distinct genius of Christianity. But an effort was made to survey the most characteristic and influential Greek theologies, if only as a prelude to an assessment of the successes and failures of Christian theologies which, in face of the epochal encounter of faiths taking place at that time, tried to exercise its inevitable discriminatory function. Needless to say, since the demonstrative (or pointing-out) function is uppermost even in the discriminatory and critical functions of doctrine, myth and theology, the successes and failures of these early Christian theologies merely reflects the successes or failures of distinctively Christian praxis in these times in attempting to swing in its own direction the prevalent Greek forms of religious praxis.

The kind of praxis in which, in very general terms, the Greeks saw the presence and power of the divine, consisted in that active relationship of, on the one side, the aching loving desire, the *eros* of the human spirit, and those fleeting appearances of beauty, of truth or intelligent order, and of goodness or graded perfection which, on the other side, this poor world afforded. The Greek spirit was empowered by this praxis at once to set out on the quest for pure and permanent truth and goodness, and the beauty which in a way is the combination of these two, and also to believe that One who was truth and goodness and beauty *par excellence* was operative within this fleeting world as the precondition of the quest and of its success. The dominant theological accounts of this distinctive praxis with its determining faith and its corre-sponding quest, at least from the time of Middle Platonism, provided its own characteristic method of dealing with the per-ennial religious problem of doing simultaneous justice to the immanence and transcendence of the absolute. This method, once again in very general terms, consisted in the construction of a descending and ascending hierarchy of truth, goodness, and beauty, in short, of being or reality as such. Partly because of the lingering Greek suspicion that materiality or sheer bodiliness was somehow the cause of imperfection, impermanence, in a word, evil, the quest could be pursued, either in an inward direction, through the recesses of the human soul or spirit to the still centre where the encounter with the One could take place or, alterna-tively, in an outward and upward direction through more objec-tively conceived grades of being. And partly, in turn, because of this ambivalence in the understanding of the quest, the hierarchy, which was at first largely binitarian but later predominantly trinitarian, could be conceived in a number of different ways. It could be conceived, for instance, as an actual account of an actual structuring of reality which was itself thought to be either per-manent or transient. Conceived as permanent, the hierarchy consisted of an actual though ineffable One, and two other real though subordinate levels of reality reaching in their interconnection down to the limits of matter, namely, Mind and Soul. In its transient form, since matter was in a sense non-being and the spiritual soul of each was destined for immortality, the hierarchy could be conceived as real, yes, but in the form of an exodus and a return both of cosmic dimensions. But yet another possibility existed and was even more fundamental for this Greek faith: since again matter was in a sense non-being, and since the human quest could be pursued inwardly through the mind rather than upward through grades of being, the hierarchy might represent no more than ways of describing the only true reality of the One, different names for the One corresponding to the human mind's more fragmentary ways of relating to It.[10] This final possibility, as has already been hinted, could be strengthened by certain analogical ways of conceiving of the task of talking about God.[11]

Different emphases on different elements of the common Greek kind of praxis would obviously correspond to these different ways of construing the hierarchy of being: to the first way would correspond a greater emphasis on ordering the world and bettering it from the resources of one's contact with the higher and deeper levels of true reality; to the second a greater emphasis on asceticism and the lure of another world; to the third a greater emphasis on the truly mystical dimension of unity with the One, to be achieved in this life as much as in the next. In fact it is probably the priority, in one's experience of the praxis, of the rational ordering or the ascetic or the mystical that determined one's way of understanding the hierarchical structuring of reality in Greek pagan theology. But, however that may be, the combination of the rational ordering, of the ascetic, and of the mystical which, with differing emphases, made up what is being termed the common Greek religious praxis, inevitably proved attractive to Christians as well as influential upon them, and provided perhaps a more basic reason, in addition to their need of a religious language in which to talk to their would-be converts, for the sometimes near-fatal ease with which they adopted the categories of Greek theology.

In short, in the encounter of Christian with pagan Greek in the formative centuries of Christian life and thought, it is primarily the struggle for human souls of two different kinds of praxis that we witness, and the successes and failures of Christian trinitarian theologies which we earlier analysed are but the reflection of the ebb and flow of the fortunes of the parties involved in this existential struggle. In the course of this promising struggle Christians were naturally determined to hold on to the absolutely central and essential place of the actual person of Jesus the Christ. And this determination had one immediate implication, but held out no unqualified guarantee of victory. The immediate implication was this: because for Christians the actual person of Jesus filled the mediating place between the One God and the world, they naturally tended to think of the hierarchical structures of Greek theology, whether binitarian or trinitarian, as corresponding to real beings existing on sequentially subordinate levels of true reality; they were accordingly prevented from adopting either of the other ways of construing the Greek hierarchies, the (Sabellian) way of transient exodus and return or the analogical/ 'negative' way of seeing the names as just different names for one and the same true Reality, accommodations to our present sojourn in the realm of unreality.

That no unqualified guarantee of victory for the Christian side followed the determination to hold on to the central place of Jesus is obvious from the way in which a Greek hypostasized Word was gradually distinguished from 'all that Jesus did and suffered' and so came to replace, at the centre of trinitarian theology at least, what we would now normally understand as the actual historical person of Jesus. Greek religious praxis did, however, hold out to Christians the prospect of developing it in their own distinctive direction – all religious praxis, even of atheistic kinds, holds out such a prospect to another faith – and Greek theology held out the corresponding prospect of being moulded to Christian purposes in the course of the ensuing encounter.

Arius and his party, like Athanasius and his party, both clearly believed that the Word which was incarnate in Jesus and through which all things were made, was in Jesus the saviour of the world,[12] but the fact of the matter is that so much of characteristically Greek religious praxis had by this time already been taken on board by Christians that the differences between Arians and Athanasians had to be found within a predominantly Greek understanding of Word. There may be differences between East and West, in that the West emphasized more the moral, if not the legal, element in praxis, and thus leant more towards the stoic contribution to the Greek divine *Logos* – Ambrose's *De Officiis Ministrorum* with its obvious echoes of Cicero's *De Officiis* is instructive here – whereas the East may have leant more towards a participation in the *Logos*, achieved by the gracious effect of the *Logos* through sacraments and other religious observances, which was more reminiscent of the contemplative or even mystical elements in Greek religious praxis. But the attraction of this Greek praxis in general can hardly be doubted, and the extent to which in general Christians willingly took it on board is all that need concern us here. For it was this as much as, if not more than, any other factor which held still within the categories of Greek religious thought the very Christian attempts, both Arian and Athanasian, to point in a discriminate manner in the essence of Christianity.

In favour of the Arians, it has already been hinted, and may now be said again, that the Greek hierarchy of descent and ascent could tolerate at its nether extreme such divine exposure to change that the life of Jesus and even his death, as described in Scripture, could with some stretching be accommodated by it. The Greek God does live, after all, as Aristotle insisted, and if only by the accident of involvement with the material sphere rather than by its own essence, as Plotinus might say, suffers change. The Arian Christian would have to strengthen considerably this element of divine exposure, of course, and there the hazards awaited him. For the sheer undeniable individuality of Jesus made the Arian also assume that the second one in the Greek hierarchical structure was a permanently real being, and although the Arian was even less inclined than was his opponent to separate the Word from what the Scriptures said about the suffering of Jesus, he shared with his opponent the common Greek tendency to look more to the Word (more to 'pre-existence') than to the flesh. The upshot of all this was, as the Arians' opponents were only too happy to point out, that the element of subordinationism endemic to the Greek schema was so exaggerated in the case of the Arian Word that it could scarcely retain its position within the realm of the divine at all.

Those who were to become the opponents of the Arians shared with them the common Greek schema, the one we have been calling emanationist and subordinationist. But they came to believe, quite rightly, not least because the logical extension of this schema by the Arians to the scriptural data on Jesus showed them, that, to put the matter quite generally, too much distance now appeared between Jesus and the highest Being (*ousia*) of God to allow Jesus to be the holding centre of Christianity which all true followers of his feel he ought to be. They sought, again quite rightly, for some formula for the oneness of God and Jesus which would enable people to confess Jesus as the very channel or instrument, indeed the very embodiment of all that God had done or would do from creation to eschaton. God, true God, highest God, they wanted to say, was in Jesus, not some divine being who was being pushed so much to the edge of the divine flat earth that he seemed in imminent danger of falling off. And yet, under the combined influence of the lingering Greek prejudice against the flesh on the one hand and, on the other, the persistent exegetical and logical attacks of the Arians, the Athanasian party was driven to insist on the substantial identity of the Word with the Father while actually driving a wedge between this Word and the humanity of Jesus. In this way, I am convinced, arose that 'immanent' Trinity as distinct from the earlier 'economic' Trinity, which has left trinitarian theology to this day with one of its most impressive red-herrings, and has left the most recent trinitarian theologians we have surveyed with the hopeless task of trying to bring together in the name of the saving God what man has put asunder. But whether that be true or false, what is surely obvious is that neither side in that ancient dispute was able to break out of the confines of Greek religious structures, and so neither was entirely successful in pursuit of the essential discriminatory function of Christian theology. The verdict of earlier pages may sound a little harsh – that they divided the Greek schema between them, the Arians taking the subordinationism to a point where no Greek could follow them, and the orthodox taking the immuta-bility of the divine being to a similar length, so that neither in the end could do justice to Jesus of Nazareth – but it is surely defensible in substance. The anxious efforts of more recent trinitarian theologians to bring the doctrine once more into contact with the actual saving work of Jesus in this world bears its own kind of witness to the justice of the verdict, and the suspicion that these theologies have as yet found only a parallellism, and no real coincidence, between the saving events of this world and events in 'pre-existence' must surely be seen to be no more than a temporary set-back in a project which they have rightly seen to be essential. How, then, can we proceed?

One way forward may be found by keeping to the theme of the primacy of praxis and the primarily demonstrative nature of doctrine, theology and myth. In the case of Christianity this will at least have the effect of focussing doctrine, in search of clarity and distinctness of content, on the life and death of Jesus of Nazareth, and on the lives (and sometimes the deaths) of those who over the long centuries have claimed to be his followers. For however people may agree or disagree with my critical assessment of classical trinitarian doctrines, there can be few who would not regret the polemical needs of the orthodox in both East and West to set so deliberately aside from their accounts of the Word of God all that Scripture had to say about the flesh, the humanity, in short, the this-wordly history of Jesus. And however people may agree or disagree with my treatment of the sources of the normative role of Scripture, at least those who truly take it as normative, rather than merely profess that it is so, must surely be impressed by the consistency with which it bends even its 'pre-existence' language in the direction of the crucified Jew, Jesus of Nazareth.

He who speaks of the Trinity, as Moltmann said, speaks of the cross of Jesus, and does not speculate in heavenly riddles. Indeed it is often said that the keys to things puzzling and mysterious are usually simple, and normally lying just under the noses of the puzzled, waiting to be seen. Certainly for Roman Catholics the key to the doctrine of the Trinity was, and is, as close as that; for practically every time they say the trinitarian formula (and they say it practically every time they pray), they make what they call the sign of the cross, passing their noses at least twice in the process.

The wrong kind of concentration on the cross of Jesus, on his death, however, can do more harm than good. When such concentration on the cross is at the expense of attention to Jesus' life, it can easily harm the proper understanding of the essence of Christianity in general and deprive us in particular of the prospect of renewing the doctrine of the Trinity. For if the cross is kept in isolation from the life of Jesus – a life which, historically speaking, led to the cross, its consummation – then the more comprehensive drama which forms the context for the cross, for which the cross is climax, is too easily located in heaven (or, to use temporal rather than spatial symbol, in pre-existence), and then we tend to get those dramatic mythical accounts of how God at once satisfied his love and his justice, in which the essential dramatic action all occurs in heaven, the decisions there taken merely being carried out on earth, often by people who know now what they do. Correspondingly, in the case of trinitarian doctrine, the wrong kind of concentration on the cross yields the kind of pre-existent drama involving Father, Son and Spirit which parallels the drama taking place on earth between the Father and Jesus. So, although Moltmann says at one point that the death of Jesus cannot be understood in isolation from his life,[13] in lieu of the thoroughly economic Trinity he so clearly seeks he himself can manage no more than a kind of parallelism of heavenly (pre-existent) dramatic relationships with those detectable through the experience of Christian faith on Calvary. The wrong kind of concentration on the cross does seem to yield, then, those pre-existent dramas which, if taken as mythical ways of telling the truth about God on earth might do no real harm, but when taken literally, simply detract from the incarnate truth, the praxis-truth, the truth which must be done, as John would say, which is the true essence of Christianity and a challenge still to the atheistic humanism of our time. It would take us too far afield to try here to search out in full detail the wrong kinds of concentration on the death of Jesus. Yet some general remarks on this delicate topic may help to secure the kind of trinitarian or binitarian theology which we now need.

Death, as Paul would have it, is the last enemy, not just in the sense that it is chronologically the last enemy which we each meet individually, but in the sense that it is the all-embracing and apparently invincible enemy, and all the other threats we face, even the fragile supports we cling to are, as in a Hitchcock film, merely the many masks it wears. Death holds a deep fascination for us; it easily becomes in itself the *mysterium tremendum et fascinans*. Like anything that is powerful and apparently invincible, it tends to make men servants. But there is a demonic and destructive form of service, just as there is a demonic and destructive form of everything which in itself might be good and benign. And since death in itself is destructive it elicits fear in its servants – one remembers the lapidary description of the human condition in Hebrews 2.15: slaves all our lives long to the fear of death – and fear is the most demonic of all human emotions. Some cynically say that love is this, not fear. But this cynical view is based on a misconception. The Freudian *eros* and *thanatos* are not twins, not equally original. *Eros* is the original driving force in human life, as Plato knew, so there is much to be said for Freud devoting most of his time to *eros*. But for those who are servants of the fear of death, *eros* is perverted. There can be no other explanation for the way in which we glorify war and enjoy the permanent portrayal of violence; for the way in which we become allies of death, and draw even religion on its side, blessing armies instead of beating our breasts for their very existence and hanging in our cathedrals the flags of battles won; for the way in which we can see peace only as the product of the balance of terror; for the way in which even economic activity, by which we secure physical life on earth, can only be seen in terms of competitiveness, and the kind of help that is given to the needy is only such that will further, or certainly not weaken, one's own global advantage. Seldom enough does love of death, perverted *eros* appear in explicit form, as it is reputed to have done during the last days of Hitler, but all concentration on death itself, rather than on life, or at least on the one who is living out the consummating moments of life, threatens to arouse or enhance this perverted *eros*, and has done more than its share to involve Christians in complicity or complacency in the deaths of others, in the very name of their badly misconceived faith.

Put in another way, it is not the death of Jesus, strictly speaking, which overcomes death, for death does not overcome death; it is the life of Jesus which overcame and still overcomes death, the last enemy. It is the life of Jesus, therefore, that reveals the true Lord of the world, the true *monarchia*, the God of the living and not of the dead, and concentration on the death of Jesus is justified only as the consummation of this life. Compared to this one God all other gods that we worship are but the many masks of death. Hence the prophetic mockery in the Old Testament of the idol-worshippers.

One must not give the impression, of course, that what is here in question is merely a matter of rational choice between options presented. Take the child, or the young adult, describe the service of the gods of death and the service of the Father of our Lord, Jesus Christ, and the corresponding consequences, and let them choose! No. The world has never been short of theories, each one more plausible than the others, but what the world has most often lacked is the power to put its better theories into practice. Even those theories which point to where the most benign kind of power is palpable do not themselves contain it except in the most indirect and diluted form. Whence we have those theories of original sin and grace, from Pelagius to Calvin, which have tried

238

to deal more adequately, though still in theory, with the troubled problem of human freedom in the presence of power both divine and demonic.

Correspondingly, neither Jesus himself nor his more credible followers have ever been reduced to words, spoken or written, to wield their benign influence; and certainly orthodoxy has never been the thing of most importance in Christian life. The primacy of praxis is undeniable in all real religion, whether theistic or atheistic, and the primacy of the demonstrative role of doctrine is correspondingly clear. Sartre's case for a human philosophy of total freedom and responsibility is vulnerable enough in its philosophical or doctrinal form, and seems relatively defenceless against the critical complaint of a Jolivet, for instance, to the effect that total freedom is indistinguishable from total determinacy.[14] And yet nothing is more obvious than the fact that the man who insists on relating to me only through the law – whatever book or code of law may be in question, human or divine – effectively constrains me to a certain impersonal type of active relationship and relegates in this manner, whether I like it or not, both his responsibility and mine. Whereas the man who takes full responsiblity at each moment even for a maxim on which he momentarily operates draws me inexorably into the orbit of full personal responsibility: for since he refuses to let any independently established maxim come between us, he leaves me with no option but to relate immediately and directly, in my own naked freedom and full responsibility, to him. There may be felt to be something missing in Sartre's philosophy which would give this freedom more concrete existential context. One might feel like making more than Sartre himself does of the desire to be God, the desire of the insatiable *pour-soi* to be also *en-soi*, to enjoy the repletion and solidity of a thing-in-itself and not be forever, as consciousness, wanting for content. And one might then suggest that there are other and better images of the God one might want, if not want to be. But what one could not fail to see from Sartre's age is that the power lies in the praxis, not in the doctrine, or even in the Scriptures.[15] And in the case of Marx one would not even have to point this out, for Marx explicitly saw and argued it himself.

It is Jesus' life that shows us the praxis and, in so far as it is continued in his followers, which enables us to encounter the power which is at the heart of Christianity. This praxis is a distinctive form of what a phenomenologist would call 'that project towards the world which we are', a project which contains in itself, as yet undifferentiated by reflection and analytic reason, the visionary, the evaluative and the actively relational and effective, a project otherwise known as a primordial faith. Hence our similar formulae for the roles of Scripture and doctrine, Scripture in its authoritative role and doctrine in its demonstrative, discriminatory and critical role: both are at once understood in the light of, and contribute to the discernment of, the life of Jesus still in the world by which alone the definitive victory over death is promised.

The life of Jesus, the power and the praxis, this distinctive project towards the world, was described, as best I could do it, in *Jesus, the Man and the Myth*: the death of Jesus was there described as the consummation of this life; the resurrection kerygma was shown to point both back to that life and forward to it, and to declare that in it and from it God's Spirit breathed and breathes still. I can only summarize this for the present context as follows.

Marx saw very clearly that the relations of production dictated by capitalism were destructive of the dignity of human kind and of the quality of human life. In order to release the free creativity of our kind to which so much of our dignity and the quality of our lives belong, he stressed instead a different set of relations of production. These new relations of production do depict a kind of praxis, a project towards the world, a living faith which is in so many ways admirable, particularly when compared to the capitalist, consumerist and truly materialist alternative which seems at times to be all that the contemporary world has to offer. But do the relations of production, even as described by Marx,[16] go deep enough? Are they sufficiently radical, *en arche*? For do I really produce my life, as Marx said? Do I truly, in the most radical sense, create rather than pro-create it? Is not the lesson of my finitude, my contingency, that all my producing and consuming kills me quietly as much as it makes me live? Are relations of production truly original, of the *arche* itself, or do they not simply illustrate the awful ambivalence of finitude and the very dominance of death which we would overcome? I do not think that Marxism records the victory over the last enemy, and I fear that those who do not win over death must always remain its servants in fear. That in itself does not mean that good Marxists are not superior to nominal Christians, and vastly superior to those Christians who have turned their own God into a dealer in arms and death, but it may help to distinguish the true essence of Christianity.

At the heart of the praxis of Jesus and of those he empowers to be his followers are relations, not of production, but of grace. That at least I believe to be clear from the variety of New Testament theologies; that I believe to shine through the shortcomings and even the mistakes of the biblical authors. To that I believe the main christological titles point – especially the title Son of God – especially when they are embedded in the resurrection kerygma. And to that, therefore, all subsequent doctrinal formulations should point also.

Jesus envisages, evaluates and actively relates to his own life, to all others, to all things great and small, as good things created and given (the faith, full-blown, of the first creation story in Genesis), in short, as graces. The sense of incredible enrichment, of pre-emptive forgiveness for the guilty, of invincible joy for all, is the first accompaniment of this praxis and its permanent undertone; the cherishing of all people and things is its persistent practice; the hope of life that even death cannot destroy is its final promise. It itself *is* the experience of the Fatherhood of God in distinctively Christian form, in the only way in which, while *in via*, we can have this experience. It makes us both the beneficiaries of life and servants of life, and so it evacuates fear from our hearts, fear which is the only real hold death can have over us. Like Sartrian freedom, or Marxist relations of production, or those relations of production characteristic of our consumerist era, its power is palpable in one's very exposure to it through the lives of those shaped by it.

The Christian faith directs us to our Source *through* the lives we live in the flesh, *through* the men and women of flesh that we encounter, or to whom we are bound, *through* the material world and all that it contains. (Greek religion directed to the Source, in the end, by directing away from the material.) Hence all Christian doctrine, even trinitarian doctrine, is meant to point to this life of Jesus, in the man Jesus and as a result in his followers, and it is not meant to point away from this to any pre-existent society of divine 'persons' or even to any self-differentiation in God which we should then presume it to describe. We may guess at self-differentiation in God, but it is not the business of trinitarian doctrine to describe this, as Barth seems to have realized on occasion. Economic trinities or binities are the only ones we possess, as the relative failures of the ancient doctrines, and the relative successes of the more recent ones, all seem to suggest. Finally, just as there were trinitarian and binitarian doctrines in the past, so there can be today. If doctrine is agreed to be essentially demonstrative, and therefore second-rate, this will be easier to accept.

If one wanted today to hold to some of the classical terms of trinitarian theology and yet to take seriously both the criticisms of classical theologies which we have encountered and the new directions suggested by their more modern counterparts, one could find in *Jesus, the Man and the Myth* one example of how to do this.[17] Undoubtedly the effort in that book to draw this example from the work of the Cappadocian fathers smacks of anachronism. For one thing, it would be difficult indeed to show that any one of the Cappadocian fathers, much less all three of them, ever consistently used the twinned terms *ousia* and *hypostasis* in the manner in which Prestige was there shown to use them, the manner which the example requires. For another thing, the Cappadocians were no more successful than were any of their patristic contemporaries in keeping together in their trinitarian theology, again in the manner which the example requires, what are called the humanity and divinity of Jesus. However, once these admissions are made, it is not at all difficult to see how those specific well-attested and ancient meanings of the two terms *ousia* and *hypostasis* to which Prestige points could be used today in a trinitarian theology which would heal the rift between the flesh and the Word in Jesus opened wide by the polemical needs of the fourth century.

So, to summarize here briefly the example from the companion volume, *Jesus, the Man and the Myth*: *ousia*, taken in the sense of Aristotle's primary substance, refers to an individual, concrete, substantial entity, but with reference to its internal structure or make-up, to the kind of thing it is. *Hypostasis*, on the other hand, refers to an individual, concrete, substantial entity, but with reference now to its being an object over against other objects, with external rather than internal reference, with reference to the way it relates to other things. To say, then, that there is one divine *ousia* and the three divine *hypostaseis* of Father, Word or Son, and Spirit, is to say, first, that in all that we shall say we are talking about one and the same being, nature or essence of the one and only God there is, that there are no other gods, and certainly no lesser divine beings beside this One. It is to say, next, that this one God objectifies himself, relates to us as Father in one manner in the Word which takes the form of the creation, in other manners in, for example, the Word which takes the forms of the Mosaic Law and Hebrew prophecy, and finally, we Christians believe definitively, in the life and person of Jesus of Nazareth who relates to us as the Son of God. The Fatherhood of God becomes definitively objectified in our world and our history in the Sonship of Jesus, that is to say, in the life and death of Jesus to which the title Son of God primarily points. The *hypostasis* of God named Father is *hypostasis* to us in the *hypostasis* of Jesus of Nazareth, the Son.

But the presence of Jesus the Christ, the real presence, the life of Christ in which we experience the Fatherhood of God in the specifically Christian sense of that term, is as a matter-of-fact 'object' to us now in our communion with those who, by the power of God which comes now in the 'shape' of Jesus, live it. That communion is found, as the name suggests, in the eucharist community, in the Holy Communion which is the centre of the existence of what we call church. Spirit – but always incarnate Spirit – is then the name for the eucharistic lives of Christians in which the Fatherhood of God through the Sonship of Jesus becomes 'object' to us in our contemporary existence.

This is certainly one way of construing the ancient formula while maintaining its trinitarian structure. It avoids the term 'person', which most modern commentators consider to be too problematic in any case. It shows the trinitarian distinctions quite clearly: the Father is distinct from Jesus, who is yet his Son and who allows us to experience his Fatherhood; the eucharistic community is distinct from Jesus while still being his body in the world which allows Jesus to be in us and we in him. And it gives us a thoroughly 'economic' Trinity which allows us to suspect some form of self-differentiation in God, in pre-existence, without tempting us to the *superbia* of presuming to describe it. It urges us to be satisfied with what we can say, and to wish only that what we can say were true if only in slight measure of our own lives.

But perhaps it may be suspected that this reconstruction of the ancient formula does not do quite as much justice to the 'one and the same divine being' element as it does to the distinctions. For if the primary reference of the word Son is to Jesus of Nazareth in his life, death, and destiny, and if the primary reference of the

243

word Spirit, in this reconstruction, is to the eucharistic community, then the question can obviously be asked: are these divine, and fully divine, in the way in which Father is divine?

Certainly, it must be conceded that the answer to the questions, 'Is Jesus divine?', and 'Is the body of Christ, the eucharist community, divine?', is; yes and no. But this is the absolutely orthodox answer. And it is instructive to notice the parallels throughout the whole history of Christian theology between the incarnation, the doctrine of the eucharist, and the doctrine about the church. Hence the answer to the suspicion just now expressed must be in two parts. First, the reference in the trinitarian formula to the 'one and the same being of God' must not convey the impression that we have any vision of the inner being or essence of God, for this we obviously do not have. The phrase is meant to express, rather, our faith that the one we encounter in Jesus and his church is the one true God, and no other or lesser one. Secondly, there is a sense in which in this reconstruction of the trinitarian formula the term Father is more purely or exclusively expressive of this divinity than are the terms Son or Spirit. But this is because of our Christian conviction that the Fatherhood of the one true God is available to us, encounters us, not directly in itself, but through what we refer to as Son and Spirit. And this sense is in any case in line with the traditional impression that the Father is not 'sent' as the others are, that Father names the 'source' accessible only through the others.[18]

As long as we remember the demonstrative function of doctrine, its role in pointing to the place where we can encounter the Fatherhood of God in the distinctively Christian form of that experience, we will suffer no danger of an exposure to heterodoxy from this reconstruction of the formula. The reconstruction resembles most those trinities of strict order in which the Spirit had to be third, and, like these also in this, it seems to place the Spirit furthest from full divinity, for not only is the Spirit incarnate in the creaturely, but the waywardness of the eucharistic community is both very far from the divine and contrary in a rather startling way to the perfection we attribute to Jesus. And yet there is now a corresponding advantage. For if we stick stoutly to the thoroughly 'economic' nature of our trinitarian formula, if we refuse to allow our religious claims to disappear into a traceless pre-existence, if we boldly insist on saying exactly where for our faith God is in his world, then we shall also gain some sort of adequate impression of the self-emptying and the suffering of God, and of the awesome extent of his patient love.

Beyond that there is probably no better way of keeping doctrine to its demonstrative role, no better way of preventing it from replacing that to which it is meant merely to point, than to maintain the most determined openness to a wide variety of doctrinal forms. It has often been said already of the Trinity of strict order that it could not claim to be the exclusive formulation of the rich variety of scriptural data, and Moltmann's social doctrine of the Trinity was praised for at least allowing for different orders of Father, Son and Spirit. It cannot be the intention here to attempt to create from the inheritance of the past, or from the present experience of living Christian faith in the world, further possible varieties of trinitarian doctrine. But, if only to do a little more justice to our past inheritance, if only further to prevent any particular doctrinal reconstruction from taking too prominent a place, if only to illustrate a little further how the rich and deep experience of the Christian life can give rise to a variety of doctrinal formulae, consider one more example, this time a binitarian reconstruction.

It is frequently said that spirit-christologies inevitably remain at the level of adoptionism, and it is sometimes suggested that this is why such christologies were dropped rather early from the repertoire of the Christian community. There is little or no scriptural support for this contention, and its theological defences are extremely vulnerable. Spirit, being a name for God, for the very being or nature of God, can quite clearly handle what is known as the divinity of Jesus just as well as can terms such as Son or Word; and if it could do so for Paul, as it almost certainly did, then there is no reason whatever why it should not do as much for his successors in the theological profession. If it is objected that Spirit was said to be in the prophets and perhaps operative in the creation, so that to use it for the divinity of Jesus would be to draw Jesus into comparison with other creatures and thus obscure his utter uniqueness, it must simply be remembered that others were also said to be God's sons and to have his Word in them, and that Word was operative in creation, and yet none of this prevented the New Testament from using these terms to say what it wanted to say about what later came to be called the divinity of Jesus.

In a reconstructed binitarian theology, then, Spirit would

function, as it normally did in the Judaeo-Christian tradition, as a term for God transcendent and immanent. The Fatherhood of God we would then be said to encounter in the Spirit of sonship which took concrete, existential form in the lives of actual people and, for Christians, definitively in the life and death of Jesus of Nazareth. Jesus would then in turn, as the very embodiment of the Spirit of sonship and its continual real presence in history, be called the life-giving Spirit, so that the term 'Spirit' could replace as their theological equivalent terms such as Son or Word by which the definitive presence of God in the history of Jesus would otherwise be expressed. The 'Binity' would then consist of Jesus and his Father, and Spirit would name that one and the same divine being or essence, at once transcendent and immanent, the fatherly *hypostasis* or objectification of which is encountered definitively in the *hypostasis* of the Spirit of sonship objectified in the life of Jesus and his continual real presence amongst us. One divine *ousia*, two *hypostaseis*. Here one could link up with those texts of the mystics in which Spirit seems to name the unity of God into which, through Jesus, God seeks to draw all that have come out from God and dispersed, each into its own path. And one could find a great deal of scriptural support, not only from Paul's use of Spirit for what is called the divinity of Jesus, but from all those Pauline texts on the fruits, effects or works of the Spirit which, as James Dunn once said in a lecture, amount practically speaking to a character-sketch of Jesus the Christ. And one could also reverse that previous strict order in which the Spirit came 'after' the Son, and so relate better to those texts of Scripture in which the Spirit comes 'before' Jesus to account for Jesus' own role and status.

Such a binitarian theology would still be thoroughly 'economic', and the demonstrative nature of its doctrinal function would be fully intact. We should be taking the risk by means of it of pointing to that in our world, to that concrete praxis, in which we believe the power of God to be active, and on which our hopes of defeating even the last enemy, death, are based. It may well be that the scattered Christian community in the world would prefer to have one doctrine which operates at the high theological level at which trinitarian doctrines have traditionally operated, rather than have a number of these. And perhaps that desirable state of affairs, if it is desirable, will one day soon come about. But for the moment it simply must be recognized that what many of us thought was a traditional trinitarian doctrine has disintegrated on us, showing its internal difficulties and its cultural obsolescence, and that the best we can do for now is to try to see, through its disintegrating forms, that life which it always meant to point out to us, if only by distinguishing this from less promising forms of life, and to let this life in turn suggest other forms to us, one of which may one day dominate.

Whatever trinitarian or binitarian doctrine we now construct in service to our living faith must respect the normative role of Scripture, at the very least by not attempting to constrict the rich variety of scriptural data within the inevitably narrow confines of its own systematic requirements; it must carry forward the long tradition of trinitarian and binitarian theology to which we are heirs, not least by noticing the changing cultural dependencies of this theology and trying always to improve upon its relative failures. And whatever trinitarian or binitarian theology we now construct, we must above all realize that it is in essence a christology, as in essence such theologies have always been. For it must attempt with whatever degree of success we can muster to express our belief, born, we hope, of our own experience of distinctively Christian praxis, that God was, is and will be in *Jesus*, reconciling the world to himself, and drawing out its astounding promise. Or, if we wish to speak of the matter from the point of view of Jesus, rather than the point of view of God – and this is always a good thing to do – we would say that we are trying to express our belief that Jesus was, is and will be, in God, the channel of unconditioned grace to us and the goal of the promise which as a result of his existence we sense in life.

In the beginning, *en arche*. The combination of spatial and temporal symbols in these last sentences, the spatial symbol in the repetition of the adverb 'in' and the temporal symbol in the past, present and future tenses of the verbs, are no more, and no less, than the plain requirements of all religious language. Bound to the forms of space and time, as all our perceptions and therefore all our language are, when we want to speak of God who transcends the conditions of our spatio-temporal continuum, we speak of a mythical time, as Eliade would say, or a mythical place, and even when we wish to relate God especially to particular people or things or places, we position these also in relation to a time above time and a place beyond all places, and we use the tenses of verbs and the spatial adverbs to this purpose. But, in

terms of our original question in this chapter, there is no doubt
that it is the existential sense of 'in the beginning', and of
comparable spatial symbolism, that we intend. The primacy of
praxis, the predominantly demonstrative role of doctrine, and the
thoroughly 'economic' nature of trinitarian theology, all point in
the same direction.

The Word of God became flesh as Jesus of Nazareth – one of the
most powerful and also one of the most verifiable religious claims
ever made. The followers of Jesus communicate his body; they
are the body of Jesus in the world. The Spirit which animates them
is the Spirit of Jesus, another term for the Word which made Jesus
what he was and is, which found its own distinctive expression as
Jesus; it is the divine power and presence which operates as Jesus
and his body in the world, in all the weakness to which human
flesh is heir, with the distinctive and invincible *eros* of which it is
thus capable.

It is impossible that a faith so thoroughly bound to human flesh
and blood and spirit should fail to speak a challenging word to
humanism ancient or modern, theistic or atheistic. It is unlikely
that there should be anything in a faith so intimately at the service
of human history, and so much at its mercy, that could automatically alienate those faiths from which it sprung and to which it at
least partially gave rise, those which belong to the same family as
itself.

Christianity does not tell us anything about a time before our
world began, or about a place beyond our world's vast extent; it
has no information about 'God in himself'; it has only the expressions of faith which it gleans from the belief that the power and
presence it experiences in its distinctive praxis – the joyful,
lived-out conviction of unconditioned grace – is the Absolute
Power and Presence operative in this universe; it has only the
on-going verification of the successive healing and happiness
which its distinctive project toward the world brings, and the
hope of definitive victory over death which it increasingly holds
out.

The Christian faith, the faith of Jesus, does not or should not
face modern humanism with a God argued from the general
structures of finite reality or human experience, a God for whom
the abstract and impersonal terms Transcendent, Ground, Horizon – to name only the contemporary preferences – provide
equivalent and satisfactory titles. And a Christian doctrine of the

248

Trinity is certainly not a way of later 'Christianizing' or further specifying a God already argued or at least presented for consideration on such general grounds, as Calvin and Hegel both knew. Though Hegel may have known better than Calvin that a doctrine of the Trinity referred most immediately to a process or project, in origin (*en arche*) divine, moving through history, becoming definitively Christian, and shaping history to its ultimate goal. In any case, the Christian faith properly understood is certainly not irrelevant to modern humanism, though whether or not it is obsolescent will only be shown in the struggle of the different kinds of praxis which, now as always, seek to influence the commitment of the spirits of humankind.

This need not be taken to mean that Christian theory or theology can do nothing but wait for the outcome of the struggle. It must continue its demonstrative service, and must carry this to the point where it is discriminatory and critical. Its discriminatory function will be exercised largely through its sensitivity to those forms of praxis which most accurately translate into action the distinctively Christian conviction of grace and its consequential generosity. It may be nonplussed to notice that when the purity of the atmosphere is threatened by experimental nuclear explosions, or the lives of baby seals by bounty hunters, people are found to go and simply place themselves between that which they cherish and those who threaten it, whereas when the lives of Falkland Islanders are threatened by oppression or death, by invaders and liberators alike, no one is found to go and be with them in the same self-sacrificing way: no one then seems to be able to think of anything more effective than the most unchristian act of war. And the critical function of theology will be exercised in the effort to catalogue, or else to envisage in that act of creative imagination, that art which is the heart of all true morality, the life-enhancing or death-dealing results of different forms of praxis, the non-Christian forms, the Christian forms, and the forms that pass for Christian though they bear none of the fruits of the Christian Spirit.

Now the task of taking that distinctively Christian form of primordial faith, the distinctively Christian project towards the world which we are, those radical relations of grace, this way of relating to our own lives, to all people, and to all things great and small as graces from God our Father, and then of saying in detail how this would enable the Christian to act towards the demands

249

of ecology, in war and peace, with respect to divorce laws or abortion, in the face of that gigantic military-industrial complex which now rules and diminishes all our lives more than we realize, against the newly-evolved consumerist form of materialism, in the presence of a Marxist-inspired struggle for social justice – this task clearly belongs to a separate volume in the system of Christian theology, the volume on Christian ethics, and it alone could show, at least in prospect, how in the concrete Christian praxis differs from, and might be superior to, those forms of modern humanist praxis which depend upon changing relations of production, or ideals of freedom, or hopes in the future of science and technology. The tast of this present volume was to show that doctrines about God which seem at first sight to take us back before the world or incredibly beyond it are in reality ways of identifying distinctive forms of power-in-praxis within the world which alone enable us to say some things in faith and hope about the God we believe we there encounter. And since the writer is a Christian of sorts, its task was to show that the Christian doctrines about God point to the life, death and destiny (particularly in his presence with his followers) of Jesus of Nazareth as that in which, in surprising joy and invincible hope, the one, true God is encountered.

Finally, with respect to those other faiths at least which belong to the same family as the Christian faith, Judaism and Islam, it very badly needs to be stressed that theological claims to superiority of one over the other, however these claims are argued, are really wide of the mark, at best counter-productive, and at worst quite destructive in their tendencies to arouse just those human reactions which each of these faiths at its best would discourage. More positively, it is in the characteristic praxis that the true promise of a faith can be seen, and in the unwelcome results of that praxis can be seen, either the failure of its devotees to live up to the faith in question, or a real imperfection in the faith itself. Efforts to see better results from the praxis should then either reform the devotees or evolve the faith. But it is by their fruits they are known, and judged, and not by any theoretical claims that can be made about them.

For faiths are not really ever primarily doctrinal systems, however much they may sometimes seem to be evolving in the direction of ideologies. And it is not in the addition of a doctrine of Trinity to the basic doctrine of God that the Christian faith, as it came to be called, differs from Judaism or Islam. Much less does it differ from these by 'adding' one or two more pre-existent divine beings to the one God who is worshipped in all three great monotheistic religions of the West, as if *that* were the point of any of the binitarian or trinitarian theologies that are found in the Christian tradition. Jesus was a Jew; that was the identity of his humanity, his 'flesh', and there is not the slightest evidence that he ever intended to found a religion other than the one in which he was born. And Muslims, in fidelity to the teaching of their prophet, accept that in Jesus true *'islam'*, true obedience to the one, true God, found expression, except of course – and this is not altogether a ridiculous thing to assert – that the followers of Jesus soon corrupted the faith of Jesus and have continued to do so ever since. It seems sensible enough to suppose, then, that it is the purity of the distinctive praxis of true followers of Jesus that will show Jews that he is indeed the fulfilment of their faith, and show Muslims that his followers can still embody, as he did, true *'islam'*. And when that is shown, if it is ever shown, then Jews and Muslims will cease to think that Christians are adding further and indefensible doctrines, or that they are adding divine beings. They will then be able to see the primarily demonstrative function of Christian doctrine; they will actually see that to which the doctrines primarily point, the praxis embodied in living relations of grace – lived towards Jews and Muslims also, of course, as they have seldom been lived in the past – and the power of love embodied in the praxis in which they might then recognize the God of love in whom they too believe.[19]

APPENDIX

Anticipatory Incompletions

The word praxis has emerged rather late in this work, to play nevertheless a rather crucial role in its conclusion, and I am very conscious of the fact that not nearly enough has been done to define it sufficiently clearly or comprehensively for this purpose. The word has been related to a phrase from some modern phenomenology, 'the project towards the world which we are', and implicitly therefore and more specifically to Heidegger's 'thrown projection'. Now if this illustratory relationship, as I hope it is, is taken in conjunction with a few specific themes argued occasionally throughout the book, it should be possible to appreciate at one and the same time the temporary validity of the book's conclusion and the directions in which this Christian theory of praxis must be continued in order to test its meaningfulness and truth in those further areas which Christian theology in its systematic forms inevitably visits – ecclesiology, for instance, and moral theology. For the thrown projection which defines our human existence is, before reflective thought breaks it up by analysis, all at once visionary (perceptive-intellective), evaluative and practical, in a very comprehensive manner; that is to say, it already ranges from those depths or heights which can reasonably be called religious, to those very superficial appreciative yet desultory attachments by which we while away, or even waste, our time. And the themes which must be joined to this understanding of this phrase are, first, that all such thrown projections, even when viewed in their communal or social, rather than individual dimensions, are always concrete and specific, never general or abstract. In its theological form, this reads: there are religions, but there is no such thing in existence (though there is

in abstract thought) as religion in general. Second and consequently, praxis in this sense of the term is truly prior to theory;
prior, certainly to that more modern kind of philosophical theory
(in which philosophy is taken to be a 'second-order' study) which
reveals the possibility and something of the nature of human
thought and imagination at a level reasonably called religious,
but prior also to theological or doctrinal types of theory whose
principal function is to point out and to distinguish from others
the particular living relationship to the empirical world and its
history, and through this to a unique God, the particular kind of
life which, far more than any doctrine or theology, creed or code,
is of the essence of the religion in question. It is worthwhile,
however, to make separate mention of the critical function of
theory. Precisely because it is through the praxis in its pre-
reflective form that the distinctive power characteristic of a particular faith comes – in the case of Christianity this is the power
characterized by the lived relations of grace, a power made perfect
in weakness, a power of love which exudes the joy of incomprehensible gratitude especially in the process of giving and giving
up – there is sometimes the danger of waywardness or excess.
The critical function of theology, therefore, must monitor the kind
of happiness and the kind of salvation which the particular faith
promises. This will be a form of eschatalogical verification, as it is
sometimes called,[1] though not in the sense that one needs to wait
for after-life in order to attempt it – the quality of life on earth
provides an on-going criterion – and it will in the end contribute
to the demonstrative function which is the overall remit of doctrine
and theology, as reflective theory at its best enhances the freedom
of choice and the quality of commitment. At its worst, of course,
it contributes to waywardness, and indulges its own peculiarly
authoritarian forms of excess.

So the book concludes with the view that the doctrine of God in
general and trinitarian or binitarian doctrines in particular must
have their sense and partial nonsense assessed from within that
material relationship that binds them to the Christian life which
gives rise to them and which they in turn attempt to point to and
point out. (A similar relationship, though at a different level of
authority, we have seen, characterizes the Scriptures.) And some
hints have been given as to how this Christian life invites refor-
mulation today of the Christian doctrines of God which we have
inherited from the past. But this very conclusion, and those hints,

press the theological task towards a fuller and more detailed account of that Christian life in which Christians believe the characteristic power of the one, true God is palpable. And that fuller account is usually thought to comprise the ecclesiastical dimension and the ethical; or, if the present book dealt with creed, the fuller account comprises cult and code. Only when that fuller account is given can we truly assess the nature of the relations of grace which are at the heart of Christian convictions (outlined in christology) concerning the sonship and the faith of Jesus; and only then can we fully assess also the adequacy of the more comprehensive doctrines of God to which christologies inevitably lead.

Obviously in this appendix it would be impossible to supply all that such a full account would entail. Yet, if only to put a little bone into our conclusion and perhaps a little flesh on our anticipation of future systematic developments, let us visit briefly two topics: eucharist and creation. Eucharist because the celebratory sacrament is more of the essence of ecclesial existence than, say, the different institutional structures by which the various Christian bodies are organized. Creation, not because, where code is concerned, the 'natural-law' morality must be taken to be specifically Christian, but because, I want to argue, creation theory is neither an independent route to the knowledge of God nor yet an attempt to satisfy curiosity about temporal origin but a statement at its best of the specific kinds of relationship to and through our empirical world which is the heart and distinctive spirit of any religious morality; and in any case, like eucharist in the case of ecclesiology, creation theology does normally sit at the centre of doctrines about God.

It might seem as if we should have had also a section on experience – as so many books on God today do – and since it has not appeared so far, that it should be appended now. But a section on experience would only summarize once again much of what has already been said, and end, perhaps, in a *caveat* against those who, in the laudable effort to keep theology close to the practical lives of real people, talk too abstractly about general structures of human experience and seem to derive from these as abstract a notion of God as any ivory-tower philosopher ever issued.

(a) Eucharist

I would not want to give the impression that I attempt here to write a theology of the eucharist in a few pages, but I would like to illustrate at least the manner in which I think attention to the Christian eucharist could show how praxis, in this case sacramental praxis, can yield doctrines and how doctrines in turn can therefore be seen as pointers to orthopraxis.

A theology of the eucharist must begin with the teaching and preaching of the New Testament on the resurrection of Jesus. This stress on resurrection is not for any crude reason of 'providing' either a victim who could continuously be offered thereafter on earth or a priest who could continue to offer in heaven his once-and-for-all sacrifice on Calvary. Such theologies usually take too literally an ancient Jewish sacrificial symbolism once used to evoke the full significance of the death of Jesus. No, the starting-point of eucharistic theology must be the New Testament resurrection-kerygma, because so very much of that New Testament resurrection-material – and by no means merely appearances stories – occurs in clearly eucharistic context, so that the meaning of Jesus' 'appearing' or becoming present after death to his followers is obviously tied to the eucharistic practice and experience of the earliest churches to an extent seldom realized by writers on either eucharist or resurrection.[2] Luke's 'they recognized him in the breaking of bread' in his Emmaus story is more characteristic of New Testament views on resurrection than minds hardened by all the apologetic argument surrounding the resurrection are normally capable of perceiving. This surely suggests that, to an extent which we are normally ill-prepared to allow, it was in the eucharistic action that earliest followers met their Lord again, and (it follows inevitably) where eucharist is truly celebrated today, we can also enjoy an 'appearance' of our Lord, or what we have come to call his real presence. It would be important to follow up this New Testament lead by paying more attention to those patristic texts in which eucharist and resurrection are quite explicitly brought together for mutual explanation.[3]

It would then be important not to lose this first point of advance in some quasi-magical interpretation of early theological thought about the food or medicine of immortality. Here again a symbolism of a fruit or food of everlasting life that is older than Babylon is at work and, as usual, we best prevent ourselves from taking it too literally by joining it to different but equivalent symbolism. And along this route we must once again encounter Spirit-language as a common heritage of both resurrection preaching and eucharistic theology. The New Testament attribution of Jesus' risen and lordly status to the Spirit and, more particularly, Paul's theology of the risen Jesus as himself the life-giving Spirit, or, closer still, to the eucharistic theme of the body, his theology of Jesus and his followers forming the one body because the one Spirit animates both him and them, though it animates him as head and them as members,[4] all contributed to the patristic theology of eucharist and should contribute to it still; it showed the eucharist as an act in which the Fatherhood of God was actually experienced in the presence of Jesus' Spirit as that Spirit was embodied and 'specified' in the distinctive eucharistic act of *taking* (as gift or grace), *blessing* (God in thanks),[5] *breaking*, and *giving* the food and drink, the bread and wine, the very necessities of life itself and hence its universal symbols.

Too urgent an interest in proto-trinitarian doctrine might restrict attention in patristic eucharistic theology to those authors and texts in which, in a manner quite similar to broader 'binitarian' strains we have already noticed, it seems a matter of indifference whether one evokes Spirit or *Logos* upon the celebrating euchar-istic community and upon the bread and wine its members share.[6] At the other extreme, such complicated historical discussion surrounds such issues as the meaning of *anamnesis* (the 'memorial' factor in the eucharist), the gradual relegation of the *epiclesis* (the invocation, usually of the Spirit) in the West, with a consequent stress on the 'declaratory' force of the words of institution ('This is my body . . .') and an unhealthy interest in the moment of consecration of elements rather than people,[7] that attention is almost inevitably distracted from the one issue which interests us here, namely, the way in which our very participatory experience of the eucharistic sacrament can yield our doctrines of the God we believe we there encounter; the way in which these doctrines at their best point to a concrete praxis, in this case Christian euchar-ist, in which we encounter the one, true God. So let us risk the following short-cut to a solution to these issues, simply for the sake of the illustration we need.

First, *anamnesis* has many meanings, one or more of which may be uppermost in any particular usage. In the words of Max Thurian:

The verb *zâkar* . . . occupies an important place in the cultic language of Judaism. Its different meanings may be summarized thus: to think of something known and past, a material something, a sin or the blessing of God; to recall a duty; in reference to God, to recall man's sin, the covenant, love and fidelity; in reference to man, to recall God or to invoke Him; to recall something in favour of someone or against him; to recall something to someone (e.g. the needs of the people of God); to utter a name (that of God); and finally, to recall before or remind God by means of a sacrifice and especially the memorial of incense.[8]

Second, Jesus himself in his life, death and destiny recollected and reminded God of the whole history of his people, and of God's history of loving-kindness to his people, and especially in his own table fellowship he dramatically recollected and reminded God of God's unconditioned grace incarnate in his own life, taken, thanked for, broken and given.[9] And those who continued his table fellowship recollected and reminded God of Jesus' life and of the death in which it was consummated, and so invoked the presence of God as the Spirit of Jesus in their midst as they again took, and thanked, and broke, and gave.

Thirdly, *anamnesis* and *epiclesis*, rather than being two separate moments in eucharist which have to be reconciled or at least given equal weight, are in reality two aspects of the same act.[10] For every human act which is referred to God is by nature invocatory. *Epiclesis* makes explicit the invocation, the plea for effective presence in the recollection-reminder (or re-presentation) which is called *anamnesis*.

Fourthly, it is in the eucharistic celebration as a whole – in the people, the people's prayer and the use the people make of the particular elements[11] – that *anamnesis* and *epiclesis* simultaneously take place and the 'appearance' of the Lord Jesus, the presence of the life-giving Spirit occurs, if it does occur, to make of the people the body of Christ extended through history, and make of the bread and wine taken, broken, poured and given in thanksgiving, the sacrament of the body of Christ, that is to say, the sign which effects this in the world.

In taking or receiving life, of which bread and wine are both staff and symbol, as grace or gift; in giving them to the point of breaking and pouring out; one is encountering in ritual act the particular power in which one believes God to be present in this world and through which one hopes God can be reached. Provided, of course – for this also is characteristic of Jesus' table fellowship – one breaks the bread and shares the cup with all without condition, enemy as well as friend. Otherwise it is not the Lord's Supper that one celebrates and one does not yet know the body of Christ. The power one encounters is God's word or spirit which takes the 'shape' of Jesus' life and person, of Jesus' death. It is a power that can be characterized in general terms as unconditioned grace, love, or more precisely joyful, giving love, self-sacrificing love, and so on. However, it is not in these general terms that it is encountered, but, ritually at least, in the act of breaking bread with the outcast and the sinner, that is to say, with everyman. Here, in cult, is the specificity of detail in Christian praxis which gives to doctrines of God their peculiarly Christian content and to which these doctrines in turn, if they are to succeed, must direct us. For doctrines of Father Gods, divine Sons and divine Spirits are themselves quite general, as the history of religions shows.

From this brief excursus on eucharist it is possible once again to see what a variety of both binitarian and trinitarian doctrines one could use to point to the power-in-praxis in which Christians believe and hope they encounter the one true God. The people encounter God in this eucharistic act as the life-giving Spirit of Jesus his Son, or as the life-giving Spirit who is Jesus, his Son, and they are thus transformed into the body of Christ in history.

(b) Creation

Patristic theology of the eucharist at times forges quite illuminating links with creation theology. Indeed creation, incarnation, resurrection and eucharist are at different times drawn together by common strands of Spirit and Word so as to make a comprehensive and satisfying pattern of religious belief.[12] We cannot, of course, afford to trace and analyse such a pattern here. But it does serve our purpose to note just this point from the pattern: that the participatory experience of the ritual act of eucharist gives access to the meaning of the theological doctrine of creation, so that the proper primacy of praxis over theory is maintained even in the case of what might otherwise seem the most primary doctrine of all.

This does not mean, however, that one must accept the thesis which Von Rad outlined in his *Old Testament Theology* and which has been accepted by many theologians since then, namely, that creation-faith arrives on the Old Testament scene as a derivative extrapolation of more primitive and quite particular experiences of God's saving acts in favour of the Israelite nation.[13] Nor is the only alternative to *this* in turn Schillebeeckx's contrary insistence that creation-faith is assumption and background to all the more specific salvation-history beliefs of both Old and New Testaments.[14] And we certainly do not wish to end up back in those dichotomous distinctions between natural and revealed theology (creation and redemption, nature and grace) which are of any real value only in obsolescent Protestant-Catholic polemics. We must continue to insist instead that the truth, as Hegel saw, is always concrete, as is falsehood, as indeed are those mixtures of truth and falsehood which are more familiar to us than either pure truth or, if this is possible, absolute falsehood. Hence the Christian doctrine of creation must take its specific content from the concreteness of specifically Christian praxis, and point to this praxis in turn. And Christians will not attempt to point, through creation, to any God other than the one to whose power and presence they point in doctrines of God such as the trinitarian doctrines.

Not even the doctrine of creation out of nothing, *creatio ex nihilo*, therefore, specifies what is distinctively Christian belief in God. The presence of such a doctrine in some pagan Greek readings of the *Timaeus*, for instance, together with the variety of meaning of which 'nothing' in patristic times was patient, sees to that. And one cannot read far in early Christian polemics against the Greeks – especially if one weeds out those arguments which seem to be based merely on misconception of what the other side is saying[15] – without coming to the conclusion that what was radically at issue between them was the extent to which they could manage to believe in the goodness of this empirical world and of all that is or happens in it. Roughly speaking, those Greeks who speculated about the uncreatedness of matter seem to have done so in an effort to exonerate a God who was good from all possible complicity in evil, for matter, they thought, was intractable to a point before good intent. And those Christian polemicists are best whose insistence on *creatio ex nihilo* is evidently a means to the confession of their faith that, since *everything* comes to us as gift or grace from the hands of God, *all* is good as the Genesis story of creation insists, and there is in this world no ontological dualism of good and evil. But such a comprehensive and radical (indeed foolhardy!) faith is itself accessible only through a specific en-

259

counter with a very distinctive kind of power or presence; it is only accessible through a very particular experience of praxis. Eucharist with its taking as grace, blessing God, breaking, and giving, is a cultic experience of just such a praxis. But the kind of living which is celebrated in eucharist and which eucharist invokes and enables, the distinctive morality of the common Christian life which holds all as gift or grace, is the more comprehensive praxis from which the Christian theology of creation arises and to which in turn it points. As this kind of living is worked out in an evolving morality which covers all the basic relationships – economic, familial, political, and so on – the Christian doctrine of creation takes characteristic flesh on its bones.

No religion can take over a creation story unaltered from another. There is no common belief in God as Creator any more than there is any other form of belief common to actual religions. The Israelites took over many of the terms of Babylonian myth, but forged from them their own distinctive creation myth, the one which now opens the Bible. The Christians in turn had the extraordinary courage and insight to point to a crucified Jew and to say that in him and through him and for him God created the world. They were thus pointing to a praxis, to a power that came to them through the crucified Jew which enabled them to cherish everything and everyone as gift from God, and they were saying simultaneously that this power (or Spirit) was God and what they believed God to be like.

In his introduction to *Being and Nothingness* Sartre wrote: 'One can conceive of a *creation* on condition that the created being recover itself, tear itself away from the creator in order to close in on itself immediately and assume its being.' It is obvious that he meant this to be a criticism of Christian belief in a Creator God, for he adds almost immediately: 'if the act of creation is to be continued indefinitely, if the created being is to be supported even in its inmost parts, if it does not have its own independence, if it is *in itself* only nothingness – then the creature is in no way distinguished from its creator; it is absorbed in him; we are dealing with a false transcendence, and the creator cannot have even the illusion of getting out of his subjectivity' (pp. 19–20). Now Sartre seemed unable to set his powerful conviction about freedom into an experience of grace – hence the other is always a threat to me – and this may be partly because he had experienced the Christian God through Christians as a dominating, pervading, and invading power. And yet one can almost see from the first sentence quoted from his work above that if he had had an experience of the radical conviction of grace in praxis, he would have easily arrived at a quite different, indeed a truly Christian theology of the God already crucified in creation. For if the Christian story of creation were retold out of the intense experience of specifically Christian praxis, it would not present a portrait of a God who *made* all things to be by the irresistible force of omnipotent will, and thereafter held them in the most intimate ontological dependence, under threat of nothing less than *annihilation*. No: for the meanest thing to which God gave being can never again be nothing to God.

Our story is that God loved. Confused, however, by the many kinds of loving which we know, we find it difficult to tell how he loves. Disappointed by the world, we tend to think that God loves one or more so utterly like (better, one-in-being with) himself, that his love has a perfection we cannot understand – but 'through' this second (and third) divine 'person', God 'afterwards' creates and loves us. Is this the Christian story? Not really. Not if we keep our eyes on the crucified Jew. Rather, in the beginning, *en arche*, God's love was creative, giving, giving existence to things that were not, life-giving. It was God's love, not another power of his, that created the world. And Sartre in his way, from his own experience of creativity, saw what that love was like, the price it had to pay, but, we may believe, paid joyfully. It had to let be and to let go. Further, since all but God himself is mortal, it had to let die. At creation itself death enters into God's necessary experience, the death of loved ones. The passion that is at the heart of the world, focussed in the death of the most insignificant mite, celebrated in the invocatory memorial of the death of Jesus, is, as much as Moltmann could ever wish, the passion of God. And a properly construed *Christian* creation-story would make that clear.

The passion of God is not a love of like for like, secure within the bounds of a pre-existent Holy Family; it is not sheltered in the slightest degree by intervening pre-existent divine 'persons' from full exposure to disintegrating creatures. Rather, in its very exposure, in the unflagging faithfulness of its loving-kindness, is its specific power, the power made perfect in weakness, the only power that can overcome death and destruction in the end. This divine *eros* found its fullest incarnation in the life and death of Jesus of Nazareth. The story of Calvary is thus the story of

261

creation. The Spirit of re-creative love, of grace, breathed on Calvary can alone bring the creature to God in this world or in any other there may be, for it alone is for God. God lives also, therefore, in hope.[16]

Notes

Introduction

1. London: SCM Press 1979; New York, Paulist Press 1979.
2. Even if one were to judge only from the controversies that have recently raged around it.
3. Martin Hengel, *The Son of God*, London: SCM Press 1976, p. 2.
4. K. Rahner, *The Trinity*, New York: Herder and Herder and London: Burns and Oats 1970, p. 42.

Part One: The Present

1. London: Pemberton 1972.
2. This last phrase forms the title of one of Schubert Ogden's essays in his *The Reality of God and other Essays*, New York: Harper and Row 1964, and London: SCM Press, pp. 120ff. Indeed the essay in question offers a short standard example of this kind of religious apologetic.
3. See A. J. Ayer, *Language, Truth and Logic*, London: Victor Gollancz 1946, pp. 114–120. A more explicit acknowledgment of the hope in science was made by Athony Flew, in 'The Presumption of Stratonician Atheism', a paper read to the Irish Theological Association in January, 1971.
4. John Dewey, *A Common Faith*, Yale University Press 1934.
5. In the epistemological order (*ordo cognoscendi*), clashes about meaning and truth are seen as the basis of clashes about commitment to particular values, and these in turn as the basis of different attitudes and active orientations in life. In the real order (*ordo essendi*) the reverse is most often the case.
6. J. P. Sartre, *Being and Nothingness*, New York: Washington Square Press 1966, pp. 19–20, 26–27.
7. See J. P. Sartre, *Existentialism and Humanism*, London: Methuen 1966, p. 56. The moral counterpart of this statement is found in Sartre's play *The Flies*, when Orestes realizes, in his scene with Zeus, that his new-found freedom makes Zeus irrelevant.

263

8. See T. B. Bottomore, *Karl Marx: Early Writings*, New York: McGraw-Hill 1964, pp. 1ff.

9. I have given here a very free paraphrase of Marx's main argument, using a very free 'translation' of some of his own technical terms, but I believe I have not misrepresented him, and I excuse the liberties taken on the grounds that I want only to illustrate briefly the predominance of his positive humanistic motives over any that were polemical and anti-religious.

10. 'The criticism of religion is essentially complete,' he wrote in his *Contribution to the Critique of Hegel's Philosophy of Right* 'and the criticism of religion is the presupposition of all criticism'. 'Religion is indeed the self-consciousness and self-awareness of man who either has not yet attained himself or has already lost himself again. But (referring to the humanistic critique of Feuerbach) man is no abstract being squatting outside the world. Man is the world of man, the state, society.' See D. McLellan, *Karl Marx; Selected Writings*, Oxford University Press 1977, p. 63.

11. Contrast, for instance, Harvey Cox and Jürgen Moltmann in their contributions to Ernest Bloch, *Man On His Own*, New York: Herder and Herder 1971. Cox in his Foreword writes, 'For Bloch, atheism is no issue' (p. 15); whereas Moltmann in his introduction declares 'There is an atheism for God's sake, like Bloch's' (p. 28)!

12. See K. Marx & F. Engels, *On Religion*, Moscow: Foreign Languages Publishing House 1955, pp.297, 298, 313.

13. The more determinist interpretation of Marx's philosophy of man is often based, for example, on the following text from Marx's critique of Hegel's *Philosophy of Right* (with its over-worked 'basis-superstructure' image): 'In the social production of their existence, men inevitably enter into definite relations, which are independent of their will, namely, relations of production appropriate to a given stage in the development of their material forces of production. The totality of these relations of production constitutes the economic structure of society, the real foundation, on which arises a legal and political superstructure, and to which correspond definite forms of social consciousness.' Nicholas Lash quotes this passage in his book *A Matter of Hope: A Theologian's Reflections on the Thought of Karl Marx*, London: Darton, Longman and Todd, 1981, p. 115, and argues very persuasively against the determinist interpretation. A useful argument for continuity between the earlier and the later Marx can also be found in Robert C. Tucker, *Philosophy and Myth in Karl Marx*, Cambridge University Press 1972, and David McLellan's lecture to the 1980 (Oxford) Conference of the Society for the Study of Theology, entitled 'Marx's Concept of Human Nature', of which I make use in this section, can also be cited in support.

14. Marx & Engels, *On Religion*, p. 41.

15. Taken from McLellan's lecture 'Marx's Concept of Human Nature', p. 6.

16. Marx & Engels, *On Religion*, p. 42.

17. See H. Desroche, *Marxisme et Religions*, Paris: Presses Universitaires de France 1962, p. 120. For a fuller account of Marx's view on religion than could be expected here, Desroche can be recommended. Also Nicholas Lash's book, *A Matter of Hope*, offers a fine critical account of the limitations of Marx's critique of religion, together with a very creative attempt to depict the kind of Christian religion which could respond to Marx's prophetic vision. One might consult also Arend T. van Leeuven, *Critique of Heaven*, New York: Charles Scribner's Sons 1972.

18. Much of Ernst Bloch's masterpiece *Das Prinzip Hoffnung*, which was published in Frankfurt in 1959, has been made available to the English speaking world in such selections of Bloch's writing as *Spirit of Utopia*, New York: Herder and Herder 1969; *A Philosophy of the Future*, New York: Herder and Herder 1970; *On Karl Marx*, New York: Herder and Herder 1971; and *Man On His Own*, New York: Herder and Herder 1971.

19. Bloch, *Man On His Own*, p. 143.

20. Bloch, *Man On His Own*, p. 144: the phrase in brackets is mine.

21. Bloch, *Man On His Own*, p. 146.

22. Albert Camus, *The Rebel*, London: Peregrine Books 1962, p. 224. These words appear in a section entitled 'Rebellion and Art', and it would be interesting to ask how many have looked to art to find an access other than the religious to the understanding of transcendence. For even those who feel the need to be shriven do not always welcome the Christian prospect of after-life. Towards the end of *Lolita* (Weidenfeld & Nicolson 1959) Vladimir Nabokov wrote: 'Alas, I was unable to transcend the simple human fact that whatever spiritual solace I might find, whatever lithophanic eternities might be provided for me, nothing could make my Lolita forget the foul lust I had inflicted upon her. Unless it can be proven to me – to me as I am now, today, with my heart and my beard and my putrefaction – that in the infinite run it does not matter a jot that a North American girl-child called Dolores Haze had been deprived of her childhood by a maniac, unless this can be proven (and if it can, then life is a joke), I see nothing for the treatment of my misery but the melancholy and very local palliative of articulate art. To quote an old poet

> The moral sense in mortals is the duty
> We have to pay on mortal sense of beauty.'

23. See Sartre, *Existentialism and Humanism*, p. 46.

24. See Sartre, *Existentialism and Humanism*. pp. 55–6.

25. Charles Hartshorne, *A Natural Theology for Our Time*, La Salle; Open Court Press 1967, preface.

26. See Barth's famous *Nein! Antwort an Emil Brunner*, in English translation in E. Brunner, K. Barth, *Natural Theology*, London: Geoffrey Bles 1946.

27. For this contemporary variation on an ancient theme see R. G. Swinburne, *The Existence of God*, Oxford: Clarendon Press 1979. Amongst the members of the group to which reference is now made the rejection of the old metaphysical approaches to God's existence is often quite

uncompromising. Ogden, for instance, describes traditional supernaturalistic theism as both 'theoretically incoherent' and 'existentially repugnant' (*The Reality of God*, p. 18).

28. Langdon Gilkey has this to say of the neo-orthodox approach: 'neo-orthodox theology presupposed a stark and real separation between the Church and the world, between belief and unbelief, between the Word of God and the secular. . . But the actual situation was by no means characterized by any such clear and distinct separation: the world was within the Church, belief was saturated by secular doubt, and no one, either in pew or in pulpit, was sure a divine Word had been heard at all or a divine presence manifested' (*Naming the Whirlwind*, New York: Bobbs-Merrill 1969, p. 102).

29. Sartre, *Being and Nothingness*, p. 29.

30. *Naming the Whirlwind*, p. 38.

31. Hans Küng, *On Being a Christian*, New York: Doubleday and London: Collins 1976, pp. 69ff.

32. Karl Rahner, *Foundations of Christian Faith: An Introduction to the Idea of Christianity*, New York: The Seabury Press and London: Darton, Longman and Todd 1978, esp. p. 53.

33. *Naming the Whirlwind*, p. 362. Facetiously once more, is this the Argument for God's Existence by Threat? More seriously, Karl Jasper's rejection of this line of approach surely applies equally to a kind of philosophy of religion which is otherwise close to his own: 'These facile alternatives of revealed faith of nihilism, of total science or illusion, serve as weapons of spiritual intimidation' (*The Perennial Scope of Philosophy*, London: Routledge and Kegan Paul 1950, p. 8).

34. *Naming the Whirlwind*, p. 362.

35. *Blessed Rage for Order*, New York: The Seabury Press, 1975. Tracy does not appear to think that this affirmative attitude in itself establishes the truth of the thesis that God exists. For this he requires the crowning efficacy of the ontological argument (which he believes will work once we adopt Hartshorne's revision of the concept of God), to complete arguments from partial intelligibility to intelligent ground and so on (*Blessed Rage for Order*, esp. pp. 184ff.). Two comments. As I have already hinted, changes in ways of describing God may make the idea of God more palatable in itself, but will not yet answer the modern question about the need or possibility to believe in God at all. And then, if we are to crown arguments from contingent existence, achieved meaning, and partial value in this way, how far are we really from the metaphysical approaches of the ancients, and what is now the credibility of the much-trumpeted demise of 'classical theism'? Classical theism, after all, contains quite a variety of reasons for belief in God, and if it were thoroughly understood rather than caricatured, could easily enough encompass the substantial arguments of books such as Tracy's.

36. *The Reality of God*, p. 37.

37. *The Reality of God*, p. 196.

38. *On Being a Christian*, pp. 69ff.

39. Rahner, *Foundations of Christian Faith*, pp. 170, 194, 246ff.

40. *The Reality of God*, p. 203.

41. *Naming the Whirlwind*, part II, section on 'Christian Discourse About God'.

42. *Blessed Rage for Order*, p. 45. He objects to Tillich's method of correlations (see Paul Tillich, *Systematic Theology*, I, University of Chicago Press 1953), partly on the grounds that it does not consider Sartre's answer to the existential question. But is there any greater reason why Tracy, for instance, should not consider more favourably Sartre's whole understanding of the experience of secularity?

43. *Blessed Rage for Order*, p. 9.

44. *Blessed Rage for Order*, p. 222.

45. G. W. F. Hegel, *Lectures on the Philosophy of Religion*, London: Routledge and Kegan Paul 1962, Vol. I, pp. 30–32. For some fuller details see my *Jesus, the Man and the Myth*, pp. 25ff.

46. Calvin, *Institutes of the Christian Religion*, Philadelphia: Westminster Press 1960, p. 122.

47. Hartshorne, *A Natural Theology For Our Time*, pp. 44–5.

48. *Blessed Rage for Order*, p. 174.

49. *The Reality of God*, p. 141.

50. See Moltmann's introduction to Bloch's *Man On His Own*.

51. I am making use of *The Holy Qur-an*, Text, Translation and Commentary by Abdullah Yusuf Ali, New York: McGregor and Werner 1946.

52. In his commentary on Sura III, 23: 'Hast thou not turned thy vision to those who have been given a portion of the Book,' Ali writes, 'I conceive that God's revelation as a whole throughout the ages is "The Book". The Law of Moses and the Gospel of Jesus were portions of the Book. The Qur-an completes the revelation and is *par excellence* the Book of God.'

53. The *Holy Qur-an* in Sura V, 76 does say: 'They do blaspheme who say: God is one of three in a Trinity: for there is no God except one God,' and in Sura IV, 136: 'Say not "Trinity": desist; it will be better for you.'

54. Geza Vermes, *Jesus the Jew: A Historian's Reading of the Gospels*, London: Collins 1973, p. 17.

55. *Jesus the Jew*, pp. 15–16.

56. *Jesus the Jew*, p. 225.

57. Joseph Klausner, *Jesus of Nazareth*, London: Allen and Unwin 1925, p. 414.

58. H. J. Schoeps, *Paul*, London: Lutterworth 1961, p. 158.

59. Samuel Sandmel, *We Jews and Jesus*, London: Oxford University Press 1965.

60. Sura II, 62.

61. Sura IV, 171. See also Sura IV, 157; Sura III, 45.

62. Sura IV, 20.

63. Sura IV, 171.

64. Sura V, 19.

65. Sura III, 59. See also Sura III, 47, where the virgin birth is treated as an act of creation.

66. Sura V, 119.

67. Sura IV, 172.

68. Sura III, 51.

69. Sura III, 55.

70. Sura VI, 19.

71. Al Shariati's *Maktab-Vaseteh* (which was published in 1955 by the Society for the Propagation of Islamic Truth) is an interesting alternative 'Marxist'-type account of the universality of the basically humanist truth of the *Holy Qur-an*.

Part Two: The Scriptures

1. For a tolerable account of differences between early trinitarian theologies, but one which is embedded in a questionable theory of development of doctrine, see B. Lonergan, *The Way to Nicea*, London: Darton, Longman and Todd and Philadelphia: Westminster Press 1976.

2. See H. Küng and J. Moltmann (eds.), *Conflicts About the Holy Spirit*, New York: Seabury Press 1979.

3. A very small sample of these differences is all that can be offered here. The Roman Synod of AD 382 used the terms *unius substantiae* and *tres personas*, though it felt the former could be helped out by *unius potestatis* (59). The creed *Quicumque* of the fifth or sixth century also uses *substantia* for the oneness and *persona* for the distinct entities within it (39). But the Lateran Council of AD 649 preferred to profess *unum Deum in tribus subsistentiis consubstantialibus* (254), and though the term *persona* for each of the Three enjoys a relatively consistent usage in Latin formulae until the more recent challenges emerge in modern times, *substantia* is sometimes replaced and very frequently supplemented. The Council of Toledo in AD 675 talked of *unius substantia, unius naturae*, as if these terms did not differ (275); the Fourth Lateran Council of AD 1215 took up Peter Lombard's phrase *quaedam summa res* (431), and the Decree for the Jacobites in 1441 ran riot with phrases it apparently thought equivalent: *una substantia, una essentia, una natura, una divinitas, una immensitas, una aeternitas, omnia sunt unum, ubi non obviat relationis oppositio (703)*. This last clause implies that the decree sees the inner divine distinctions in terms of the oppositiness of relationships. And so on. Numbers in brackets above refer to H. Denzinger, *Enchiridion Symbolorum*, Rome: Herder 1965.

4. See G. Van Noort, *De Deo Uno et Trino*, Holland: Brand 1954.

5. F. Ceuppens, *De Sanctissima Trinitate*, Taurini 1949.

6. E. Brunner, *The Christian Doctrine of God (Dogmatics*, Vol. I), London: Lutterworth Press and Philadelphia: Westminster Press 1950, pp. 206–7.

7. *The Christian Doctrine of God*, p. 216.

8. *The Christian Doctrine of God*, p. 223.

9. *The Christian Doctrine of God*, p. 224.

10. *The Christian Doctrine of God*, p. 226. More recently Cyril C. Richard-

son has gone as far as Brunner, though from a different starting point and in a different direction. Scripture, he maintains, makes no genuine distinctions between the work of Logos, Wisdom, Son, and Spirit. All refer interchangeably to God's activity and revelation in creation. Trinitarian theology is therefore quite unnecessary, although its symbolism may be of some use in worship and devotion: *The Doctrine of the Trinity*, Nashville: Abingdon Press 1958.

11. K. Barth, *Church Dogmatics*, I, 1, Edinburgh: T. & T. Clark 1936, p. 355; 'We designate the doctrine of the Trinity as the interpretation of revelation, or revelation as the ground of the doctrine of the Trinity.' Also, 'we find revelation itself so attested in Holy Scripture that our understanding of revelation (which is related to this testimony), i.e., of the self-revealing God, must be this very doctrine of the Trinity' (p. 359). This leaves us free, of course, in Barth's view, to pick and choose amongst, and to improve upon, the various theological formulations of the doctrine which Christian history has left us.

12. See Barth's section on *Vestigium Trinitatis* in *Church Dogmatics*, I, 1, (1936), pp. 383ff.

13. Barth, *Church Dogmatics*, I, 1 (1936), p. 368–372, 381.

14. *Church Dogmatics*, I, 1 (1936), p. 348.

15. I am not sure if this is *the* teaching of the Bible (if the Bible ever claims that God reveals *himself*) or, if it is, how far it excludes the possibility of any thing, person, or event in this world being itself or intrinsically a revelation of God, but I find illuminating the following combination of sentences from E. Jüngel, *The Doctrine of the Trinity: God's Being is in Becoming*, Grand Rapids: Eerdmans 1976. pp. 24 and 22: 'God corresponds to himself. In actuality Barth's *Dogmatics* is basically a detailed exegesis of this proposition'; 'the doctrine of the Trinity in Barth's theology has the same function as the programme of demythologising in the theology of Rudolf Bultmann'.

16. *Church Dogmatics*, I, 1 (1936), p. 344.

17. See Barth's section on Appropriation, *Church Dogmatics*, I, 1 (1936), esp. p. 429.

18. A great deal has been written on this disputed topic, but for a balanced Roman Catholic view of the matter one could do worse than read G. Tavard, *Holy Writ or Holy Church*, London: Burns and Oates 1959, or, better still, Tavard's two chapters in Joseph E. Kelly (ed.), *Perspectives on Scripture and tradition*, Notre Dame: Fides Publishers 1976.

19. How many other Calvinists, one wonders, would accept Barth's reasons for acknowledging the normative role of Scripture? See his *Church Dogmatics*, I, 2 (1936), pp. 485–6, 508–9, 515–519.

20. Although the image of divine dictation is sometimes used to give striking expression to the normative status itself and to the manner in which it is to be respected, it is not thought to offer an account of the manner in which the Bible's normative status arose, or of the manner in which the Bible itself arose. See E. A. Dowey, *The Knowledge of God in Calvin's Theology*, Columbia University Press 1965, p. 102. Also on the

general point made in this paragraph see J. K. S. Reid, *The Authority of Scripture*, London: Methuen 1957, p. 63.

21. *Jesus, the Man and the Myth*, pp. 147ff. See also the chapter on 'Christian Faith and Human History'.

22. J. D. G. Dunn, *Jesus and the Spirit*, London: SCM Press and Philadelphia: Westminster Press 1975, p. 325.

23. I dealt all too briefly with some of these distinctions in *Jesus, the Man and the Myth*, pp. 75–82, 214–17, though in the latter pages, as Nicholas Lash kindly pointed out to me, I engaged in some very uncritical uses of the word 'literal', uses which in fact did not accord with my own earlier image of the spectrum of human perception and expression, a spectrum which ranges from the most concrete to the most abstract with, by implication at least, most human perception and expression falling somewhere in between.

24. See below, p. 153.

25. Hengel, *The Son of God*, p. 3.

26. *The Son of God*, p. 1.

27. *The Son of God*, p. 15.

28. Main texts on 'Son of God' in Paul's letters noted here are: Rom. 1.3, 4, 9; 8.3, 29, 32; Gal. 1.15f.; 4.4f.; II Cor. 1.18f.; I Cor. 1.9; 15.28.

29. *The Son of God*, p. 15.

30. Ibid.

31. *The Son of God*, p. 60.

32. Ibid.

33. *Jesus the Jew*.

34. Gen. 6.2, 4; Deut. 32.8; Ps. 29.1; 89.7; Dan. 3.25.

35. Ex. 4.22; Jer. 31.20; Hos. 11.1; Deut. 32.5–6, 18–19.

36. II Sam. 7.14; Ps. 2.7; 89. 26–27.

37. *Jesus the Jew*, p. 195. Texts include Ecclesiasticus 4.10; Wisdom 2.17–18; Book of Jubilees 1.24–25; Psalms of Solomon 17.26–27; some texts from Philo and some rabbinic material.

38. *Jesus the Jew*, p. 200.

39. Oscar Cullmann, surely one of the more conservative of modern exegetes, thought that, though Jesus was certainly conscious of bearing the title (he refers to the scenes of baptism and transfiguration), it is not at all certain that he ever applied it to himself. Jesus' probable reticence in this respect can be explained, Cullmann suggests, by the common use of the title, its sometimes spectacular overtones, and by the fact that he was conscious of bearing it in a very special way. See his chapter on this title in *The Christology of the New Testament*, London: SCM Press 1959.

40. *Jesus the Jew*, p. 211.

41. Ferdinand Hahn, *The Titles of Jesus in Christology: Their History in Early Christianity*, London: Lutterworth Press 1969, p. 311.

42. *The Son of God*, p. 63. Hengel weakens his case, however, by offering as evidence of this unique filial relationship, not Jesus' life as evidenced for instance in his identification with sinners and the oppressed, but the alleged uniqueness of Jesus' use of 'Abba', the unique-

ness of which Vermes quite correctly challenges: see *Jesus the Jew*, pp. 210–11.

43. More detail on this life of Jesus, which was his lived faith, can be found in *Jesus, the Man and the Myth*.

44. *Jesus the Jew*, pp. 201ff. Hengel, with acknowledgment of the work of Vermes, also points to this root of the title in Palestinian Judaism: *Son of God*, pp. 41ff. So does Hahn, except that he develops the material in terms of the relationship of Son and Spirit, a relationship which must occupy our own attention soon: *The Titles of Jesus*, p. 294.

45. *The Titles of Jesus*, p. 288. His main texts for this use of 'Son of God' are Mark 14.61f.; Luke 1.32f.; I Thess. 1.9f.

46. *Jesus the Jew*, p. 211.

47. *Jesus the Jew*, p. 199.

48. *The Titles of Jesus*, p. 288.

49. Hengel thinks one of the historical reasons for the application of the title 'Son of God' to Jesus may have been that it was possible to translate the Hebrew *ebed* by the Greek *pais* and then interpret the latter as 'son': *The Son of God*, p. 66. This is another indication of the life of obedience unto death as the primary source and meaning of the title.

50. Hengel even finds a Jewish parallel to this idea of exaltation and transformation into a heavenly being in the so-called Third Hebrew Book of Enoch, but allows that pre-existence is still not present at this point: *The Son of God*, p. 47.

51. Hengel, *The Son of God*, p. 71; Hahn, *The Titles of Jesus*, p. 304. Hahn, however, in this context, and quite inexplicably in my view, regards Rom. 8.3 – God sending his Son in the likeness of sinful flesh (Hahn leaves out the word *hamartias* when he quotes the Greek) – as a text which adds the idea of incarnation to the idea of sending thus giving the latter 'an entirely new accent'. I cannot at all see how he can say of this text: 'What is put allusively in Gal 4.4. . . is made plain in Rom. 8.3. . . in such a way that the divine and human natures are set in an appropriate relation to one another.' Reading a two-nature doctrine into such texts is surely as proud a piece of eisegesis as anyone could easily envisage.

52. *Jesus the Jew*, p. 137. Hengel also appeals to this notion in his attempt to explain the derivation of the pre-existence of his alleged divine figure who became man: *The Son of God*, p. 71.

53. *Jesus the Jew*, pp. 138–9.

54. *The Son of God*, p. 69.

55. R. H. Fuller, *The Foundations of New Testament Christology*, London: Lutterworth Press 1965. See his section on Hellenistic Gentile titles for Jesus, which he believes do contain the idea of pre-existence, but then he adds that this is myth and is thus, presumably, not to be read as if a 'real' pre-existent figure were in question.

56. *The Son of God*, p. 72. Hengel even suggests an analogy between Ben Sira 24 and the hymn in Philippians.

57. Hahn talks even more strongly about divine sonship in the physical sense and, as we saw in a previous note, about divine and human

natures, and sees pre-existence texts as a major step towards sonship of nature rather than of function in the New Testament: *The Titles of Jesus*, pp. 299ff. The eisegesis at this point is truly massive.

58. London: SCM Press 1980.

59. Mark 1.11; 9.7; 12.6 and parallels.

60. John 1.18; 1.14: 3.16, 18: I John 4.9.

61. Schillebeeckx, *Christ*, p. 875 n. 57.

62. And it is significant that in Revelation this is obviously just a name by which, as Schillebeeckx puts it, 'we Christians call him' (*Christ*, p. 444), for the previous verse in Revelation insists that 'he has a name inscribed which no one knows but himself'. Only at the parousia shall we really know who Jesus is to God. Here again we are dealing with Jesus in God's mind or eternal plan, ideal or eschatalogical pre-existence, as it might be called. That which will be consummated through Jesus is to us future, but ever-present to God in his eternity, or, as we are forced to express such things, before us and before all things like us created. So does Revelation relativize even the title 'Word' to our transient ways of knowing Jesus' 'name' or 'being' *vis-à-vis* what Jesus ('already') is and is known to be to God.

63. Philo in particular proves the feasibility of this model. See Hengel, *The Son of God*, p. 53; Schillebeeckx, *Christ*, p. 353.

64. *Christ*, p. 363.

65. *Christ*, p. 323.

66. See, for example, Schillebeeckx's summary section on 'The Person of Jesus in Johannine Theology: the son', *Christ*, pp. 427–32.

67. Schillebeeckx's efforts to find parallels in Jewish literature for these Johannine texts (*Christ*, pp. 384ff.) are rather diffuse and eclectic and in need of much more precision in order to be fully convincing. For a brief treatment of 'I am' texts and an indication of further relevant literature see David Mealand, 'The Christology of the Fourth Gospel', *The Scottish Journal of Theology* 31, 1978, pp. 464–5.

68. Schillebeeckx, *Christ*, pp. 168–77. The case for the pre-existence interpretation of the Philippians hymn – where it is thought necessary to put a case rather that simply assume a conclusion – usually centres on the phrases *en morphe Theou* and *to einai isa Theo*, and on the double sequence of self-emptying followed by self-humbling. But there is scarcely enough difference between the Greek words *eikon* and *morphe* to prevent us from seeing in the Genesis creation and garden stories the source of our two phrases: man created in God's image and likeness and grasping after some status of equality with God ('become like one of us', 'be like God': Gen. 2.5, 22). Messiah Jesus, the subject of the hymn, by contrast with kingly Messiahs and in particular with their traditional Adamic imagery, empties himself in this life (see the temptation stories) of such god-like status and, appearing as the most ordinary, indeed the most obscure of mortals, he humbles himself further to die a slave's death. The hymn itself gives rise to no need to contrast a pre-existent emptying with an 'existent' self-humbling (and it is not irrelevant to remark that no kenotic

theology along such lines has ever quite succeeded) – though I admit that this conclusion follows best on a certain punctuation in the translation of the hymn. I have punctuated by following most slavishly my Greek text of the New Testament.

69. Hengel is right to maintain that no intrusion of a Hellenizing concept of a 'real' pre-existent Son of God destroys the continuity of the biblical traditions. But this conclusion follows, not, as he argues, because such a concept emerges extremely early in the traditions, but because it still has not emerged at their end.

70. Perhaps if the section of Barth's *Church Dogmatics* (III, 1) which intrigues Hendry and in which Barth suggests that the *discarnate* Word as Second Person of the Trinity is an abstraction which, while indispensable to trinitarian theology, barely appears in the New Testament, were fully integrated into his trinitarian thought, he might be brought very close indeed to the proposal now being made. See George S. Hendry, *The Holy Spirit in Christian Theology*, Philadelphia: Westminster Press and London: SCM Press 1956, p. 49. On this general theme of pre-existence in christology see also F. B. Craddock, *The Pre-Existence of Christ in the New Testament*, New York: Abingdon Press 1968.

71. If that last phrase makes any sense, it is one obvious way of paraphrasing the questionable term 'pre-existence'.

72. Oxford: Clarendon Press 1977. 'In order, then, to interpret God's saving work in Jesus we do not need the model of a descent of a pre-existent divine person into the world' (p. 33). Lampe, it should be said, finds the idea of pre-existence in the New Testament in much the same way as do some of the authors studied in the last section. He traces the introduction of this idea to Paul's combination of Wisdom motifs with the title 'Son of God', strengthened by subsequent references to 'sending', and clinched by the hymn in Philippians which, Lampe suggests, made Christ himself the subject of the decision to come on earth (pp. 123ff.). If the last section above is correct in arguing that such belief in pre-existence is not of quite such substance in the NT, then Lampe might have found a way of integrating the Wisdom-Word-Son material and not have had to treat it as an alternative to be finally rejected.

73. To Lampe the theology of the incarnation of a pre-existing Word or Son of God implies an intrusion into human history which he at one point compares to an invasion from outer space (p. 41). It is, he thinks, linked to an Augustinian-cataclysmic assessment of the Fall which virtually destroys the sense of the continuity of God's Spirit in human history (p. 22–3). It owes its origin to a confluence of quite varied factors which range from a tendency of analytic reason to hypostasize the referents of images and symbols (p. 39), to a 'two-way projection' of the personhood of Jesus on to the pre-existent Logos-Son, and then of the resulting personhood of this pre-existent divine being back on to the historical figure of the Gospels (p. 141). It can scarcely avoid Arian or ditheistic implications (p. 41).

74. *God as Spirit*, p. 118, cf. also pp. 22–3.

75. *God as Spirit*, p. 33.

76. *God as Spirit*, p. 208–9. Lampe's major text here is Romans 8.

77. *God as Spirit*, pp. 11, 12. On pp. 210ff. Lampe lists patristic texts in which 'Spirit' is still used, not in a restrictive sense in reference to a third divine 'person', but with the meaning of 'deity', to refer to the 'stuff' of divinity, and consequently to refer to the divinity of the Word made flesh (e.g. in commentaries on Luke 1.35).

78. *God as Spirit*, p. 179.

79. P. Grant, *Six Modern Authors and Problems of Belief*, London: Macmillan 1979, p. 145.

80. See George T. Montague, *The Holy Spirit: Growth of a Biblical Tradition*, New York: Paulist Press 1976, for examples of such references of *ruach* taken from different strands of the Old Testament.

81. Barth would no doubt insist that *analogia fidei* is the only kind of analogy which can be in question here, not *analogia entis*. This means that our words can refer to God, not by any intrinsic power of words or of the things they name to make reference to God possible, but because God himself lays hold on our words to enable them to refer to him. Since, however, the only ones we ever see laying hold on words are human beings like ourselves, such assertion is empty rhetoric and does nothing whatever to alter the human condition of all our religious faith or of any of its myriad expressions.

82. S. T. Coleridge, *Lay Sermons* (Collected Works of Samuel Taylor Coleridge, 6), London: Routledge 1972, p. 30. To paraphrase George Watson's comment on this passage: whatever Keats' nightingale may 'stand for' it always refers to the actual bird. George Watson, 'Beckett's *Waiting for Godot*: A Reappraisal', *The Maynooth Review* I, 1975, p. 25.

83. *God as Spirit*, p. 206. Most theological heads nod wisely at such a statement and with good reason. One could wish, however, that more people would keep it in mind in the course of their often facile criticisms of the Stoa. As M. E. Isaacs points out, *pneuma* was one favourite stoic term for the divine, but because the Stoa, for reasons which their critics might do well to notice, refused to treat of spirit as opposed to matter, many try to locate the difference between Judasim (with Christianity) and Stoicism in the latter's alleged inability to talk of anything other than immanence. M. E. Isaacs, *The Concept of Spirit: A Study of Pneuma in Hellenistic Judaism and its Bearing on the New Testament*, London: Heythrop Monographs, 1976, p. 19.

84. See, for instance, Hendrikus Berkhof, *The Doctrine of the Spirit* London: Epworth Press 1965, p. 28. Much of this type of reference has to do with the 'Christianized' Spirit, the Spirit of Jesus, and much of it is combined with the extremely questionable distinction, not between transcendence and immanence, but between objective and subjective, where the Spirit becomes 'the subjective condition for the apprehension and recognition of the objective self-manifestation of God in Christ' (Hendry, *The Holy Spirit in Christian Theology*, p. 34). We shall, of course, have nothing to do in the context with such a volatile distinction as that

of subjective/objective and, though he acknowledges its presence in his tradition, we may welcome Berkhof's criticism of it on exegetical grounds (op. cit, pp. 22–3).

85. M. E. Isaacs, *The Concept of Spirit*, pp. 18–26; see also p. 108, pp. 137–8. She also indicates from Josephus the affinity in rabbinic teaching between 'spirit' and 'shekinah'. In addition, for many other such affinities with 'word', 'power', 'angel', 'finger', see Lampe, *God as Spirit*, pp. 35ff. Further, though the gift of prophecy was later described almost universally in terms of spirit, much of the prophetic literature in the Old Testament itself avoids the term spirit, possibly because of its use to describe more bizarre types of ecstatic behaviour in war or peace, and uses instead the term 'word' to describe this particular form of God's effective presence. The terms are, then, clearly equivalent. See Montague, *The Holy Spirit*, pp. 35ff.

86. See, for instance, Rom. 8. 12–27.

87. See, for instance, the role of *eros* in the Platonic Dialogues.

88. This is not only the case with older Roman Catholic exegetical studies such as that of Ceuppens, already referred to above, but also with more recent books such as Lindsay Dewar's *The Holy Spirit and Modern Thought*, London: Mowbray 1959, which attributes to the farewell discourse in the Fourth Gospel 'what must be described as the classical statement of the personal work of the Spirit' (p. 35), not, of course, as personification of a divine attribute, function, or activity, but as a distinct divine personal being.

89. M. E. Isaacs, *The Concept of Spirit*, p. 84.

90. Isaacs, *The Concept of Spirit*, pp. 51, 135.

91. C. K. Barrett, *The Holy Spirit and the Gospel Tradition*, London: SPCK 1958.

92. C. K. Barrett, *The Holy Spirit*, pp. 52–3, 99, 120.

93. Barrett's approach is certainly preferable to that of J. D. G. Dunn, whose book *Jesus and the Spirit*, London: SCM Press 1975, on other topics contains much valuable material for this area of research. But as far as the life of Jesus is concerned Dunn's presentation is marred by a kind of naiveté (touching at times) in assessing the historicity of scenes like the baptism of Jesus (and Luke's Pentecost in Acts), and more so by a persistent tendency to look for the distinctiveness, and perhaps the uniqueness of Jesus in what must be considered subjective qualities of his consciousness when he acted as exorcist, healer, prophet. Jesus was conscious of a spiritual power whose source was self-evident to him (p. 53); he believed himself empowered by the Spirit (p. 63); and his sense of power was 'so overwhelming in his consciousness' (p. 89) that he concluded that the end was present in his ministry; he had a sense of being inspired like Moses, but in his case 'its immediacy and numinous quality transcended all that went before' (p. 90). Such persistent harping on overwhelming consciousness of the numinous as the key to Jesus' mission is a very shaky platform on which to build the kind of historical basis for Christianity which Dunn so rightly requires ('unless there is

some correlation between Christian claims for Jesus and Jesus' own self-awareness, these claims lose touch with reality. It is the transcendent otherness of Jesus' experience of God which roots the claims of Christology in history', p. 92), and it seems a little too like certain nineteenth-century thinkers to come from the pen of a man who uses nineteenth-century liberalism as a term of complaint. Further, in sentences such as 'His awareness of being uniquely possessed and used by divine Spirit was the mainspring of his mission and the key to its effectiveness' (p. 54), combined with statements to the effect that Christians stood in a dual relationship to God as Father and Jesus as Lord and attributed this relationship to the Spirit (p. 326), there is an assumed hypostatizing of the Spirit, the kind of assumption about which I have complained above, and which the New Testament texts, when read without crumbling systematic presuppositions, may not support.

94. This is not to deny the actuality or the possibility of discrete numinous experiences, with their train of adjectives such as overwhelming, transcendent, self-evidencing; but it is to remove them with quiet determination from the centre of the stage on which the Christian drama has been played out from the day that Jesus was born. It is to say that, compared to the public life and death of Jesus, in which the essence of Christianity is found, compared to his followers' experience of that life in themselves, these are both secondary and distressingly fragile before the critical historical intent of the present era.

95. M. E. Isaacs, *The Concept of Spirit*, p. 64.

96. E.g. by preference for *psyche* or *thumos* in Jewish Hellenistic translation where the original reference was to human reason or emotion, thus leaving *pneuma* to refer more exclusively to God; also comparison of Matthew and Luke with Mark and 'Q' shows a growing tendency to refuse to use the word *pneuma* for evil or demonic forces, a tendency again in line with the usage of Paul, the LXX, and general Hellenistic Jewish usage. M. E. Isaacs, *The Concept of Spirit*, pp. 105–6.

97. See H. Berkhof, *The Doctrine of the Spirit*, pp. 19ff., for possibilities of designing 'christology from a pneumatological viewpoint', some early attempts at this and their early abandonment in favour of Logos christologies.

98. See especially Ingo Hermann, *Kyrios and Pneuma*, München: Kösel 1961; and for other references Berkhof, *The Doctrine of the Spirit*, pp. 23ff.

99. Writers such as J. D. G. Dunn ('2 Cor. III, 17 "The Lord is the Spirit" ', *Journal of Theological Studies* 21, 1970, pp. 309–20) and M. E. Isaacs (*The Concept of Spirit*, p. 113) believe that the Lord here is Yahweh rather than Jesus. But in view of the argumentative sequence of II Cor. 3, as Herrmann outlines it in the opening chapter of his book, and in view of Paul's statement a few verses later on that he preaches not himself but Christ Jesus as Lord, I find such a neat distinction difficult to accept.

100. Dunn, *Jesus and the Spirit*, p. 322.

101. Dunn, *Jesus and the Spirit*, p. 323.

102. Dunn, *Jesus and the Spirit*, p. 325; this after noticing how Spirit is

used like other OT concepts such as Wisdom and Word to denote the revelatory activity of God in Jesus, and concluding that such hitherto impersonal, though sometimes personified concepts gain 'character and personality', the character and personality of Jesus.

103. Berkhof, *The Doctrine of the Spirit*, pp. 28–9; the phrase *modus existendi* is clearly meant to anticipate the *tropos hyparxeos*, one of the ways of distinguishing the 'persons' in classical trinitarian doctrine.

104. M. E. Isaacs, *The Concept of Spirit*, p. 114.

105. Luke in particular, especially in Acts, handles the missionary expansion of the faith of Jesus in terms of spirit.

106. Raymond Brown, *The Birth of the Messiah*, London: Chapman 1977, pp. 291, 313–14, 432.

107. Brown, *The Birth of the Messiah*, pp. 312–14.

108. Hahn, *The Titles of Jesus*, pp. 303ff. He also refers to Ignatius' phrase about Jesus in *Eph.* 7.2 'sarkikos te kai pneumatikos . . . . ek Marias kai ek Theou'.

109. From this point of view the sentence of C. F. D. Moule is rather startling: 'It seems to be intended, literally and exclusively, that it was from no man, but from the very Spirit of God that the semen came (Matt. 1.18, 20; Luke 1.35)', *The Holy Spirit*, London: Mowbray 1978, p. 55.

110. J. G. Davies, *The Spirit, the Church and the Sacraments*, London: Faith Press 1954, p. 20, gets over this by cobbling on to the Lucan narrative a Logos christology which it does not possess. 'The descent of the Spirit was for the creation of a new nature which was assumed by a pre-existent Person.' And he had just explained: 'But this creative act, it should be noted, did not bring into being a new person – the *Person* of the God-man, i.e. the subject of all the human experiences, was already in existence, viz. the Logos' (pp. 19–20). With this kind of cobbling – with hindsight, of course – any theological conclusion whatever could be 'proved' from Scripture.

111. See also, e.g. Luke 4. 18–21; compare Luke 7.22.

112. *Jesus, the Man and the Myth*, pp. 108ff.

113. See, for example, R. E. Brown, 'Paraclete in the Fourth Gospel', *New Testament Studies* 13, 1966–67, pp. 113–132; C. K. Barrett, *The Gospel According to John*, London: SPCK 1955, p. 76; Barnabas Lindars, *The Gospel of John*, London: Oliphants 1972, p. 478.

114. The following material is taken from a paper on 'The Prophetic Spirit in the Fourth Gospel' read to the British-Irish Theological Society at Maynooth on 8 September 1980.

115. It is just such a questionable form of hindsight, no doubt, which allows Hendry to write: 'The presence of the Spirit is always secondary to, and consequent upon, the presence of the incarnate Christ . . . The function of the Spirit is essentially subservient and instrumental to the work of the incarnate Christ' (*The Holy Spirit*, p. 23). But in actual fact, such sentences are as little obvious from a reading of the New Testament as they are difficult to harmonize with later trinitarian theology.

116. In this conclusion I come very close to M. E. Isaac's views in *The*

Concept of Spirit, p. 123. Indeed, if I do in fact reproduce them, this merely extends my acknowledgment for so much of the material of the present section. But I am not sure that she would follow exactly the line I have taken with the material. In any case let me add this: if it is possible to talk of the statement about 'another paraclete' in terms of personification of intermediaries and not in terms of a separate *hypostasis*, there should be no difficulty at all in taking 'trinitarian formulae' such as II Cor. 13.14, 'The grace of the Lord Jesus Christ, and the love of God and the fellowship of the Holy Spirit be with you all' in terms of a poetic triplet, rather than a reference to three distinct *hypostaseis*. As J. D. G. Dunn says of I. Cor. 12. 4–6, 'As the whole range of spiritual gifts can be described alternatively as charismata, services, activities, so their source can be described equivalently as "the same Spirit", "the same Lord", "the same God" ' (*Jesus and the Spirit*, p. 324.)

117. II Cor. 1. 22; 5.5; Rom. 8.23.

118. Barnabas Lindars (*New Testament Apologetic*, London: SCM Press and Philadelphia: Westminster Press 1961, pp. 55–7), for instance, has an interesting commentary on a New Testament *midrash pesher* of Psalm 68.18 which makes it speak of the ascended Lord (originally Yahweh) giving gifts to men. Usually gifts refer to gifts of the Spirit, but since the risen Lord is said to send the Spirit (as in Acts 2.32), Luke, according to Lindars, either misunderstands or rationalizes, and begins to talk of 'the gift of the Spirit' (Acts 2.38; 8.20; 10.45; 11.17) and this, he thinks, contributed to the hypostatizing of the Spirit.

119. Michael Ramsey, *Holy Spirit*, London: SPCK 1977, p. 118, writes: 'critical opinion, even of a very moderate kind, would question the authenticity of the saying in Matthew 28.19 in its present form'.

120. *The Holy Spirit*, p. 103.

121. See Ian T. Ramsey, *Models for Divine Activity*, London: SCM Press 1973.

Part Three: The Past

1. E. Husserl, *The Idea of Phenomenology*, The Hague: Martinus Nijhoff 1964, p. 13.

2. S. Kierkegaard, *Concluding Postscript*, Princeton University Press 1941, p. 182.

3. See my 'The Theology of Faith: A Bibliographical Survey', *Horizons* 2, 1975, pp. 207–38.

4. M. Merleau-Ponty, *Phenomenology of Perception*, London: Routledge and Kegan Paul 1962, p. 405.

5. *Phenomenology of Perception*, p. xviii. Gadamer's reading of Heidegger on the original nature of human understanding is similar. For Heidegger, according to Gadamer, understanding is 'the original form of the realization of There-being, which is being-in-the-world. Before any differentiation of understanding into the different directions of pragmatic and theoretical interest, understanding is There-being's mode of being, in

that it is potentiality-for-being and "possibility".' H. Gadamer, *Truth and Method*, London: Sheed and Ward 1975, p. 230.

6. Merleau-Ponty, *Phenomenology of Perception*, pp. 343, 409.

7. *Phenomenology of Perception*, p. XVI.

8. For it does seem odd that in dealing with such as Marx and Sartre I insisted that their indifference to divine transcendence be taken seriously and I doubted that the newer apologetic of Gilkey and Küng had really met their case, yet, when in search of an epistemology of faith and doctrine, I should pick up Husserl and Merleau-Ponty and ignore their indifference to a transcendent God. There is, however, a difference in the present context which should more than cancel this impression of oddity. For it is one thing to produce an entire philosophy of existence (as Marx and Sartre tried to do) and to maintain throughout that belief in a transcendent God was obsolete or irrelevant. It is quite another thing to produce an epistemology and already, at the epistemological level, to try to rule out or to avoid the issue of faith in a transcendent God. For epistemology has to do with the nature, structures, and processes of all human knowing, and, especially if it is sufficiently comprehensive as to include human faith, its proponents can certainly be taken to task for attempting to say, before the structures and processes even go into action, that there are some things that people can never know or in which belief will always be impossible. There is therefore nothing inherently inconsistent about the view that some modern philosophical challenges to faith in divine transcendence have not been met, whereas other epistemological attempts to rule out the very question of belief in divine transcendence are not to be tolerated.

9. E. Husserl, *Ideas, General Introduction to Pure Phenomenology*, New York: Humanities Press 1931, p. 74.

10. Consciousness, for Husserl, is absolute in the sense that, when we 'bracket out' the question as to whether what we are aware of in our consciousness exists as objectively real or not, we come upon the *ego-cogito-cogitatum* (Husserl, *Cartesian Meditations: An Introduction to Phenomenology*, The Hague: Martinus Nijhoff 1960, p. 50), a conscious ego with all its real and possible objects of consciousness regarded simply as such. This is absolute in the sense that everything else 'exists for me only as *cogitatum* of my changing and, while changing, interconnected *cogitationes*' (op. cit., p. 37). In another place he writes: 'cognition itself is a name for a manifold sphere of being which can be given to us absolutely' (*The Idea of Phenomenology*, p. 23). In short, if the phenomenological method leads you as its first and most substantive move to 'see' consciousness and its objects purely as objects of consciousness then, on this method, that is the most basic or absolute thing you will see.

11. Merleau-Ponty, *Phenomenology of Perception*, p. 40. It is interesting to note how the author combines empiricist and idealist epistemologies in this complaint about their ultimately unacceptable implications (see my own 'Making Room for Faith: The Gospel According to Kant', *The*

Maynooth Review 3, 1977, esp. pp. 28ff.). For other challenges to a divine Logos-divinity see, e.g., pp. 393–5, 424, 430.

12. Those who need immediate assurance that this is not the only, or even the best, way to conceive of the God of Christians could consult Charles Hartshorne's self-surpassing God who, though unsurpassable by another, is nevertheless 'receptive, enriched by his creatures, perpetually transcending himself', in part consequence of this receptivity and interaction: *A Natural Theology for Our Time*, La Salle: Open Court Press 1967, pp. 44–5.

13. There is obviously here an echo of the previous discussion of apologists such as Küng, Tracy and Gilkey. And since Gadamer has already been mentioned the point may be repeated here in his terms. Gadamer is well aware of the power of the argument of what he calls 'reflexive philosophy'. At least since Plato it has been said that to assert the truth of anything whatever is to imply access to an ideal of truth by which such assertion can be made. As Gadamer puts it: 'The insistence on immediacy – whether of corporal nature, of the Thou which makes claims, of the impenetrable factuality of historical chance, or of the reality of the relations of production – is always self-refuting in so far as it is no immediate attitude but a reflective activity' (*Truth and Method*, p. 308). Yet to Gadamer, 'experience is experience of finitude' and 'true experience is that of one's own historicality' (*Truth and Method*, pp. 320–1). Reflection is an inescapable part of our conscious activity, and it leaves us with questions about ideal forms which its exercise presupposes in making any judgment or evaluation, but this leaves us no more certain than Plato was as to whether such forms actually exist, or how, or where, or what it could mean to say that they exist. Since we may be dealing in fact with no more than empty formalism, we are certainly not entitled to conclude without further ado that the reflective activity of the mind by which it judges, evaluates and creates, require grounding in the infinite knowledge of some absolute mind.

14. Gadamer reports this remark of Heidegger's from a theological meeting at Marburg: *Philosophical Hermeneutics*, University of California Press 1978, p. 198.

15. See, for instance, *Phenomenology of Perception*, pp. 198–9, and *passim*.

16. Professional turn-watchers tend to locate Heidegger's turn somewhere round the time of the publication of his *Was Ist Metaphysik?* (Bonn 1929).

17. The Argument for God's Existence from Capital Letters (e.g., the A of absolute, the T of transcendent and the B of being) is probably the most common form of argument used in modern apologetics.

18. Heidegger, *Was Ist Metaphysik?*, p. 52.

19. The contention that faith is the comprehensive term, and knowledge (hypothesis, theory, doctrine) the included one, a contention as old as Augustine (*credimus ut intelligamus*) and as recent as Polanyi's tacit dimension, can also be reached by an historical account of relations between *pistis* and *gnosis*. To illustrate briefly this line of access let me

refer to a paper by Raoul Mortley to the Center for Hermeneutical Studies in Hellenistic and Modern Culture at Berkeley, to which during my California years I belonged. Despite Mortley's insistence both in the paper and in the course of the ensuing colloquy that 'Faith is only belief, after all, and to offer the possibility of belief rather than knowledge is to offer something less,' and that in the case of those early Christians who 'could only offer credence' instead of 'knowledge or proof', their attackers naturally 'selected the epistemology of faith as a prime embarrassment', neither the paper itself nor the discussion could support any such clear distinction, much less such alleged inferiority of faith before knowledge.

For if in Plato himself, as Mortley points out, *pistis* refers to the knowledge we have, by persuasion or 'proof', of things 'sensible', in our changing world, towards the end of the great ancient philosophical tradition of the Academy Proclus placed faith at the pinnacle of knowledge where it named that union with the source of all, and crowned the whole course of knowledge which until then is partial and taken up with pluriformity. Aristotle used the word to refer to the way in which presuppositions or axioms are grasped from which all reasoning begins, and he used it also for that acceptance of conclusions or results which follow logical demonstrations. It was for him, in a very literal sense, a very inclusive term, for it was within its boundaries that ratiocinative processes took place. During the course of the discussion John Dillon quoted a sentence of the Neo-Platonist Porphyry: 'For one must have faith that one's sole salvation lies in turning towards God, and, having acquired this faith, one must strive as far as possible to know the truth about him, and, having acquired such knowledge, to love what one knows; and having loved, to nurture one's soul on good hopes throughout life.' There were influences of a Chaldean triad of faith, truth, and love here, as in the case of Proclus there may have been Christian influence. But I quote this brief selection of views from the founding philosophies of Western culture simply to illustrate the great epistemic range of which the concept of faith was capable, and how easily it could encompass knowledge within that range. See Edward C. Hobbes (ed.), *Protocol of the Thirty-Third Colloquy*, Berkeley: Center for Hermeneutical Studies 1978.

20. Merleau-Ponty, *Phenomenology of Perception*, p. xix.

21. F. Schleiermacher, *The Christian Faith*, Edinburgh: T. & T. Clark 1928, pp. 30ff. See also his insistence that God-consciousness is always in company of specific determinations of it, such as the distinctively Christian determination, in a way analogous to that in which self-consciousness in general accompanies every particular determination of it and is never found in general or abstract form: *The Christian Faith*, pp. 131–2.

22. Brunner and Barth, *Natural Theology*.

23. Berkhof, *The Doctrine of the Holy Spirit*, pp. 114–15.

24. K. Barth, *Church Dogmatics*, I, 1, Edinburgh: T. & T. Clark 1975, pp. 358–9.

25. Quoted from an as yet unpublished manuscript of Gerard Watson entitled *The Theology of the Later Greek Philosophers*, which I have previewed by courtesy of its author and to which I am indebted for much of the substance of this present section. Werner Jaeger produced *The Theology of the Early Greek Philosophers*, Oxford University Press, in 1947, leading up to Socrates, and since, as Watson says, the areas linking philosophy and patrology 'are so vast that the non-specialist is intimidated by the bulk of the introductory reading required in order to gain some familiarity with the questions, and is appalled at the obscurity of even some of the names of the philosophers, not to mention the highly scholastic issues which are occasionally debated', a complementary volume such as this manuscript provides is highly desirable.

26. The conventional view that it was the philosophical leanings of Arius that caused the trouble is challenged quite successfully in a recent book which will prove most useful in succeeding sections: R. C. Gregg and D. E. Groh, *Early Arianism: A View of Salvation*, Philadelphia: Fortress Press and London: SCM Press 1981. Jaroslav Pelikan, in his recent history, *The Christian Tradition*, University of Chicago Press 1975, even generalizes this conventional view: 'In the development of both dogmas of the early Church, the Trinity and Christology, the chief place to look for hellenization is in the speculations and heresies against which the dogma of the creeds and councils were directed' (p. 55).

27. Watson traces these themes in his first chapter, and in much more nuanced form, to Xenophanes, the Pythagoreans, Heracliteans and Parmenides.

28. Watson, p. 11: the notion was popular in fifth century Athens. See W. D. Ross's edition of Aristotle's *Metaphysics*, London: Oxford University Press 1924.

29. Watson, p. 13.

30. For this see A. Festugière, *Personal Religion Among the Greeks*, Berkeley: University of California Press 1960.

31. Watson, pp. 19–20.

32. Watson, pp. 14–15.

33. Other questions connected with creation in Plato, and with the *Timaeus* in particular, do not concern us directly here. I take Watson's view that the issue of creation in time (and also out of nothing?) is indecisive in the Middle-Platonic period; and in general his view that though some passages in Plato's later work may sound dualist – e.g. the two controlling souls of *Laws* 896E – dualism is not really the issue with Plato. 'Plato was primarily concerned, as so often, with defeating the materialists, and thought he had done so when he established the priority of soul. After that, he felt, all things would fall into their proper order, and among them evil would take its place. Human freedom will take a large share of the responsibility for evil in the universe' (p. 16).

34. Philosophy is literally the love of wisdom, and so philosophy and religion in this tradition are basically coterminous.

35. Watson's suggestion is also to be accepted, I believe, that the faith

and hope in the God and in universal justice in which Socrates died 'gave a weight to Plato's arguments for the immortality of the soul which they do not merit in themselves' (p. 17).

36. There was a tradition that in a lecture or lectures on the One Plato had dealt more didactically with the God-question, or at least supplemented the dialogues on this issue. But it is unlikely that his dialogues leave us without any key elements in his religious thought. On this see Gerard Watson, *Plato's Unwritten Teaching*. Dublin: Helicon Press 1973.

37. See my *Jesus, the Man and the Myth*, ch. 4, passim.

38. The central theological text in Aristotle is found in Book Lambda of his *Metaphysics*, chapters 6–10. For fuller detail on the few points I make here see again Watson's chapter on Aristotle in *The Theology of the Later Greek Philosophers*.

39. Watson points out that chapter eight of Book XII of Aristotle's *Metaphysics*, the chapter in which the intractable issue of the number of prime movers emerges, is in any case suspect as to its authenticity (Watson, p. 31).

40. Watson, p. 31.

41. Watson, p. 32.

42. The *homoiosis theo* is, of course, as central a theme in Aristotle as in the Platonic *eros*. In ch. 7 of Bk. 10 of the *Nicomachean Ethics*, he recommends the purely contemplative life as our highest happiness even here on earth.

43. For this material on the Stoa, I am again heavily indebted to Watson's chapter on 'Hellenistic Philosophy', in which he deals with Stoics and Epicureans. And I may mention at this point that I have not raised the issue of polytheism or monotheism with the Greeks on which he also touches in this chapter. I think that at the very least he shows that the positions were not as contrasting as the terms make them seem. And I'm not at all sure, in any case, that Christians who are shortly to produce three divine 'persons' while maintaining as stoutly as ever their much advertised monotheism, are in any position to open a case for the prosecution.

44. Watson, p. 42b.

45. Jaroslav Pelikan, *The Christian Tradition*, p. 32: 'The apologists' use of the idea of the Logos in their dispute with classicism certainly helped to establish this title in the Christian vocabulary about Christ.' And more generally: 'as the apologists came to grips with the defenders of paganism, they were compelled to acknowledge that Christianity and its ancestor Judaism did not have a monopoly on either the moral or doctrinal teachings whose superiority Christian apologists were seeking to demonstrate. To some extent this acknowledgment was a tacit admission of the presence within Christian thought of doctrine borrowed from Greek philosophy' (p. 31).

46. See John Dillon, *The Middle Platonists*, London: Duckworth 1977, esp. p. 45.

47. Watson, p. 61.

48. Watson, p. 57.

49. Watson, p. 61.

50. Watson, p. 62. Indeed, as these samples show and many more would confirm, and as John Dillon advised me in correspondence, 'Middle Platonism is rather more binitarian than trinitarian.' The Moderatus, incidentally, in this selection of authors was Pythagorean by professed allegiance. Apparently his reaction to the assimilating tactics of the Platonists of this period was to advance the counter-claim that Platonism itself was Pythagoreanism plagiarized! *The Cambridge History of Later Greek and Early Medieval Philosophy* (ed. A. H. Armstrong, Cambridge University Press 1967) describes his views on God as follows: 'There is a first, a second, and a third One. The first One is beyond all being and *ousia*. The second, i.e. that which is actually being and intelligible, equals ideas. The third One, viz, the psychical, participates in the first One and in the ideas. These three are followed by that which is sensible . . . a shadow of the first non-being which appears in quantity' (p. 93).

51. As illustrations of Philo's influence on the development of Christian theology (the most influential forms of which occurred in any case in Alexandria), one might mention Andrew Louth's assertion that Philo's material was preserved by Christians and that he was not even mentioned by another Jew until the fifteenth century AD (*The Origins of the Christian Mystical Tradition: From Plato to Denys*, Oxford: The Clarendon Press 1980, p. 27); and Henry Chadwick reminds us that Eusebius preserves a legend to the effect that when Philo visited Rome, he met Peter! See Chadwick's chapter on Philo in *The Cambridge History of Later Greek and Early Medieval Philosophy*.

52. See Louth's chapter on Philo in *The Origins of the Christian Mystical Tradition*, in which he allows Philo some claim to be regarded as the Father of Apophatic Theology.

53. Though Louth maintains, in the chapter just referred to, that God's word (*logos*) manifested in Scripture brings us closer to God, according to Philo, than do the powers and their works. This is most likely true, but it does not immediately concern us at this point.

54. Maurice Wiles, *Working Papers in Doctrine*, London: SCM Press 1976, pp. 1–3.

55. *The Cambridge History*, p. 144. There are obviously interesting parallels here with the anti-Mosaic revelation polemics which we noted in the scriptural section of this work, and with the use of the *Logos* to express the divinity of Jesus in the theology we are about to meet later.

56. *The Cambridge History*, p. 143. Chadwick's assertion that 'Philo is the earliest witness to the doctrine that the Ideas are God's thoughts' is perhaps a bit extreme, though he does add: 'The notion . . . is certainly earlier than Philo', and is right in suggesting that it 'could naturally arise from a fusion of Platonism either with the Stoic doctrine of seminal principles (*logoi spermatikoi*) in nature or with the Aristotelian conception of the divine self-thinking mind' (p. 142).

57. Watson, p. 60.

58. Lampe, *God as Spirit*, p. 141.

59. See A. H. Armstrong and R. A. Markus, *Christian Faith and Greek Philosophy*, London: Darton, Longman and Todd 1960, pp. 1–2, on the image of generation as one of the earliest Greek symbols for origin.

60. I do not, of course, mean to detract from the point of which Maurice Wiles reminds us, and which is habitually under-represented in accounts of the origin of Christian doctrine, namely, that the needs and habits of common Christian worship affected doctrinal development as they did – see his chapter on 'Lex Orandi' in *The Making of Christian Doctrine*, Cambridge University Press 1967. But we are dealing here with the manner in which the doctrine came to be formulated, and the finer points of that task, then as now, can hardly have been very intelligible to the man and woman in the pew.

61. See above p. 280, n. 19. R. T. Wallis recounts the manner in which, as the 'faith' nature of the Neo-Platonism movement came to be stressed, some leaders wished to restrict even the reading of the faithful (*Neo-Platonism*, London: Duckworth, p. 101). Religious establishments never really change much, do they?

62. We are not concerned here with the question of the creation of this matter itself, with creation out of nothing. For this is an additional question to the question of creation in time. Aristotle argued for the indestructibility of motion and time – and hence of matter. But Middle-Platonists were selective in what they used of Aristotle, and I get the impression that the Middle-Platonists who were anxious to stress the creation of matter were just the ones who came closest to being theological dualists – for matter had always been considered somewhat intractable before the good intentions of the demiourgos, the maker (see Watson on Plutarch and Atticus, pp. 63ff.). In any case, since both the terms 'matter' and 'nothing' are elusive, to say the least – later thinkers in the Platonic tradition will describe 'prime' matter precisely as 'nothing' – it is doubtful indeed if writers should try to gain quite as much theological mileage out of the idea of creation out of nothing as Louth, for instance, does in his *Origins of the Christian Mystical Tradition*.

63. Louth, *The Origins of the Christian Mystical Tradition*, p. 27.

64. *Christian Faith and Greek Philosophy*, p. 19.

65. There is even a passage in the *Enneads* in which Plotinus makes *Logos* accountable for evil in the world. Evil he attributes mainly to the Fall of Soul at its lower level into body; yet not just that, for that is necessary for its action in the world, but also to its self-will, its weakness, its tendency to indulge its own motion away from God who is its goal and towards nothingness. Evil in the overall view is for good; it is an indispensable part of the total rational order: 'The Reason-Principle (Logos) is the sovereign, making all: it wills things as they are and, in its reasonable act, it produces even what we know as evil: it cannot desire all to be good: an artist would not make an animal all eyes . . . We are like people ignorant of painting who complain that the colours are not

beautiful everywhere in the picture: but the artist has laid on the appropriate tint to every spot (*Enneads* III, 2.11).

66. I have deliberately used this phrasing in order to take issue with such premature cases for the superiority of Christian mysticism as Andrew Louth presents. Reacting against Festugière's point that the mysticism of the Fathers is essentially independent of their Christianity, that when the Fathers 'think' their mysticism they simply Platonize without originality, Louth is anxious to depict Plotinus' One as 'unconscious either of itself or of the soul' and to say: 'The One has no concern for the soul that seeks him; nor has the soul more than a passing concern for others engaged on the same quest; it has no companions. Solitariness, isolation; the implications of this undermine any possibility of a doctrine of grace – the One is unaware of those who seek it, and so cannot turn towards them (*The Origins of the Christian Mystical Tradition*, pp. 51, 176, 191ff.). Without commenting on Plotinus' 'more than passing concern for others engaged on the same quest', and while allowing that Plotinus is anxious to stress that the One lacks nothing and seeks nothing (*Enneads* V, 2.1), one must still question the fairness of Louth's description, not only to the general ungrudging goodness of the One in giving existence to all, but to the kind of language in which Plotinus talks of the final rapture of the unitive way, of which the following few examples must here suffice: 'Suppose the soul to have attained: the highest has come to her, or rather has revealed its presence; she has turned away from all about herself and made herself apt, beautiful to the utmost, brought into likeness with the divine – by those preparings and adornings which come unbidden to those growing ready for the vision' (*Enneads* VI, 7.34); 'The Good spreading out above them and adapting itself to that union which it hastens to confirm is present to them as giver of a blessed sense and sight; so high it lifts them' (VI, 7.35); 'Suddenly, swept beyond it all by the very crest of the wave of Intellect surging beneath, he is lifted and sees, never knowing how; the vision floods the eyes with light, but it is not a light showing some other object, the light is itself the vision (VI, 7.36). See also VI, 7.22, where such phrases are used of the Good as, 'source of those graces and of the love they evoke', and the 'giver of that love'. The grace, the free gift, of the One is at the origin of all existence and at the consummation of every quest. That is not to say that Plotinus has a *Christian* concept either of God or of grace; merely a caution against finding the uniqueness (and possible superiority) of Christianity too soon and in too general a type of consideration.

67. *Enneads* I, 6.6, for instance, or V, 1.7; 'so far we deal still with the divine'.

68. *Enneads* II, 3.18.

69. Or, perhaps, Existence, Life and Intelligence. *Enneads* V, 6.6: 'Being is entire when it holds the form and idea of intellection and of life. In a Being, then, the existence, the intellection, and the life are present as an aggregate.'

70. Using the translation of the *Enneads* by Stephen McKenna (4 vols,

London: The Medici Society 1916–1930), I retain his 'Intellectual-Principle' for *Nous* where I sometimes use 'Mind'. On the 'teeming' of this text see also VI, 7.12: 'To ask how those forms of life come to be There is simply asking how that heaven came to be: it is asking whence comes life . . . and the answer is that There no indigence or impotence can exist but all must be teeming, seething, with life. All flows, so to speak from one fount not to be thought of as some one breath or warmth but rather as one quality englobing and safe-guarding all qualities – sweetness with fragrance, wine-quality and the savours of everything that may be tasted, all colours seen, everything known to touch, all that ear may hear, all melodies, every rhythm.' Or, as he says in a context in which he described Mind wandering through the Meadows of Truth which it itself is: 'To a traveller over land all is earth but earth abounding in difference: so in this journey the life through which Intellectual-Principle passes is one life but, in its ceaseless changing, a varied life' (VI, 7.13).

71. This is the case at the beginning of the Fifth Ennead where he outlines the nature, origin, and relationships of the three *hypostaseis* (Nous, incidentally, is offspring and image of the One); and see the quotation in n. 69 above.

72. Though R. T. Wallis writes 'for pagans . . . the triad in question was situated at the level of the *Second* Hypostasis', he also notes that the commentator on the *Parmenides* 'agrees with Porphyry, against Iamblichus, in identifying the first moment in the triad, that of Existence, with the One itself' (*Neo-Platonism*, pp. 106, 116).

73. I used Arius's reliably reported belief that the *Logos* replaced at least the *nous* and probably the human soul of Jesus as a clinching point in the case against him, though I knew then, and said, that Athanasius shared substantially this Apollinarian view. This argument I think I must now drop, though I still believe that the Apolliniarism did particularly suit Arius's purpose.

74. Even in Aristotle this teaching on primary substance occurs only in the *Categories* and is only used of embodied creatures which are individualized by prime matter; though it does have a history in later philosophy: a version of it can be found, for instance, in Plotinus, *Enneads* VI, 2–3.

75. I 'solved' the problem in precisely the same terms as the christology of the book itself developed (in terms of the identity of the Jesus of history and the Christ of faith), by insisting, for instance, that the second '*hypostasis*' through which the '*hypostasis*' of the Father became definitively revealed in history was the Word-made-flesh, that is to say, the Jesus of history.

76. See G. L. Prestige, *God in Patristic Thought*, London: SPCK 1952; his first chapter on terms for God, and particularly the term 'One'.

77. See C. Stead, *Divine Substance*, Oxford University Press 1977, pp. 180ff., on the complex concepts underlying the terms *unus*, *unitas*, *unio*, and *monas*.

78. See Pelikan, *The Christian Tradition*, p. 53, for the patristic agreement

287

on 'the concept of an entirely static God, with eminent reality, in relation to an entirely fluent world, with deficient reality'.

79. See, for example, Maurice Wiles, *The Making of Christian Doctrine*, pp. 27–8; C. Stead, *Divine Substance*, p. 187; Prestige, *God in Patristic Thought*, the section already referred to, on the 'One'.

80. Stead, *Divine Substance*, p. 187.

81. *In Joh.* 13.25. See Prestige, *God in Patristic Thought*, pp. 151ff.

82. Quoted in Gregg and Groh, *Early Arianism*, p. 7.

83. A sample of texts can be found in *Jesus, the Man and the Myth*, p. 224. And see T. E. Pollard, *Johannine Christology and the Early Church*, Cambridge University Press 1970, pp. 56ff. Also Tertullian, *Adversus Hermogenem*, 22, where the Word is called both minister and intermediary of the Maker.

84. Tertullian, *Adversus Praxeas*, 5–7.

85. G. L. Prestige, *Fathers and Heretics*, London: SPCK 1940, p. 173.

86. Lonergan, *The Way to Nicea*, sec. VI.

87. I have to say that neither at this point nor later in the patristic era do I find any clear preference for *creatio ex nihilo* over emanation in the matter of the concepts and images used to describe the origins of all things from the one unoriginate Source, and I shall later try to say what I think the main theological point of the explicit insistence on the *creatio ex nihilo* was. Andrew Louth (*The Origins of the Christian Mystical Tradition*, p. 167) wants to say that Pseudo-Denys, for instance, believed in creation out of nothing, not in emanation of being, yet he finds himself noting these words of Denys: 'being Goodness Himself He extends His Goodness, simply by being God, to all that exists' and commenting: 'This going out (Louth refers to *proodos*, emanation) of Himself in will and power is the creation of the world out of nothing.' For Tertullian's view on creation out of nothing see his *Adversus Hermogenem*, 1 (and see 21 for his admission that the Scripture did not clearly proclaim that all things were made out of nothing).

On the main point made about Tertullian's relative use of 'economy' and 'person' in his case for distinctions in the Deity, see Prestige, *God in Patristic Thought*, pp. 97ff.

88. See J. N. D. Kelly, *Early Christian Doctrines*, London: A. & C. Black 1958, p. 96.

89. Kelly seems to see it, a little prematurely perhaps, already installed in the Old Roman Creed which saw its final redaction in the late second century: *Early Christian Creeds*, London: Longmans 1960, p. 143.

90. Wiles, *Working Papers in Doctrine*, p. 21.

91. See Prestige, *God in Patristic Thought*, pp. 130ff. (section on Origen), and Tatian, *Address to the Greeks*, 5; Novatian, *On the Trinity*, 31; Eusebius of Caesarea, *Demonstratio Evangelica* IV, 3, 7. And so on.

92. The identification of the one who became incarnate with the Spirit is probably present in the *Shepherd of Hermas* (Sim. V, 5, 6; IX, 1), certainly in the *Second Letter of Clement to the Corinthians*, IX, 5, and in the oft-quoted words of Justin Martyr on Luke 1.35: 'The Spirit and Power which is from

God must not be thought to be other than the Logos, who is God's first begotten . . . and who, when it came upon the Virgin and overshadowed her, made her pregnant (I *Apol.* 7.33). Irenaeus also calls the pre-existent Son the Spirit of God (*Ad. Haer.*, III, 10, 3). See also Tertullian, *Adversus Hermogenem*, 18, 45. Though attempts are often made to identify the Spirit as the one who foretold Christ through the Old Testament prophets, quite often – as in Theophilus, *Ad Autol.* 2, 10; Justin, II, *Apol.*, 10; Hippolytus, *Contra Noet.*, 11, 12; Clement, *Paed.*, 1, 9 – this function is attributed to the Word. Even the function of pervading all things, which has again helped to identify or distinguish the Spirit, is by Eusebius of Caesarea, for instance, attributed to the Word (*Dem. Evang.* IV, 13, 2–3).

93. The lowest place in the divinity is often very firmly insisted upon for the Spirit in the theology of the pre-Nicene period. We shall see this in the section on the Spirit below. For the moment we may refer simply to Novatian's use of the inferiority of the Spirit (who is yet, to him, divine) to secure the divinity of Christ: '*minor autem Christo paraclitus Christum etiam deum esse hoc ipso probat, a quo accepit, quae nuntiat, ut testimonium Christi divinitatis grande sit, dum minor Christo paraclitus repertus ab illo sumit, quae ceteris tradit*' (*De Trinitate*, 16).

94. Gregg and Groh, *Early Arianism*, p. 97.

95. *Early Arianism*, p. 2.

96. These texts are everywhere in the New Testament and liberally presented by Gregg and Groh.

97. Two favourite texts of the Arians which gave Athanasius and his followers great trouble, and forced them to insert into their exegesis distinctions between the divinity and the humanity of Jesus signally absent from the texts themselves (with the sorry results which we must notice later), were Hebrews 3.2, 'who was faithful to him who made him', and Luke 2.52, 'Jesus advanced in wisdom and in stature, and in favour with God and man'.

98. *Early Arianism*, p. 53.

99. *Early Arianism*, p. 91. The contrast with Athanasius which the authors imply is almost a reversal of the conventional judgment that it was Arius who was over-influenced by philosophical theology: 'the tendency repeatedly encountered in orthodox argumentation to deflect or direct Arian soteriological assertions in the direction of concerns which might more precisely be called theological or cosmological in character' almost says as much (p. 64). But an even more balanced account may still be required of the relationship of both the Arian and the Athanasian parties to both the Scriptures and the prevailing philosophical climate of Greek culture.

100. Some have suggested that it was adopted by the opponents of Arius precisely because the latter rejected it: see, for instance, Wiles, *The Making of Christian Doctrine*, pp. 35–6.

101. *Early Arianism*, p. 97.

102. Tertullian's *una substantia* is not really equivalent, and he attributes *consubstantialis* only to his opponents: see Stead, *Divine Substance*, p. 202.

103. Stead, *Divine Substance*, p. 248: 'Homoousion guarantees very little; it can be used of things which resemble one another merely in belonging to the created order, or to the category of substance; it can relate collaterals to each other, or derivatives with their source; it does not exclude inequality of status or power. . . However the term is often used to indicate a relationship which is in fact closer than mere membership of the same species or similar material constitution, for instance, that of a stream to the actual fountain from which it flows, or that of an offspring to his own parent. To call a son *homoousios* with his father implies more than merely their common membership of the human race; and the further implication need not be merely that of their physical linkage, the term can evoke their whole biological and social relationship.' He adds two further meanings: an identical thing with different names or functions, and one thing which is constituted from a number of things; neither quite apt for the Christian Trinity.

104. Stead, *Divine Substance*, pp. 209ff.

105. Stead, *Divine Substance*, pp. 227, 244–5. Gregg and Groh, *Early Arianism*, p. 91, suggest some texts from I Timothy as the inspiration of these 'repeating *monon*' formulae of the Arians, and comment: 'Of a purposeful depreciation, demotion, or assault upon the honour and status of the Son there is no real evidence – at least no more than can be found in I Tim. 2.5.'

106. Stead, *Divine Substance*, p. 266.

107. Hence their phrase 'a creature promoted to the status of a god' is not fair to Arius: *Early Arianism*, p. 2. And note their own account of the scriptural origin of Eusebius of Nicomedia's terms for origin – creation, formation, begetting – in Proverbs 8.22 (p. 97).

108. Only a much fuller history of doctrine could afford to trace the various forms of so-called dynamic-type (Sabellian) monarchianism. And we may suspect, despite the usual lack of sufficient historical data, that the so-called adoptionist form may have had more going for it in the New Testament spirit-christologies than its opponents will now allow us to see. In any case, the point here is that 'adoption' is a totally inadequate term to describe the origin, admittedly by God's will, of the Framer of the universe and the consequent saviour of the human race. For both Arius and Athanasius our salvation is guaranteed by the work of the pre-existent Word, hence for *both* the Word is divine: *Early Arianism*, pp. 8, 25.

109. C. Stead, 'The Thalia of Arius and the Testimony of Athanasius', *Journal of Theological Studies* 29, 1978, p. 30. See also *Early Arianism*, p. 113. For the attribution to Arius of an Origen-like view that the Father is *Logos*, Wisdom, and so on, pre-eminently, and the Son has these attributes by participation, see C. Stead, 'The Platonism of Arius', *Journal of Theological Studies* 15, 1964, p. 20.

110. Kelly, p. 22.

111. *Working Papers in Doctrine*, p. 9.

112. See above p. 66.

113. *Early Christian Creeds*, p. 23.

114. *Working Papers in Doctrine*, p. 10. Wiles comments: 'We are therefore bound to conclude that the ante-Nicene Fathers did not adopt a trinitarian scheme of thought about God because they found themselves compelled to do so as the only rational means of explanation of their experience of God in Christ. Rather they came to accept the trinitarian form, because it was the already accepted pattern of expression, even though they often found it difficult to interpret their experience of God in this particular threefold way' (p. 11).

115. Basil, *On the Holy Spirit*, 4. In view of Gregg and Groh's work and especially their insistence that Arians and their opponents were deeply divided precisely on the issue of the type of language applicable in this area of theology, Athanasians preferring 'essentialist' language and Arians language of will, it must be a matter of some doubt as to whether Arians would themselves choose to have the difference of status of Father, Son, and Holy Spirit described in terms of difference of nature or whether it was their opponents who insisted on or even forced this way of describing the difference.

116. Athanasius, *First Letter to Serapion*, I, 10 ('But those Tropici, true to their name, having made a compact with the Arians and portioned out with them the blasphemy against the Godhead'), 21, 22.

117. An interesting example, perhaps, of Maurice Wiles' dictum: 'The real fault is to be seen in the spirit (characteristic especially of the later periods of the patristic age) which gave to some of the early formulations of christology an absoluteness of authority to which in view of their nature they had no right to aspire or to claim' (*Working Papers in Doctrine*, p. 39).

118. See above n. 93.

119. See Prestige, *Fathers and Heretics*, p. 157: 'The problem of the Trinity is the one theological question of absolutely fundamental importance which has even been pressed to a positive and satisfactory answer.' This judgment may now seem premature.

120. Athanasius, as usual, is making very selective use of the differences between divine and creaturely generation when answering the question of the Tropici; Why not say God has son and grandson, or that he generates two brothers? (*First Letter to Serapion*, 16). Athanasius appeals to two old favourites, the immutable and incomposite nature of divinity, in order to argue in this context that there must be one Father always such and one Son always such. But these qualities, in a system which now has no room for different levels of divinity, with the consequent possibility of composition entering in at a lower level, could just as easily argue that no generation whatever could take place in divinity, and that no distinction at all could be allowed.

121. That language, in a manner uncomfortably reminiscent of Humpty-Dumpty, too often means what it does by *fiat* of the user rather than by any intrinsic factor is already too painfully obvious from the tortuous history of the *homoousios*. It would also be obvious from the

history of the word which the Cappadocians gradually introduced to denote inner divine distinctions, *hypostasis;* and doubly obvious from the fact that *ousia* and *hypostasis* can sometimes be used with identical meaning. See Kelly, *Early Christian Doctrines,* p. 254; *Early Christian Creeds,* pp. 214, 241; Prestige, *God in Patristic Thought,* pp. 179ff., 201ff., 219, 233–4.

122. Athanasius, *De Synodis,* 54. See J. H. Newman, *Select Treatises of St Athanasius in Controversy with the Arians,* London: Longmans, Green and Company 1903, p. 144.

123. See in Newman, *Select Treatises,* the *Epistle of Athanasius in Defence of the Nicene Definition,* 10; also the text already referred to, *First Letter to Serapion,* 16.

124. *God in Patristic Thought,* p. 233.

125. See also, for instance, Hilary of Poitiers, *De Trinitate,* VII, 14: '*Anne naturalis nativitas non est ubi per nomen patris proprii naturae aequalitas demonstratur.*'

126. See his *First Letter to Serapion,* 27.

127. That the use of the modern term 'person' is not alone in trinitarian theology in causing impressions of tritheism should be clear from the Cappadocian habit of relating *ousia* and *hypostasis* as the general is related to the particular (see Basil, *Epistle* 214, 4). Gregory of Nyssa in his *Answer to Ablabius,* attempting to prevent impressions of tritheism emerging from the formula, goes to the length of insisting that we should not call Peter, James and John three men since human nature is one (E. R. Hardy, *Christology of the Later Fathers,* Philadelphia: Westminster Press 1954, pp. 256–67); and other Fathers make equally determined, if not altogether convincing attempts to reverse the normal impressions conveyed by language designed to contrast the general and the particular (see H. Bettenson, *the Later Christian Fathers,* Oxford University Press 1970, p. 11). Here again, of course, the idea that true unity is found at the very height of reality, and composition, number and so on found only lower where lesser beings participate after their manner in the life and existence that flows from this One seems about to be replaced by a schema for unity in distinction which at first sight at least does not seem to be quite so successful.

128. Prestige, *God in Patristic Thought,* p. 233. Prestige uses Basil to illustrate how gradually the *homoousios* came to be accepted with its full implication of identity of substance. John McIntyre quite rightly expresses some hesitation about the phrase 'identity of substance' and finds it characteristic of Gregory of Nazianzus ('The Holy Spirit in Greek Patristic Thought', *The Scottish Journal of Theology* 7, 1954, pp. 357–8). All we need to note here, however, is that the inherent tendency of the *homoousios* to telescope the levels of the older model also reduces the distinctions which that model secured.

129. 'The Holy Spirit', p. 358 (I should say that in references to this work of McIntyre's I am using a revised and expanded edition which I have by courtesy of its author).

130. References to the theology of Gregory of Nyssa are to the Greek text of W. Jaeger, ed., *Gregorii Nysseni Opera*, Leiden: Brill 1960 (in this case vol. I, pp. 236ff.). Readers should note that what the English translation of some of Gregory's works in the Library of Nicene and Post-Nicene Fathers, vol. V, treats, following Migne, as Book II of *Against Eunomius*, Jaeger considers to be and edits as a separate work of Gregory entitled *Refutatio Confessionis Eunomii*. Correspondingly Jaeger edits as Book II of *Against Eunomius* what the English translation lists as the *answer to Eunomius' Second Book*.

131. *Against Eunomius* II, 3 (*Gregorii Nysseni Opera* II, p. 319).

132. Ibid.

133. *Against Eunomius* X, 3.

134. *Against Eunomius* I, 42.

135. *Against Eunomius*, II, 2.

136. *Against Eunomius* I, 22.

137. The only positive phrase used to distinguish the Holy Spirit, 'being manifested through the Son', is precisely the phrase which it is feared in another context may make us confuse the Holy Spirit with creatures: *Against Eunomius* I, 22.

138. For a representative sampling of this material from the Cappadocians see: Basil, *Epistle* 214, 4; *Epistle* 38, 4; *On the Holy Spirit*, 46; Gregory of Nazianzus, *Oration* 25, 17; *Oration* 42, 15; Gregory of Nyssa, *Against Eunomius* 1, 22.

139. On Gregory's own account of the matter, Eunomius the Arian believed – and it is not in itself an unreasonable belief – that being ungenerated or generated made a real difference to the substance or being (*ousia*) of the divine *hypostasis* concerned; or if they did not, then the distinctions which were secured by their usage would be reduced to a mere matter of verbiage (*Against Eunomius* IV, 8). Indeed, Eunomius' position would gain some support from the following consideration: words like unoriginate or ungenerate were, after all, capable of theological use because of the (apophatic) contrast they expressed with the condition of creatures. Hence it was bound to be embarrassing for the orthodox Fathers to use these sets of contrasting terms in order to distinguish divine 'persons' while insisting against their opponents on the complete dichotomy between the divine and the creaturely. That this embarrassment is real rather than conjectural would be obvious to any reader of Gregory of Nyssa not blinded by total enthusiasm for what has come down to us as the Cappadocian solution.

140. *Against Eunomius* II, 9.

141. *Against Eunomius* I, 36. Previous writers had also been at times uncomfortable with inherited emanationist imagery: see Wiles, *Working Papers in Doctrine*, p. 22. Incidentally, at the beginning of this passage where the English translation has 'this one First Cause, as taught by us,' the Greek text reads: *to tes monarchias dogma*.

142. *Gregorii Nysseni Opera*, III, pt. 1, pp. 319–20.

143. See *Gregorii Nysseni Opera*, III, pt. 1, p. 56. The passage talks about

'the interposition of the Son' (*tou huiou mesiteias*) in the divine origin of the Holy Spirit, which does not however shut out the Spirit from his relation by way of nature to the Father, but though it asserts that the *mesiteia* does not cast doubt upon the *'ek tou patros'* of the Spirit, it does not lessen the *mesiteia* either. (The Greek text contains an additional phrase when compared to the translation of this passage in the Library of Nicene and Post-Nicene Fathers, Vol. V, p. 336, but this does not alter the logical balance of the point made.) For a similar attempt, explicitly now, to 'preserve intact the godly doctrine of the monarchy', see Basil, *On the Holy Spirit*, 47.

144. Examples: Athanasius, in *De Synodis* 55, argues from the Son's eternity, his title of Lord, and so on. And Basil, *On the Holy Spirit*, 19, 48 argues from such titles of the Holy Spirit as Spirit, Holy, Good.

145. For an example of the dogma at work in this precise context see Gregory of Nyssa, *On the Holy Spirit*, as in Müller's reconstruction of the text in *Gregorii Nysseni Opera*, III, pt. 1, p. 90, lines 28–9.

146. Many accept that the significance of the partial delay in confessions concerning the Spirit is expressed in a theory put forward by Gregory of Nazianzus, *Or.* 31, 26: the old dispensation revealed the Father, the new the Son, but only as the Spirit dwells in the church does its nature become successively clear (see Kelly, *Early Christian Doctrines*, pp. 255ff.) But this theory is far too artificial. As far as the Testaments are concerned, the Spirit was active from the very beginning, long before the incarnation. I suspect, therefore, that patristic hesitations about the Holy Spirit point to a deeper source, a sense that the case for yet a third co-equal divine *hypostasis* was more innovatory than anyone was prepared openly to admit.

147. *On the Holy Spirit*, 19, 23, 24.

148. *Or.* 33, 16: 'The Father is God, the Son is God, the Holy Spirit (if you will not be exasperated by this) is God.' He also shows his sensitivity to the innovation that is now going on when he suggests 'procession' (*ekporeusis*) as the specific mode of origin of the Spirit: *Or.* 39, 2.

149. *First Letter to Serapion*. 23–4.

150. As examples of patristic statements on this 'co-ordination and unity', as Athanasius calls it, of the Three in action on the world, see Athanasius, *First Letter to Serapion*, 31; Basil, *On the Holy Spirit*, 51; *Gregorii Nysseni Opera*, II, p. 317 (*Refutatio Confessionis Eunomii*).

151. See *Gregorii Nysseni Opera*, III, pt. 1, p. 11; *te tautoteti tes energeias*. For more detail see John McIntyre, 'The Holy Spirit', p. 355; 'Since the Holy Spirit is indivisibly united with the Father and the Son in the Divine Activity, His own Divine Nature is thereby guaranteed.'

152. 'The Holy Spirit', p. 358 (although my quotation is taken from the fuller version).

153. 'The Holy Spirit', p. 366 (again I use the revised version).

154. Sample texts may be found in Athanasius, *First Letter to Serapion*, 28, 31; Gregory of Nyssa, *On the Holy Spirit* (Library of Nicene and post-Nicene Fathers, V, p. 322); Basil, *On the Holy Spirit*, 47.

155. I have not dealt in the course of the preceding pages, though at times the material seemed to clamour for it, with the distinction between immanent and economic trinities. I personally consider the distinction to be one of the largest red-herrings ever drawn across the confused pages of the history of trinitarian doctrine. The only sensible distinction between God in himself and God as he appears to us in the economy of salvation/revelation is the one drawn in the old subordinationist model (and still obtruding in the new model) between the highest level of God, or the innermost being of God, which is unknown, and (or, except in) the lower levels or more composite forms of divinity which are to some extent known. Now, as I begin to suspect, once the *homoousios* approaches its logical conclusion of one identical essence in three *hypostaseis*, it can no longer provide any rationale for this particular order of Father first, then Son, and finally Spirit (nor does Scripture give exclusive endorsement to such an order). So the sensible distinction of the obsolete model is unavailable. All we can now say is that we can only know of trinities or binities in God to the extent that God reveals and saves, and even though we must always confess that God is not quite as we know him, we should not express this either in the terms 'the immanent trinity (or binity) is distinct from the economic trinity', or 'the immanent trinity is the economic trinity'. For the imperfection of our knowledge would tend to falsify the latter, and the former would convey the impression that we had an independent standpoint from which we could compare God in himself with his economy of salvation/revelation, which is absurd. I personally believe that when people talk in terms of a distinction between immanent and economic trinities they really have in mind the distinction between the homoousiite trinity and the older, subordinationist one and, as usual, they want to have both without bothering to show any good reason as to why they should have either.

156. *The Origins of the Christian Mystical Tradition*, p. 146.

157. A more thorough and detailed critique than I could here provide of the implications for trinitarian theology of Augustine's substance language is well presented in Joseph O'Leary's 'Dieu-Esprit et Dieu-Substance chez Saint Augustin' *Recherches de Science Religieuse* 69, 1981, pp. 357–91.

158. 'The Doctrine of the Holy Spirit in the Latin Fathers', *Scottish Journal of Theology* 7, 1954, p. 132. Burleigh includes in this remark Augustine's effort to find scriptural authority for 'naming' the Holy Spirit as 'Love', a point we must also consider in due course.

159. Thomas Aquinas, *Summa Theologiae*, I, 30, 1–2.

160. See in addition the question put by Augustine to himself in *De Trinitate* I, 8, as a result of his insistence in I, 7, that only the Son was born, died, and was raised, only the Spirit descended as a dove and as fire, only the Father spoke of Jesus as his beloved Son at baptism and transfiguration. See also Aquinas, *Summa Theologiae*, I, 47, 7, ad 3.

161. Aquinas, extremely Augustinian in his theology of the Trinity, follows Augustine's preference for the internal or invisible mission of the

'persons' in the very structure of his Question on missions, *Summa Theologiae*, I, 43. See especially articles 3, and 6, ad 2.

162. The fear of a 'natural theology' approach haunts all of Karl Barth's pages, but more particularly those on the *Vestigium Trinitatis* in I, 1, of his *Church Dogmatics*. See Brunner's critical remarks on this influence on Barth: *The Christian Doctrine of God*, pp. 235ff.

163. *Beyond Personality: The Christian Idea of God*, London: Geoffrey Bles 1944 is a good example of the mistaking of tentative psychological analogies for the substance of Christian orthodoxy, all the more danger-ous because its author, C. S. Lewis, was such a powerful popularizer.

164. Once again it is difficult to accept Louth's suggestion of 'Augus-tine's use of the doctrine of the Trinity to gain a greater understanding of the soul' (*The Origins of the Christian Mystical Tradition*, p. 160). Apart from seeming to place the cart before the horse, this ignores the damage undoubtedly done to Augustine's otherwise penetrating introspection by the now strident demands of *homoousios* language.

165. I refer to books such as R. Garrigou-Lagrange, *The Trinity and God the Creator*, St Louis: Herder 1952, which says of Augustine 'whatever difficulties still remained were attributable not to deficiencies of method but to the sublimity of the mystery' (p. 197); and M. Schmaus, *Die Psychologische Trinitätslehre des hl. Augustinus*, Münster: Herder 1927, which calls the *De Trinitate* simply 'the grandest monument in Catholic theology to the august mystery of the most Holy Trinity' (p. 2).

166. I do not refer here to such 'alternative' trinitarian theologies as were suspect later of having been heretical, either as Arian, or in some other direction. Since I am not attempting to write a history of the doctrine, I feel no need to include such people as Eusebius of Caesarea and Marcellus of Ancyra. Anyone who would wish to study a subtle and resourceful trinitarian theology which combined acceptance of the Nicene *homoousios* with a tolerable degree of subordinationism could begin with Colm Luibhead, *Eusebius of Caesarea and the Arian Crisis*, Dublin: Irish Academic Press 1978. And the chapter in that work on Eusebius and Marcellus provides a balanced introduction to the intriguing trinitarian theology of that other much-maligned theologian of the fourth century, Marcellus of Ancyra.

167. See above p. 122.

168. See above p. 144.

169. *The Divine Names* II, 4 and 6, and especially *The Mystical Theology*, 5. The phrase about philosophically unravelling and unfolding so as to guide the mind to the truths of Scripture must be one of the few honest accounts from the ancient world of what was really going on in trinitarian theology.

170. John Scotus Eriugena, *De Divisione Naturae*, ed. H. J. Floss, Paris 1865, 614C.

171. *De Divisione Naturae*, 614B.

172. The jump forward to this medieval mystic must again be justified on the grounds that I am following theological trends rather than writing

a history of dogma. And it may in any case help to answer those who complain that the mystical dimension is often inexcusably absent from works on the Trinity. For one is sometimes told – and at times a little haughtily – that if, instead of treating men like Gregory of Nyssa and Augustine as mere logicians, one looked to the mystical depth of their own expressed spiritual experiences, one would be less critical of their achievement and see more of its perennial value. However, only a very simple-minded logician would concede that men who showed such great confidence in their own logic should not have its strength tested at every point; and none but the most desultory of historians could fail to notice that mystical or apophatic noises are sometimes made only when a logical battle in which a man has up to that point engaged with gusto seems unlikely to result in victory or even in the avoidance of defeat. Some logic must rule all that one has to say, for otherwise even that degree of truth which is accessible to human endeavour is distorted. So we shall probably do more justice to the mystics by carefully selecting the contributions they seem to have made to our topic than by any general appeal to mysticism in order to seek to excuse the occasional, but the very real, weaknesses in the logic of classical trinitarian theologies.

173. It is important to note that this idea of 'double creation', the first an ideal creation in the divine mind which coincides with the birth of the Word, the other the consequent creation in or with time, is a common borrowing of early Christian theologians from Greek culture in their theology of creation, as characteristic of Athanasius and Augustine as of Clement and Origen.

174. John of Ruysbroek, *The Adornment of the Spiritual Marriage* III, 3. (Page reference will be to *the Adornment of the Spiritual Marriage, The Sparkling Stone, The Book of Supreme Truth*, Westminster: Maryland 1974.) For a view of the creation of all things, in ideal or intelligible form, in the Word or Son, compare John of Ruysbroek, *Adornment*, ch. 3, with John Scotus Eriugena, *De Divisione Naturae*, 609A–B.

175. Ruysbroek, *Adornment* III, 2 (p. 170).

176. Ruysbroek, *The Book of Supreme Truth* X (p. 240).

177. Ruysbroek, *Adornment* III, 4 (p. 177).

178. Ruysbroek, *The Book of Supreme Truth* XII (p. 245).

179. One or two quotations from Eckhart, perhaps: 'In this way the soul enters into the unity of the Holy Trinity, but it may become even more blessed by going further, to the barren Godhead, of which the Trinity is a revelation. In this barren Godhead activity has ceased and therefore the soul will be most perfect when it is thrown into the desert of the Godhead where both activity and forms are no more.' 'No one can strike his roots into eternity without being rid of the concept of number . . . God leads the human spirit into the desert, into his own unity which is pure One' (*Meister Eckhart*, trans. R. B. Blackney, New York: Harper and Bros 1941, pp. 98–9).

180. See Marius Victorinus, *Ad Candidum Arrianum* I, 13: I, 19; III, 2.

(Marius Victorinus, *Traités Théologiques sur la Trinité*, 2 vols, Sources Chrétiennes 68, Paris: Éditions du Cerf 1960).

181. *'Idem ergo motus, duo officia complens, vitam et cognoscentiam. Logos autem motus est, et Logos filius. Filius igitur unicus in eo quod filius. In eo autem quod Logos, geminus. Ipse enim vita, ipse cognoscentia, utroque operatur ad animarum salutem'* (*Ad Candidum* III, 8).

182. *Ad Candidum* I, 58.

183. *Ad Candidum* I, 41. He suggests instead: *'de una substantia, tres subsistentias esse'* (*Ad Candidum* II, 4; see also I, 10).

184. See *Ad Candidum* I 13, his comment upon Jesus' statement that 'the Father is greater than I'. He may be more historically accurate to the minds of some at least of the Fathers at Nicaea in not taking the *homoousios* to mean total equality of status. See his own nuanced reflections on whether we should speak of the one identical substance (*eadem*) in Father and Son (*Ad Candidum* I, 41).

185. See, for instance, Ruysbroek, *Adornment* II, 43 (p. 115).

186. Ruysbroek, *The Book of Supreme Truth* X (p. 242).

187. Ruysbroek, *The Sparkling Stone* III (p. 186).

188. John Scotus Eriugena places the faith by which Peter, for instance, could confess Jesus during his life, even lower than Augustine, for to John it is lower than both science and contemplative wisdom: see Jean Scot, *Honélie sur le Prologue de Jean* (Sources Chrétiennes, 151), Paris: Éditions du Cerf 1969, III. Also *Ad Candidum* I, 34, 44.

189. *Ad Candidum* I, 32.

190. See the phrase *'dei filius . . . opere quo vita est, Jesus existens, opere autem quo cognoscentia est, spiritus sanctus et ipse existens'* (*Ad Candidum* III, 8).

191. Ruysbroek, *Adornment*, II, 51ff. (pp. 118–122).

192. *Summa Theologiae*, Part 1, Question 40, Article 3.

193. *ST* I, 28, 1, ad 3.

194. *ST* I, 31, 3, ad 1.

195. *ST* I, 36, 1.

196. *ST* I, 37, 1; 38, 1.

197. Compare *ST* I, 30, 2 with I, 36, 2–4.

198. The case reveals a certain dependence on Anselm's *De Processione Spiritus Sancti*.

199. I refer to conferences of Eastern and Western theologians on the *filioque* such as that held under the auspices of the Faith and Order committee of the World Council of Churches at Klingenthal in October 1978.

200. As an illustration of this point one need only read, I think, the rather tortuous suggestions of J. Moltmann in his *The Trinity and the Kingdom of God*, London: SCM Press 1981, pp. 178ff. For a slightly fuller treatment of the issue than I can offer here see my 'The Holy Spirit: Relativising the Divergent Approaches of East and West', *The Irish Theological Quarterly* 49, 1982, pp. 256–67.

201. V. Lossky, 'The Procession of the Holy Spirit in Orthodox

Triadology', *Eastern Churches Quarterly* 7 1948, pp. 31–53; *The Mystical Theology of the Eastern Church*, London: Anthony Clarke 1957.

202. See John of Damascus, *De Recta Sententia*, 1; *De Fide Orthodoxa* I, 8, 12, 13.

203. André de Halleux made this point in his paper to the Klingenthal conference, 'Towards an Ecumenical Agreement on the Procession of the Holy Spirit and the Addition of the Filioque to the Creed'. Indeed he argues throughout that paper that the Western insistence on the *filioque* never, even at Lyons and Florence, ruled out the *per filium* position, but always assumed and accommodated it. I would add only that Augustine's 'traces' are, on Augustine's own showing, weak premises for such solid conclusions as the *filioque* position tries to draw from them, and indeed that another passage from his treatment of the 'traces' could as easily support the contention that the Son proceeds from the Father through the Holy Spirit. See my 'The Holy Spirit', p. 265.

204. *ST* I, 36, 2 and 3.

205. John of Damascus repeats the ancient formula to the effect that the Spirit is image of the Son, as the Son is image of the Father (*De Fide Orthodoxa* I, 13); neither of them being the *arche*, the *fons et origo*, the original, as we might say, and the Holy Spirit being third in the order of image or representation of the original.

206. The threat of quaternity is as real for others as it is for Aquinas, though it emerges from different places in their logic. For Aquinas it emerges from the logic of processions and relations. For Gregory of Nyssa, for instance, it emerges from the logic of the relationship of the one *ousia* to the three *hypostaseis* – a fact which gives one more reason for challenging the vastly over-simplified view that the Greeks find the unity of the Trinity in the Father while the Latins find it in the divine substance. For some details of Gregory of Nyssa's problems in relating the one to the three without having them add up to four see above p. 144, and also my 'The Holy Spirit', p. 262.

207. It is interesting that Aquinas appropriates the terms Spirit and Love for the third 'person' on the grounds that they suggest a certain vital movement and impulse: *ST* I, 27, 4; I, 36, 1.

208. For example Moltmann tries to have it both ways without really showing that he can have it either way in *The Trinity and the Kingdom of God*, pp. 119ff.

209. K. Rahner, *The Trinity*, New York: Herder and Herder and London: Burns and Oates 1970, p. 16.

210. This may be why Rahner's own fundamental theology begins with the one God and why it is that what he has to say about the Trinity in that large volume is very little and very late indeed: see his *Foundations of Christian Faith, An Introduction to the Idea of Christianity*.

211. The main reference for this short section on Calvin is his *Institutes of the Christian Religion*, Bk I, ch. 13.

212. E. A. Dowey has shown that the *duplex cognitio Domini* is the real principle of organization of Calvin's *Institutes*. The knowledge of God the

creator is dealt with in Bk I; the knowledge of God the Redeemer, the sole source of which is Christ, is dealt with in Bks II–IV; and the Trinity is discussed mainly in Bk I. See Dowey, *The Knowledge of God in Calvin's Theology*, New York: Columbia University Press 1965, pp. 43ff.

213. On this rather difficult issue of the source of our knowledge of the Trinity according to Calvin see Dowey, *The Knowledge of God*, pp. 45, 127: 'The doctrine (of the Trinity) does not include Calvin's Christology. Nor is it meant to establish the divinity of Christ, but rather of the Eternal Son or Wisdom of God who became incarnate in Christ and of the Spirit.'

214. Perhaps this is why, as Dowey points out, Calvin interprets the Johannine 'I and the Father are one' as follows: 'he does not speak simply of his divine essence, but he is called one as regards his character as Mediator'. Dowey, *The Knowledge of God*, p. 15.

215. *ST* I, 28, 2.

216. *ST* I, 29, 3, ad 4.

217. C. F. D. Moule, *The Holy Spirit*, London: Mowbray 1978, p. 46.

218. *The Holy Spirit*, p. 51.

219. *The Holy Spirit*, p. 56.

220. A. M. Ramsey, *Holy Spirit*, London: SPCK 1977, p. 119.

221. A further possible exception here is H. Berkhof, who seems willing to settle for a trinitarian theology based on an improved version of Marcellus of Ancyra.

222. See above note 155, p. 295.

223. Rahner, *The Trinity*, p. 24.

224. *The Trinity*, p. 22.

225. *The Trinity*, p. 28.

226. *The Trinity*, p. 32.

227. *The Trinity*, p. 33.

228. *The Trinity*, pp. 100–1.

229. *The Trinity*, p. 65.

230. *The Trinity*, p. 76 n. 30.

231. K Barth, *Church Dogmatics*, Edinburgh: T. & T. Clark 1975, vol. I, part I, ch. 2.

232. Barth, *Church Dogmatics*, I, I, p. 372.

233. Ibid.

234. For some information on others who proposed a social doctrine of the Trinity, see, for instance, the article on 'Trinity' in the *New Dictionary of Christian Theology*, London: SCM Press 1983 (forthcoming).

235. J. Moltmann, *The Trinity and the Kingdom of God*, London: SCM Press 1981, I, sec. 2.

236. *The Trinity and the Kingdom of God*, p. 17.

237. J. Moltmann, *The Crucified God*, London: SCM Press 1974.

238. *The Trinity and the Kingdom of God*, p. 64.

239. *The Trinity and the Kingdom of God*, p. 94; for fuller expressions of various forms of the Trinity see also pp. 75, 83, 88.

240. *The Trinity and the Kingdom of God*, p. 95.

241. *The Trinity and the Kingdom of God*, p. 175.

242. *The Crucified God*, p. 207.
243. *The Trinity and the Kingdom of God*, p. 83.

Part Four: The Future

1. See the section on Eucharist in the Appendix.
2. E. Becker, *The Denial of Death*, New York: The Free Press 1973. A comparison of Becker's book with Philip Rieff's *The Triumph of the Therapeutic*, New York: Harper and Row 1960, would offer an interesting 'replay', on the pitch of psychology, of the contest between those who argue for theistic belief of a general nature on general structures of human experience and those who insist on some form of atheistic humanism. For the psychologist Rieff the shape of the humanist future is as follows: 'The brief historic fling of the individual, celebrating himself as a being in himself, divine and therefore essentially unknowable, could be truly ended . . . Men already feel freer to live their lives with a minimum of pretense to anything more grand than sweetening the time . . . Affluence achieved, the creation of a knowing rather than a believing person, able to enjoy life without erecting high symbolic hedges around it, distinguishes the emergent culture from its predecessors. The new anticulture aims at . . . release from the inherited controls'. p. 23.
3. I do not mention Deism here since I tend to think that its emergence in eighteenth-century Europe, for instance, was, as someone said, late, literary and artificial.
4. See *Jesus, the Man and the Myth*, pp. 75ff.
5. See Barth, *Church Dogmatics* I, 2, (1936), p. 519.
6. References to Philo's *Life of Moses* are to the text and translation found in the Loeb Classical Library's *Philo*, Vol. VI, London: Heinemann 1935.
7. If I have tended to overuse the terms power and praxis, it may help at least to say, since I am here dealing with Philo, that they correspond to Philo's *dynameis* and *energeiai* as names for that of God which is palpable as and in our world.
8. *Life of Moses*, I, 28: *autos egineto nomos empsychos te kai logikos Theia pronoia*. Compare John 1.14, *logos sarx egeneto*, and remember that the word we translate reincarnation is *metempsychosis*. See also the symbolism of the High Priestly Vestments in *Life of Moses* II, 23–24.
9. One might ask Moltmann, for instance, why Jewish theologies of a suffering God do not yield a Trinity long before the specific cross of Jesus comes into view. See his *The Trinity and the Kingdom of God*, pp. 23ff.
10. That the One and Intelligence are really two ways of viewing the same thing emerges for instance in the anonymous *Parmenides Commentary*. See Wallis, *Neoplatonism*, p. 117.
11. See above p. 168.
12. Gregg and Groh, *Early Arianism*, pp. 8, 25.
13. Moltmann, *The Crucified God*, p. 127.

14. R. Jolivet, *Le Problème de la Mort chez M. Heidegger et J.-P. Sartre*, Abbaye St Wandrille 1950.

15. Some artistic forms of words have the power to evoke an experience or a creative vision which more analytical or ideological forms lack; so that the relative powerlessness of verbal expression and the corresponding predominance of its demonstrative role – whereby it points away from itself – is not equal across the verbal board.

16. See above p. 14.

17. *Jesus, the Man and the Myth*, pp. 235–40.

18. For some support for this reconstruction see ch. 3 of Carl E. Braaten, *The Future of God*, New York: Harper and Row 1960.

19. If one wished to consider Christian Trinitarian doctrines in relationship to world religions other than Judaism and Islam, one could begin to tackle the problem through R. Panikkar, *The Trinity and the Religious Experience of Man*, London: Darton, Longman and Todd 1975.

Appendix

1. See John Hick, *Philosophy of Religion*, Englewood Cliffs: Prentice-Hall 1973, pp. 90ff.

2. M. Kehl, 'Eucharistie and Auferstehung' in *Geist und Leben* 43 1970, pp. 109–207.

3. Two exemplary texts must suffice here: Irenaeus, *Adversus Haereses* V,2,2 and Theodore of Mopuestia, *Mystagogical Catechesis* V,10–11.

4. I follow here Ingo Hermann's exegesis, which opens Part Two of his *Kyrios und Pneuma*, Munich: Kösel 1961, of I Cor 12.4–27.

5. Louis Bouyer, *Eucharist*, University of Notre Dame Press 1968, p. 86.

6. Hippolytus (*Apostolic Tradition*, in any case), Addai and Mari, the Anaphora of Serapion, Justin, and Irenaeus are usually mentioned in this connection.

7. For a comprehensive historical and critical treatment of these and related Eucharistic issues see John H. McKenna *Eucharist and Holy Spirit* (Alcuin Club Collections 57), Great Wakering: Mayhew-McCrimmon 1975.

8. Max Thurian, *The Eucharist Memorial*, I, Richmond: John Knox Press 1962, p. 25.

9. See Bernard Cooke, *Christian Sacraments and Christian Reality*, New York: Holt, Rinehart and Winston 1965, p. 135.

10. This point was made well in a doctoral thesis I once examined: William M. Cieslak, *Gabriel Marcel's Notion of Presence and Paul Tillich's Concept of Religious Symbol: Towards an Ecumenical Understanding of Eucharistic Memorial and the Manifold Presence of Christ*, Berkeley: Graduate Theological Union 1979, p. 315. See also Gabriel Marcel, *Présence et Immortalité*, Paris: Flammarion 1959.

11. Gregory Dix, *The Shape of the Liturgy*, London: Dacre Press 1964, p. 238.

12. See McKenna, *Eucharist and Holy Spirit*, pp. 49, 51–2, 67ff., for a selection of patristic examples.

13. L. Scheffozyk, *Schöpfung und Vorsehung*, Freiburg: Herder 1963, pp. 2–3.

14. Schillebeeckx, *Christ*, pp. 515ff.

15. From the fact that matter is uncreated, for instance, it does not follow automatically that it is also a God (especially since to some Greeks matter is a 'nothing' which is at the opposite extreme to the creative effusive 'nothing' that is God!); any more than from the fact that the Word can be said to be created or 'out of things that are not', it follows for an Arian that the Word is not divine. Polemics in these cases characteristically overlook admissible differences in the definition and use of theological terms. The question of orthodoxy cannot usually be solved as simply as all that!

16. Ending on a footnote undoubtedly contravenes some artistic canon or other. Yet, since baptism looms so large in much classical theology of Trinity, someone might wonder why I did not choose it over eucharist. Well, first, because there is a sense, as Aquinas knew, in which eucharist is all-sacrament, the full light of which is refracted through other sacraments partially (however many others there be). And, second, because consideration of baptism would change none of the conclusions to any noticeable degree. The baptismal formula was christological in apostolic times, and only later became trinitarian. When the trinitarian form or formula did arrive, it was an *epiclesis* (only later still did the declaratory form take over), and it was in fact part of a 'double *epiclesis*', the other member of which was the recipient's profession of faith, so that, as in eucharist, elements and people were sanctified in the one integral act. This particular connection of the form or formula with the profession of faith means that the form or formula, far from yielding immediately a Trinity of the fourth-century types, coincides rather with the content of a very 'economic' creed and tells us no more about, for instance, a distinct Spirit than does the following example of such a confession of faith from Irenaeus: 'God the Father, not made, not material, invisible; one God, the creator of all things: this is the first point of our faith. The second point is this: the Word of God, Son of God, Christ Jesus our Lord, who was manifested to the prophets according to the form of their prophesying and according to the method of the Father's dispensation; through whom all things were made, who also at the end of the age, to complete and gather up all things, was made man, among men, visible and tangible, in order to abolish death and show forth life and produce reconciliation between God and man. And the third point is: the Holy Spirit, through whom the prophets prophesied, and the fathers learned the things of God, and the righteous were led into the way of righteousness; who at the end of the age was poured out in a new way upon mankind in all the earth, renewing man to God' (see Kelly, *Early Christian Doctrines*, p. 89; on the development of baptism see E. Schillebeeckx, *De Sacramentele Heilseconomie*, Antwerp 1952, pp. 240–83).

Index

Index

307

Index